HERBS

Their Culture and Uses

HERBS

Their Culture and Uses

By

ROSETTA E. CLARKSON

Illustrated by
TABEA HOFMANN

Foreword by
GERTRUDE B. FOSTER

WINGS BOOKS
New York • Avenel, New Jersey

This 1996 edition is published by Wings Books,
a division of Random House Value Publishing, Inc.,
40 Engelhard Avenue, Avenel, New Jersey 07001,
by arrangement with Macmillan Publishing USA,
a division of Simon and Schuster, Inc.

Wings Books and colophon are trademarks of
Random House Value Publishing, Inc.

Random House
New York • Toronto • London • Sydney • Auckland
http://www.randomhouse.com/

Printed and bound in the United States of America

Library of Congress Cataloging-in-Publication Data
Clarkson, Rosetta E.
Herbs, their culture and uses / by Rosetta E. Clarkson ;
illustrated by Tabea Hofmann ; foreword by Gertrude B. Foster.
p.   cm.
Originally published: New York : Macmillan Co. , 1942.
Includes index.
ISBN 0-517-18243-2
1. Herbs. 2. Herb gardening. 3. Herbs—Utilization. I. Title.
[SB351 . H5C49 1996]
635' . 7—dc20   96-31293
CIP

8 7 6 5 4 3 2 1

Foreword

Rosetta Clarkson's path to the study and growing of herbs was a circuitous one. Although she had earned a degree in chemistry at Vassar College, her father, who was a superintendent of public schools in Pough-keepsie, New York, persuaded her not to take a job in a laboratory. At the time, 1914, he felt that a woman had no future in chemistry. As a result, she took an assignment teaching English in a high school in New Rochelle, New York.

It was in pursuit of an advanced degree in English at Columbia University that Rosetta Clarkson spent a good part of 1931 in England. A trip to the countryside took her to the Herb Farm, Seven Oaks, Kent, and while in London she would pass Culpeper House, which was a supplier of herbs for culinary and medicinal purposes. The fragrance that emanated when its door was opened spelled enchantment to Rosetta, the scent bringing with it a strong remembrance of her grandparents' farm in upstate New York. Upon returning to the United States, she started the hobby of growing herbs, studying the old herbals she ordered from London. Over the next years, she assembled an outstanding collection of rare editions, including *Theatrum Botanicum* (1640) by John Parkinson and *De Materia Medica* (1558) by Dioscorides. These were donated to the Yale University Library after her death.

Rosetta Clarkson shared her hobby with a number of friends and students, but the keenest of her herb admirers was her husband, Ralph P. Clarkson, a journalist, patent lawyer, inventor, and writer. He typed up the reams of notes she had brought back from her studies of the Eliz-abethan period. These notes interested him so much that it was his idea to publish the relevant extracts as *The Herb Journal*. The first edition of the monthly was sent out in 1936, and, as were all ensuing editions, it was free of charge. The subject matter she covered in the next three years of its publication became the basis of her first two books, *Magic Gardens* (1939) and *Green Enchantment* (1940). Both volumes tell the story of herb gardens through the ages, drawing heavily from the old herbals.

Herbs: Their Culture and Uses was a departure from the first two books and was written in response to the overwhelming demand for a practical guide to growing herbs and creating herbal products. The book was an enormous success. It became a cornerstone of the commercial herb business, offering ideas for herb products and packaging that have since become ubiquitous in their popularity and success.

Though Rosetta Clarkson never had a business of herbs, she did have an immense herb garden that served her as a laboratory of sorts. "My so-called herb farm was always an avocation," she wrote to Vassar in 1949, "a means of study in connection with my writing and a demonstration for the hundreds of herb lovers who came to 'Salt Acres' [her garden in New Milford, Connecticut] in the summer months. We had a little garden with a little cottage facing it, in which were shelves of herbs dried and prepared for use.

"In the garden at the edge of the salt pond were several of the old-fashioned bee skeps, and around a tree was a wattled garden seat, as in Elizabethan gardens. One plant of each of perhaps a hundred herbs formed a border; in the center was a sundial surrounded by many varieties of mint; and geometrically spaced were bushes of old-fashioned roses: the apothecaries' rose, Rosa Mundi, and the Tudor Rose. Another part of the grounds was fenced in with some three hundred or more herb varieties in raised beds.

"We had a bed of sage, one of coriander, one of dill, one of sweet marjoram, one of thyme, one of basil, etc., etc. We even grew cumin, to the amazement of the U.S. Department of Agriculture, which had given up in despair trying to get it started. During the early forties, we helped restock the English seed houses . . . sending over some skirret seed to one of the famous firms, who wrote me there was none in England. We still have visitors from near and far who ask questions, and, even when modern medicine seems to have failed . . . hope that I may know some ancient cure for body or for soul. Most, however, are interested in the culinary herbs or in the multitude of commercial uses in wines and liqueurs, in perfumes and toiletries, in toothpastes and in drawing ink, dyes, and liniments, in tobacco and cigarettes—even in paints for which perilla was used."

My husband and I had the pleasure of meeting Rosetta Clarkson and her husband after she had contributed the lead article to the first issue of our new venture, *The Herb Grower Magazine,* in 1947. We had corresponded with her for years but, until that day, had feared we would never see Salt Acres while she lived there, for by that time she was suffering from a very serious heart condition which would eventually take her life. It was on that first visit that Ralph Clarkson handed me a huge box of correspondence that Rosetta had accumulated by answering the literally thousands of letters that came to her in response to her newsletters. This was the beginning of a happy collaboration that lasted until Ralph Clarkson's death, some fourteen years after that of Rosetta.

It was an honor to have known and worked with Rosetta and Ralph Clarkson and it is my sincere hope that this new edition of *Herbs: Their Culture and Uses* will bring her a well-deserved new generation of readers.

GERTRUDE B. FOSTER
Falls Village, Connecticut

Introduction

What is an herb? An herb is a plant that has been cherished for centuries because of its usefulness in cooking, in medicine, in household preparations and in industry. It is upon the basis of usefulness that I have chosen the herbs discussed in this book. Most of them, however, are as ornamental as they are useful and garden lovers will do well to turn their attention to some of the herbs discussed here. Many I shall mention only in passing because they are too coarse, too rampant spreaders, or too free in self-sowing to be of interest, although some are grown commercially as, for example, burdock, dandelion, licorice, nettle and dozens of others.

Again, unless the herbs have been used in the home, in industry, or in medicine in recent years, they have been rejected in this book even as they were in olden days from the narrow limits of castle gardens, where no plant was admitted until it had proved its usefulness. Of the medicinal plants there are many but here I have gone little beyond the herbs that are officially recognized as drugs by the United States or British Pharmacopoeia and by the National Formulary. I have included a few herbs long used as drugs unofficially in home remedies and professional practice and which are still of great interest to research workers.

Neither have I included in this book the vegetable herbs such as onions, leeks, asparagus, beets, all grown more for their medicinal value than for their culinary worth in ancient times. Even now green vegetables are sources of our modern vitamins, and beets are grown widely for sugar. Nor have I here included many flowers, such as the dozens of varieties of irises, roses, lilies, unless they still are valued for their great practical usefulness. Again, there are many beautiful, decorative, but not utilitarian, varieties of the most useful foliage plants, such as mints, artemisias, thymes, each of which would afford possibilities of a garden in themselves for the collector.

Such are my limitations for these pages, but the herbs that have been chosen will be found to be of the utmost importance both for use and ornament. In the body of the book the cultural advice applies in general to all herbs mentioned, but in the back are tables and outline paragraphs which indicate special peculiarities and requirements of some hundred herbs of maximum value. Only a few of the best known herbs are indigenous to the United States, most of them originating along the Mediterranean Coast. It would be expected that they might flourish best under the growing conditions of their native habitat, but the plants and seeds you get will be hundreds of generations removed from those early field herbs, and you will find that they accommodate themselves wherever they are planted. I have indicated the best conditions for each plant and have recorded what I have observed in many herb gardens north of Washington, D. C., particularly in my own herb gardens in suburban New York City and in Connecticut along the coast. These recordings apply to all annuals wherever grown, except where the growing season is very short, and in isolated cases where some adjustments must be made for warmer climates. Sweet marjoram, for example, is a perennial botanically and will be such where there is no frost, but in the cooler zones must be treated as an annual.

Herbs for centuries have been the backbone of the garden and of many industries. Although they are used more in modern times for commercial products than ever before, these fragrant useful plants for a while were driven from private gardens in favor of showy flowers. Now their worth is more and more appreciated and Americans are eagerly restoring herbs to their gardens both for ornament and use. A little herb patch, like a small vegetable garden, is making life happier for many a cook. Here and there it has been extended to market-garden size as a source of pin money, and a favored few, by hard work, persistent effort and a deep knowledge of marketing methods, have built up successful herb farms.

Table of Contents

CHAPTER 1

Why Have Herbs in Your Garden?

Today herbs are more popular than they have been in many generations. In past years we came to rely on imported herbs from the Balkans and Russia, and to a large extent, from Europe. These imports have almost ceased and our reserves are fast dwindling away. We are faced with the fact that we in the Americas must grow our own herbs. The little herb garden which has been fashionable for several years is more in vogue than ever but now the growing of herbs on a large scale is going to be profitable for many. We cannot all grow herbs for profit but each one of us with a little piece of ground can grow some of these magic plants so satisfying in fragrance and in flavor.

The herb garden is truly a magic garden in that it satisfies the spirit, mind and body of every type of person—gardener, housekeeper, artist, botanist, aesthete, dreamer and searcher for peace. Begin with a mere dozen herbs, basil, savory, lavender, rue, thyme, hyssop, sage, tarragon, sweet woodruff, rosemary, wormwood, sweet marjoram, all used in cooking, medicine and in household preparations. In the garden of flowers, for weeks the whole interest lies in the anticipation of bloom which, unhappily, is gone in a few days, but in the herb garden, you will find more lasting interest. Here our interest is held from day to day in the unfolding of fragrant leaves, the grouping of plants, the gradual changes that take place from seed time to harvest. Herbs do not depend on their flowers for their beauty; yet they may be very colorful, as are the orange calendula, red bergamot, blue chicory, the characteristic lavender flowers, and when they bloom it is not for a day or a week, but frequently for week after week.

We find an ever new delight in the texture of the leaves, from furry to smooth; in the color of the leaves, varying from a bright

1

yellow green or the light grays to rich dark greens; in their fragrances from the pungent santolina, clovelike basil, penetrating lavender to piny rosemary. In the house at all times, beautiful aromatic bouquets are lasting, and refresh the mind and spirit. Teas made from chamomile, mints and thyme are a pleasing and satisfying variation from the ordinary tea. The culinary herbs, basil, savory, thyme, marjoram and a dozen others, lift many a commonplace dish to gastronomic heights. A whiff of lemon verbena, of rosemary, of lavender can carry us back to childhood where for a few minutes we are far away from troubled times and nervous tension, and even though we must return again to the present, those moments of relaxation have helped to restore our equilibrium.

Many a doubting Thomas has asked, "How can you make an herb garden attractive?" That reveals a lack of fundamental garden knowledge for most of the elaborate garden designs which have come down to us from the sixteenth century have been planted with herbs as, for example, the much reproduced knot gardens. Only the herbs permit of complicated garden patterns that stir one's admiration, and some of the most strikingly beautiful herb gardens are those designed in the English tradition with simple, orderly, rectangular plots. Herbs give permanence and form, low soft borders, neatly trimmed hedges, soft green or flowering carpets, tropical backgrounds, ground covers, massive clumps or prim little individual settings.

Some people say they have no space to devote to a special herb garden. Yet in every garden there is some spot just waiting for the right plant and among the herbs that need can be found. Some herbs fit into rock gardens; others make pleasing edgings for the vegetable plot, for bordering garden paths or roadways, for surrounding the sundial or for tucking in among the flowers of beds or borders. The suggestions in this book are to stimulate your imagination, but do not follow any design slavishly. The plan you lay out must suit your garden, your location, your individuality.

Many people believe they must grow a great many herbs for their use. As a matter of fact, a half dozen plants of the foliage herbs will supply the average family. Others say they have grown vegetables and flowers but know nothing about growing herbs, but it is only within the last two hundred years or so that any distinction has been made between herbs and vegetables or between herbs and flowers. If you have a garden, it is almost certain that you have grown herbs.

Begin with a few herbs and really get acquainted with them by growing them and by using them. You will find yourself wondering how you ever did without them and will be eager to become familiar with more and more of these ancient plants.

Chapter 2

Herb Arrangements in the Garden

As you read of herbs here and there, the impression may be given that a whole garden must be devoted to them alone, but this is not so. Herbs may be combined with other gardens wherever you have space or where they will add color, beauty, form or fragrance. For every part of the garden there are herbs that will grow especially well in the heat of summer. Along paths, around the pool and sundial, through the rock-garden, in beds and borders, around the vegetable plot, their fragrant, volatile oils greet you, and the plants themselves are at their best on those July and August days that wilt human beings.

If flower beds and borders are raised and edged by boards or metal strips, you have found no doubt that just inside the boundaries you face the problem of hard lines, a little bare and ragged. If the spot is in shade or partial shade, parsley or sweet woodruff will fill in for a softening effect. Parsley may be clipped to a suitable height, and woodruff with its whorls of starlike, deep green leaves and tiny white blossoms in late spring, may be kept from spreading by cutting back the runners. The runners, of course, may be rooted elsewhere or given to a friend. Thrift, which resembles a low cushion of grass, and has rose pink tufts of flowers in early summer, falls gracefully over hard edges. Another edging is calamint which spreads delicately into six-inch-high mats.

A very striking edging is the prostrate variety of bugle-weed (*Ajuga reptans*), which settles comfortably along hard boundaries. Variety *atropurpurea*, with tiny vivid blue flowers and bronze leaves, variety *multicolor*, with leaves spotted and variegated with yellow, brown and red; variety *rubra*, with dark purple leaves—all are so attractive that any one would make a most effective edging.

For a gray garden or as a foil to green foliage plants, beach wormwood with gray leaves like soft felt is attractive as a soften-

Triangular Herb Gardens at Salt Acres

ing effect for hard edges. To keep it from encroaching on plants within the border, slide down through the roots with a turfing tool at the desired width, and remove the unwanted parts with a spade. Here again, the discarded roots may be planted elsewhere to lengthen the border or fill in a bed.

If the bed or border is at ground level with a row of stones, either whitewashed or plain, marking the separation of grass and soil or if nothing at all has been used to define the edge of the garden, any of the above low edgings are suitable. If plants directly back of the edge of the bed have little foliage near the ground, or are inclined to burn off in the heat of summer, a higher, less sprawly edging plant would take away the bareness. A suggestion is ordinary garden thyme with small grayish green leaves, clipped from time to time to prevent plants from becoming woody. Another suitable edging is winter savory, with flowers resembling a light fall of mauve-colored snow. This is particularly good if there is an artificial boundary upon which it may incline. Although the stems may grow a foot long, they are flexible and fall softly over any boundary. I have used it for edging a raised bed containing clary sage which has coarse lower leaves and stalks.

Germander, with small, glossy, deep green leaves shaped like oak leaves and beautiful rose-colored flowers in summer, makes a pleasing edging for any bed. It is under one foot high and can be clipped just as any hedge, but I never do clip it because the flowers are so pretty and I enjoy the graceful informality of the natural plants.

For trim, precise edgings, there is dwarf basil, called bush basil, in two varieties, green and purple. The green will grow a foot high but the purple seldom rises more than six or eight inches in height. These basils have a clove-pepperish odor so they are especially pleasant along a walk, for when you brush by a spicy fragrance greets you. Another edging plant, erect and tiny, strong with minty, aromatic odor which needs merely a touch to be released, is the American pennyroyal. The leaves are small and the plant is covered with a cloud of tiny bluish white flowers. This pennyroyal reseeds so freely that each spring you will have to dig up the undesired seedlings, either to discard or to place where you want more plants.

Chives are surprisingly effective edgings, especially in late spring when the rosy-lilac flower pompoms, an inch across, wave gracefully above the slender pencillike leaves. An edging of primroses is colorful for a flower garden and after the blossoms have gone, the yellow-green foliage is still decorative.

Surely you will enclose the flower or herb garden with a hedge which will be determined by the size of the area. If you live where the weather is mild the year around and plants can be left to grow where they have first been set, a hedge of rosemary would be the first choice. Here, in southern New England, rosemary has to be taken indoors for the winter. In a beautiful garden on Cape Cod, where there has been a rosemary hedge for many years, the taking up is quite a task, for the roots of each plant must be carefully packed with soil, wrapped in burlap and set in a cold greenhouse. Each ball of root and dirt of these great bushes now weighs some two hundred pounds. Most of us know rosemary as only a small bush with light blue flowers resembling a tiny orchid, while the narrow leaves, dark green above and gray beneath, have a warm, piny taste and fragrance.

A much lower hedge would be of lavender, with its delicate blossoms and soft gray foliage a beautiful foil to the gay garden flowers. In the coldest northern climate no lavender would be hardy, but here in Connecticut a hedge of true lavender (*Lavandula vera*) would be hardy and spike lavender (*L. spica*) in a protected spot would be almost sure to survive the winter, if covered.

Hyssop is perfectly hardy, most practical for northern climates, and resembles in appearance the much desired yet slow growing and expensive box. If seeds are sown in spring in well prepared soil, in a row around the area to be hedged, you will have a foot-high growth the same summer. The second summer you will see a well established hedge eighteen inches high. Thin out the plants so that they stand about fifteen inches apart, and use the discarded specimens elsewhere, for hyssop transplants readily.

To make the hyssop hedge formal, clip it and shape it as you would a box hedge. Let the plants flower in spikes of blue, pink and white, and you will have the most beautiful, informal, flowering hedge imaginable. I never clip my hyssop hedges until after they have flowered and I have collected the seed. Since the white flowering variety is rarer than the blue or pink, I carefully mark those plants and save the seed separately. The blue flowering hyssop is the usual variety, but in any packet of seeds you are likely to get some of the pink and rarely a few seeds of the white. By noting these and saving seeds separately, you can multiply any one of the varieties many fold in a year or two and have separate hedges of different colors.

Rue, with its lacy blue-green foliage and small yellow blossoms, makes a hardy, yet dainty, hedge about two feet high. These plants also grow readily from seed, are easily transplanted and may be clipped to form. They show to best advantage after the second year when you have thinned out the weaklings and arranged the sturdy plants to stand about fifteen inches apart. For a most striking effect, try an inner border of annual, dwarf harmony marigolds against the rue.

Southernwood, also called lad's love and old man, makes a wide gray-green hedge for a large garden. It grows some three feet tall with spreading branches, if not trimmed rigorously; is perfectly hardy, and readily multiplied by layering the bent down branches.

Gray santolina, also called lavender cotton, with flower heads of small lemon-colored balls, is a gray pungent plant resembling tiny coral. It is suitable for hedges, is hardy, and may be trimmed. To avoid the center portion dying out, it must be kept free from melting snow.

Germander is a fine bordering plant for a small garden, but do not clip it as closely as for an edging. Pungent feverfew with its daisylike flowers, growing a foot and a half high, is a striking border, and Roman wormwood, a gray-green feathery plant, is pleasing if severely restrained by a sharp turfer and spade to limit its width. It is likely to become untidy in late summer unless carefully looked after.

The vegetable garden possesses great possibilities for studies in form, in colors, in shades of green, all contributing to a garden as decorative as any flower gardener could wish. Yet this plot is usually relegated to the back of the house or drying yard, and our imaginations seem to go no further than long row upon row, all very useful, very efficient and very dull. Those old Tudor kitchen gardens, on the other hand, were charming. They were filled with potherbs, salad herbs, herbs for seasonings and always edgings and hedges of herbs, small or great as the spot demanded. Berry bushes or southernwood might well form a hedge for a large, pretentious garden, but if your vegetable plot is to be in a smaller area, what could be more appropriate than a hedge of culinary herbs? There is perennial sage, about eighteen inches high, with grayish green foliage, or annual sweet basil of a similar height, either the green or purple leaf variety. You might sow seed of the annual red orach, an old-time potherb and a most colorful border for vegetables with green foliage. For a high, informal hedge, tender pineapple sage, with spikes of red flowers late in the fall, delights the eye. For a high boundary, there is stately lovage with stalk and leaves tasting like celery and often growing as high as seven feet.

Unless you have a truck farm or are raising vegetables on a large scale where cultivation must be made simple with beauty sacrificed to utility, I suggest fewer long rows and more and cosier vegetable plots. In the small space, your imagination may be boundless. Each plot should be rectangular, of course, for economy, but around each one have a low border made by herbs of contrasting colors and types of foliage with a taller plant at each corner. A lettuce bed, for example, could be bordered by the emerald-green parsley and at each corner an eggplant with its purple fruit. For the onion bed, have a border, not of chives, but of dwarf basil, while chives would make a most attractive border for the feathery carrot foliage. Curled chervil around the dull green foliage of radishes, softly drooping dark green foliage of winter savory around prim rows of cabbages; grayish garden thyme bordering the vivid green broccoli and New Zealand spinach; all these arrangements would set off smartly otherwise dull vegetable plots.

Through herb, vegetable and flower gardens the main path and various cross paths must be distinguished. For the latter, use low-growing herbs and reserve taller herbs for the main walk. To make a fragrant walk, choose those herbs that will give out their odors as you brush past them or stoop to work among them. The most fragrant are garden thyme or caraway thyme, the latter spreading over the bricks, boards or stones that line the path. Erect garden thyme, some ten inches high, particularly suits the main path, and behind it plant higher fragrant herbs, ranging from the spicy dwarf basils, both the purple and the green variety, to lavender, santolina, lemon balm, costmary, pineapple sage, lemon verbena and the lemony southernwood. All of these will be so near the path that you may readily pluck a spray in which to bury your nose and breathe in refreshing odors on a sweltering day.

If you use stepping stones through the path, choose irregular

pieces that do not fit to one another but leave spaces that must be
filled with soil. In these spaces set in hardy caraway thyme which
forms a low, spreading mat on which you may walk and be greeted
by its fragrance. A similar walk can be made with bricks laid regularly or in crazy pattern, allowing about an inch between them in
which you can plant the roots of any carpeting thyme. No special
precautions are taken with thick stones or bricks, but where thin
slabs or tiles are used, old gardeners tell me that they always place
a handful of lime beneath the stone to sweeten the soil.

A roadway leading from the street to the garage or a drive
around the house may be treated in a manner resembling that of the
garden paths. Along this path you will not often walk, so the fragrant herbs for the border should be those that appeal particularly
to the eye. I remember vividly a roadway bordered on both sides
with a wide band of bee balm (red bergamot), a most spectacular
sight in late summer. Tansy with its brilliant flower heads of
orange "buttons" is striking. Other herbs with colorful flowers, that
will bloom all summer if the old blossoms are continually removed,
are the old-fashioned, single calendula, the red, pink and white
flowering varieties of hyssop and blue cornflower. Many herbs, with
foliage lovely in texture of leaf and in shade of color, are well
suited to line a roadway or a path. Such are the silvery gray Roman
wormwood, the dull gray santolina, the bronzy red perilla, or the
blue-green rue which, if not clipped, flames into brilliant yellow
bloom.

Nearly all the flowers now in the flower border have been and
still are medicinal herbs, such as hollyhock, rose, lily-of-the-valley,
cornflower, foxglove, to name but a handful. Why not add other
herbs of striking color or beauty of form? For the back of the border I suggest white mugwort with fragrant panicles of white blossoms, wild senna with axillary racemes of yellow flowers and whose
leaves are formed of a dozen or more oval shaped leaflets, both
flower and leaves resembling the locust. There is lovage and angelica; both are handsome, tropical-looking plants with large, deeply
cut leaves and yellowish white umbels of florets. There is also
elecampane producing huge leaves and shaggy orange flower disks
like small sunflowers, and butterfly weed with orange flower heads.
Another decorative plant is the marsh mallow, three and a half feet
tall, with pinkish white flowers three-quarters of an inch across and

many footstalks on which are soft, velvety, greenish gray leaves. For a colorful background, use red bergamot. For a lighter, less conspicuous color arrangement, I suggest a row of clary sage, both the light blue and the white flowered varieties.

For those who think of herbs as dull, green plants, let me recommend for flower bed or border the blue and orange combinations, or either against a red background. For the blue, choose larkspur, aconite, chicory, blue-flowered hyssop, speedwell, cornflower. For the orange, choose elecampane, butterfly weed, tansy. For the red, you may have red bergamot or red yarrow. All of these plants are still used medicinally.

Then there are many close harmonies for those who do not like brilliant contrasts in the garden. A group of catnip, lavender, sage, santolina mixed with flax, chicory, blue-flowered hyssop, common spiderwort and any of the gray artemisias such as either Roman or common wormwood, offers a delicate symphony of blue, lavender and gray. A blush-rose combination is achieved by grouping anise, coriander, summer savory, dwarf green basil, pink-flowered hyssop; all will blossom in July north of Washington, D. C. In these combinations, before some stop flowering others will take their place for color.

Perhaps the garden path leads beyond the herb and flower gardens to a shady spot where there is a pool. Arrayed against the light greens of angelica, lovage and costmary, with bee balm in front, the taller mints will curve around from the back to the sides of the pool. You will enjoy English and American peppermints, woolly mint, curly mint and spearmint. In front of the pool and curving around to meet these, plant the three sweetest smelling and tasting of all the mints—the orange mint, striped-golden apple mint and water mint.

Around the sundial, we may have the fragrance of the orange mint and peppermints or, perhaps, more colorful herbs in a low arrangement, such as violets, primroses, the bronzy or purple bugle-weed, lungwort, calendula or Johnny jump-ups. If you prefer taller plants so that the flowers reach the face of the dial, you may have larkspur, bee balm, aconite, butterfly weed, or if you wish the tall fragrant herbs with inconspicuous blossoms, choose lemon verbena, sweet wormwood, meadowsweet, ambrosia (Jerusalem oak).

In the rock-garden, herbs offer many lovely additions to the other

plants. A pleasing background is the orange butterfly weed, safflower, cardinal flower and bee balm. Tuck in among the other plants
dainty thrift, lungwort, winter savory, sweet marjoram, rosy-
flowered germander and borage on the highest spot so that the
drooping clusters of heavenly blue flowers are seen from below.
Pasque flower, houseleek, thymes, sea lavender, chamomile and
dead nettles are natural rock-garden plants. Gray dittany of Crete,
beach wormwood, silvery gray Roman wormwood, fringed wormwood and many more will suggest themselves as you run through
the lists of herbs.

To carpet the ground delightfully, one must turn to the herbs.
Several of them spread into mats, some thin and flat and others
unbelievably thick. Frequently they thrive where grass will not
grow. You already know the spreading habit of the shade-loving,
running myrtle with blue or white flowers. Others which thrive in
shade are lily-of-the-valley, sweet woodruff and various varieties of
Ajuga reptans, called carpet bugle-weed. For sunny places, give first
thought to caraway thyme, and for a brighter, yellow-green, con-
sider fragrant lemon thyme. Calamint and beach wormwood are
excellent for dry sandy soils. Remember, too, the old-fashioned
Johnny jump-ups and sweet violets, both of which have spreading
habits that can be put to useful service.

A particularly good use for calamint or caraway thyme is found
in the bulb border. If bulbs are planted among these ground covers,
you will be enchanted to see how they take away from the bareness
of the lower stalks of tulips, hyacinths, daffodils and jonquils. These
ground covers help support the stalks, especially the taller, weaker
stems and during hard rains protect the lower flowers from being
mud-spattered.

CHAPTER 3

Propagation of Herbs

All of the annuals and a great proportion of the perennials are best produced from seed, especially if any considerable crop is to be harvested. Oftentimes, however, mature plants may be had sooner by means of layerings, cuttings or root division, than would be possible from seed. These are especially important methods in producing mature plants to sell or in reproducing a particularly choice strain of some plant, for you cannot be sure of getting it from the seed.

Layering is an easy and certain method of propagation which is almost ignored by the average gardener who has no contact with commercial growers. It is a simple way of increasing sage, thyme, winter savory, perennial marjoram, lemon balm, santolina and many more perennial herbs. Bend a supple branch to the ground or choose a branch lying along the earth, peg it down firmly with a large hairpin or a bent wire and cover the pegged down portion, preferably a joint in the branch, with an inch or two of soil firmed down and kept moist. Peg down every available branch, if you wish, and within three or four weeks roots will form at each covered joint. As soon as the root system is considerable, cut the new plant from the parent plant, and transplant it to another place where it may be treated the same way, as sufficient branches form. In time, a limitless number of plants, all mature, are produced from a single original plant, which is still left.

Layering is not only the easiest method of propagation but it is the only absolutely certain method, because the new plant-to-be is nourished from the parent plant until a root system is developed, and a root system will develop in time from every covered joint. Many herbs layer themselves naturally. If you wish to cut off and transplant newly rooted plants outdoors, layering cannot be done much later than the middle of summer since you must allow time for rooting and also time, after transplanting, for new plants to become established before frost. You can however, continue to layer old plants until four or five weeks before frost if you take the newly rooted plants indoors or if you leave them attached to the parent plant until spring.

Perennial herbs are also propagated by cuttings or "slips." Of late years, producing roots on cuttings has been made easier by the root inducing substances, commonly called hormone powders. Roots are produced from any joint that is kept in rather moist soil, if the slip is not taken from too new growth. A cutting that snaps when it breaks is best.

If you have never taken "slips," try a cutting of mint. Cut it with a razor-sharp knife just below a joint, take off the lower leaves, and put it in a glass of water for a week or so. Do not change the water, although it may be added to in order to make up for evaporation. Keep it in a shady, but not dark, place and watch the roots form from day to day. Mint is one of the easiest plants to root, and the glass of water method is the simplest for rooting many cuttings. I have rooted rosemary slips in water, and any herb bouquet left for a considerable period will no doubt show a number of cuttings taking root.

Cuttings are commonly made from soft wood plants such as lavender, lemon balm, feverfew, or from hardwood plants such as winter savory, pineapple sage, rosemary, southernwood. In taking cuttings, be sure not to check the growth of the main plant by too vigorous pruning. Tip cuttings seem to be best, and although slips can be taken any time, late spring slips seem most successful. Any slip, however, three or four inches long is usually satisfactory. Cut the end to be rooted with a razor-sharp knife just below a node or joint, strip off all but the topmost one or two leaves, and lay the cutting aside for three or four hours or more, but keep it moist by sprinkling a paper on which it lies and covering with another wet paper, or it may be rolled up in moist paper. The purpose of laying the slip aside is to permit the cut end to heal over.

If you use a hormone powder, follow the instructions given in the circular. If you do not use such an aid, the slips may be propagated in a moist, sandy bed in the garden, in flats or other containers. Drainage must be provided and the material in which the slip is propagated must be kept moist. The slip itself must not dry out.

Sharp sand is best for cuttings. They should not be kept in the dark nor in full sun. The period of rooting runs from five or six weeks for most herbs to several months for hardwood cuttings. The slips are buried to half their length in moist sand which is packed as firmly as possible around them.

The flat, sand and water should all be sterilized but seldom are. After a root system has formed, the slip should be potted in sterilized soil in a sterilized pot. This, too, is seldom done. Sometimes and in some places it is not necessary but the greatest loss of slips is not through lack of roots but through disease-action after potting, just as the greatest loss indoors from seed is not failure to germinate but death of the seedling through "damping off." Commercial growers fight damping off by preparations sold for that purpose, in which the seeds are coated before planting. I know of no such preparations for cuttings and the only safeguard is sterilization of sand, soil and equipment.

There are several refinements to the process of propagation by slips or cuttings. One is the provision of bottom heat for the flats which shortens the rooting period and when combined with some form of transparent covering for the flat, as by setting it in a discarded aquarium or inverting a glass jar over each cutting, helps to insure a high percentage of plants. Some growers give the flats an hour or so of full sun each day, but it is questionable whether this is of any value whatever unless the flats are in the open air.

A third way of propagation of perennial herbs is by root division, usually done in early spring when the plants have come to life and are active. Some perennial plants, marjoram, betony, lemon balm, hyssop, winter savory, thyme, are divided by cutting through the roots with a sharp spade, and transplanting a part of the plant, but this may retard the growth considerably through shock. It is much better to dig up the entire plant and carefully separate the tangled roots by hand, using a sharp knive to divide the plant into portions about three inches square. This not only multiplies the number of plants but is usually beneficial to their growth. Many plants, as chives, can be divided easily without any cutting. Skirrets are amusing to separate as the roots are like tiny parsnips and with no entangling fibers.

Where herbs are grown out-of-doors, it is amazing how you can aid the natural processes of propagation by allowing a number of plants to go to seed. Watch them carefully until the time is just right and then, instead of letting the wind blow the seed, shake the plant vigorously or run your hand over the seed pods to release the seed and cultivate about the plant where the seed falls. In the spring, do not weed or cultivate in seeded areas until you can distinguish the nature of the seedlings. Frequently you will find almost a solid sod of seedlings you want and can lift up the mass, separate the sturdy little plants and either pot them or set them out in a prepared bed. Often they will number dozens or even hundreds.

Unless you raise herbs for seed or desire to have on hand early in the spring a stock of plants for sale, there is little or no advantage in sowing seed indoors. You get an earlier start but by mid-season the plants grown out-of-doors will have caught up with those set out from flats, although the latter will flower and seed earlier. For a foliage crop or for a summer and fall garden, I advise sowing seed in the open as soon as the ground can be worked and danger of frost is past.

In those localities, however, where the growing season is not long enough for seeds to mature and you wish seeds, it is essential to start plants indoors. If you wish to supply plants to gardeners in the spring, you must have plants ready when they have their ground prepared and, therefore, indoor planting of seed is essential. The average gardener may ignore both possibilities. Then, through the long summer and fall, he may enjoy the herb garden in all its beauty and fragrance, long after the flower garden has almost passed away.

CHAPTER 4

Outdoor Planting

As natives of the Mediterranean Coast, most herbs grow best in poor soil, with good drainage, in full sun, in a protected spot. Under the hot, devastating sun herbs generate their essential oils and in some manner these form a protective blanket around the plants to prevent their drying out. Upon the oils of the plants depend the flavor and fragrance which we enjoy in our household preparations, herbal teas and culinary dishes. When given too much water, fertilizer and shade, most herbs will produce little oil, though frequently the water and fertilizer will cause a luxuriant, lush foliage. Herbs, more than any other plants, ask to be let alone in poor, well drained soil and in full sun. A few do need partial shade or protection from the sun during the hottest part of the day. If these can be placed to receive the shade of a tree at noon, all requirements will be met. If not, shade-needing plants are best protected by a lattice or hedge or by the shade of taller plants placed to the south of them.

Determine whether the spot chosen for the herb bed already has good drainage by watching it after a heavy rain. If the water stays long on top of the ground (and the ground is not frozen), the drainage is poor and this condition has to be corrected if you want a really satisfactory herb garden. The remedy is simple. If the area is not too large, dig out the bed to the depth of twenty inches and supply drainage. The first foot or so of depth is topsoil, frequently good, loamy earth with plenty of soluble minerals and decayed vegetable matter. It may be too clayey and tend to cake and crack. The addition of a few bushels of sand or sifted ashes will improve it tremendously, and give good growing soil for your plants.

Below this layer of topsoil, the subsoil is solid and heavy and must be made porous. You will probably find it easiest to discard a few wheelbarrowfuls of this subsoil, and replace it with gravel or ashes or sand, well worked into the remaining subsoil before the topsoil is put back in place. Then the roots of plants can go down as far as they wish and will not be affected by droughts, while heavy rains will no longer leave a puddle of water to evaporate from the surface but will sink into the soil and help to keep it moist. The soil should be well pulverized, and the clods broken up by a spading fork. If the ground is plowed, it should also be harrowed and afterward gone over with a heavy iron rake.

Of course, in large areas of ground, deep digging is not practiced. The same effect is obtained by deep plowing, frequent cultivation and the use of either drainage ditches or tile drains laid with open joints. Clay that bakes and cracks offers a problem which requires a crop to be chosen suitable for the land, rather than the expense of changing the nature of the soil in order to grow a preferred crop.

For small herb garden spaces, after the soil has been dug out and prepared, the edges of the bed may be kept trim and sharp by a boundary. This may be either sheet iron six inches wide and one-eighth of an inch thick, well coated with graphite or other rust-resisting paint, or boards about four inches wide and seven-eighths thick, well painted with creosote to preserve them. A cheap grade of lumber is suitable, and normally costs about two cents a running foot. The iron edging costs about four times as much.

By the use of either form of edging material, sunk slightly into the ground, one inch for the boards or two inches for the iron, your herb beds may be filled with soil, crowning over from the top of the borders, and thus raised three or four inches. The rectangular shape is most economical for a small space and such shaped raised beds have been in the English tradition from medieval days. Neither peat moss nor any great amount of fertilizer is advised, if herbs are grown for either flavor or fragrance, but if plants are grown merely for garden effect, follow the usual procedure that you have found satisfactory. A few herbs have special requirements which are set forth in the tables.

Along in February slow-germinating seeds must be started indoors—for an early crop of marjoram, or any appreciable growth from lavender or rosemary seeds the first season. If you are not sure your seeds are viable, test them and save time. By the per cent of germination, you will be able to tell whether or not you should sow the seed more thickly than usual. There are many devices to test seeds but they all reduce to the idea of keeping the seed moist and warm for a period of time long enough to insure germination. The simplest device is a brick, set in a pan of water. The top of the brick should project at least an inch and a half above the water. There need be no more than one-quarter to one-half inch of water in the pan, but it must not dry out. Divide the face of the brick into as many sections as you have kinds of seeds to test; put ten seeds in each section. Place the brick in a warm place, and invert a box over it to keep the light out, hold the moisture in, permit air to enter and protect the seeds against accident. The number of seeds that sprout, multiplied by ten, gives the percentage germination and is a guide in their use.

These seeds, if caught just as they sprout, can be planted. Our grandmothers, more economical than we are, put a layer of earth on top of the brick and planted the seeds, thus not only testing the seed but providing for seedlings which, in due time, could be potted and later transplanted to the garden. Nowadays we use flats, shallow boxes of any size convenient for handling. Standard flats, of course, can be purchased. There are flats available, fitted with tiny bricks of pressed peat moss, or similar material, requiring only that you slit each one, drop in a seed, and later the brick is removed and planted in the ground where it crumbles as the plant takes root. Ordinarily, the average gardener sticks to the less expensive flat prepared with earth.

The preparation of a flat for planting seeds is a chore, and once again, warning is given that germination is but a small part. The seedlings must be prevented from damping off, that is, decaying at the surface of the soil because of some fungus effect heightened by the use of excess water or too high a temperature or, rarely, lack of air. The first step to prevent this fungus is careful sterilization, particularly of the soil. There are many compounds available to sterilize both the seed and the soil, and these are essential when seeds are precious. Home gardeners may sterilize the soil or sand for flats by baking from three to four hours and dusting the seeds with any of the preparations sold for the purpose.

The proper soil for flats is equal parts of loam, sand and leaf mold, well mixed and sifted. At the bottom of the flat put drainage material—broken flower pots, gravel, crushed stone or ashes, and many people add a layer of sphagnum moss. Fill the flat with the soil mixture and firm the soil down compactly, leveling it with a board. Soak the flat in water and let it drain for several hours. Mark out shallow rows for the seeds, sow them very thinly and evenly. Thick sowing results in crowded, spindling, leggy seedlings, which are difficult to prick out and transplant. Technically, no seed should be planted at a depth much greater than twice the diameter of the seed. Practically, the best way of covering the seeds is to sift over them a light layer of sand which has been sterilized by pouring boiling water through it. Such a porous covering must be thin but can be more than if soil were used.

Label the flat clearly and cover, preferably with a pane of glass and a newspaper to keep out the light. Glass is not essential for darkness but it retains the moisture, protects the planting and permits inspection by lifting the newspaper. As soon as growth appears, remove the paper to permit light; otherwise the seedlings will be leggy.

It is essential to keep the seeds moist, so that if a glass cover is not used, you may have to soak the flat in water again. Do not attempt to water from the top until there is a distinct row of seedlings. A fine spray between the rows may be used but care must be taken not to overdo the watering. Moderate temperature and freedom from gas fumes are essential, just as with your house plants.

The first two leaves are seed leaves which help to nourish the seedling. When more leaves appear, the seedling can be "pricked out" carefully into another flat prepared just as the first one was. Many gardeners prefer to fill the second flat with nests of paper or wooden forms, each about two inches square. The seedlings are pricked out of the first flat, and each is put into a separate form in the second flat. This form, the equivalent of a pot, can be handled without disturbing the others, and permits the contained seedling to be wrapped for sale or taken to the garden for transplanting.

When the second flat is prepared, remove a small clump of seedlings from the first flat. Use a pointed pencil as a dibble; poke holes about two inches apart in the rows, which also should be about two inches apart. Separate a seedling from the clump, put it in the hole, and firm the earth about the delicate roots, and repeat. Handle the seedling by its first leaves very carefully, and do not let the roots dry out. If you cannot complete the separation and transfer of the whole clump at one session, return the remainder to the first flat and carefully cover it into place. Usually a second transplanting is made into pots or another flat before transplanting to the open ground.

As has been stated before, any of the herb seeds can be started in open ground after danger of frost is over. The only reasons for starting herbs indoors are to have plants ready for the market when spring planting begins or to give slow-germinating plants a start where the growing season is short.

Many perennials come so readily from seed that a small crop is obtained the first year from seed sown out of doors. Catnip, thyme and horehound are striking examples. Most perennial seeds may be planted out of doors late in September; the following spring the seedlings will come up as well established little plants and considerable time will be saved. Those plants which self-sow in the fall will provide spring seedlings which are much stronger and usually finer plants result than from the first sowing. A particular example is borage.

Do not expect to find all the herbs you want in the catalogue of any one seed house or nursery. If you do, it is mere luck that your particular requirements coincide with the assortment that particular firm happens to have available in some one year. Almost any of the larger catalogues lists the herbs commonly used, but the others you will find here and there by exploring many catalogues and by exchange with other herb lovers. The chase is half the fun, and often a grand garden adventure leading to many friendships and pleasures.

Before you buy seeds or plants, learn something about them, not only so that you will select intelligently those that you want but also that you may recognize them when they arrive and be able to correct any errors in the shipment before it is too late. Then, too, by the time the garden is made, you will know what to expect about their height, spread of foliage, and whether they require full sun or part shade. Do not buy packets of mixed seed, either annual or perennial mixtures. The various seedlings will appear at different times, from five days to five weeks after planting, and you will not know one from another. By some certain law, which I call the general cussedness of nature, the large plants will be sure to come up in front of frail little seedlings, or too close to those which cannot be transplanted, such as dill, coriander, fennel or chervil. Some plants will need but slight space between them, as marjoram, or will need a foot or so, as basil. You might just as well mix sunflower, sweet pea, grass and cucumber seeds and expect to be able to sort that mixture, and get good results.

In making the layout of the garden and preparing the beds, give especial care to the area for perennials. That spot will not be dug again, unless you renew the plants some years hence when they become woody, while the beds for annuals will be dug each spring and corrections can be made. If annuals and perennials are planted together, it will be most confusing; as you prepare for the annuals, some perennials may not be above the ground at that time. Keep the annuals markedly separate from them, preferably on the other side of a path or in a section marked off from the perennial bed.

When the time has arrived for sowing, water the beds well and leave them for some hours before planting the seeds. No seed will sprout in dry soil.

As the seed packets are opened, notice how they differ in size, from the long, flat seeds of sweet cicely which take eight months to germinate, to the dark brown, round seeds of garden sage which come up in eight days or so. The depth of planting and amount of covering depend on this difference in size and on the time of sowing. Most people plant too deeply and cover too heavily. Some experts state that the covering should be five times the diameter of the seed, but considering the difference in shapes and the minute size of some seeds, the process of solving this problem would certainly baffle most of us. Also, the nature of the covering, whether heavy soil or porous sand, plays a part. A good general rule is not to cover the small seeds at all but firm them down into the earth with a flat board, and sift only enough earth over the larger ones to be sure they are covered and firm that down with a flat board. Seeds sown in the fall, however, should be well covered, much more heavily than those sown in the spring. All seeds sown in the spring should be protected from the light until they germinate. Newspapers can be used but burlap is best as it stays in place, and the seed bed may be watered through the burlap by a fine spray, if it is necessary because of drought. The thickness of sowing depends, not only on the germination test mentioned, but also on seed size, the larger ones being sown more thickly than the smaller ones.

Seeds slow to germinate—parsley, lemon balm and sweet marjoram—can be hastened in their action by soaking them in lukewarm water for twenty-four hours before sowing. This helps them to start to swell and burst. In general horticultural practice even more drastic measures are taken with some seeds, especially those with a hard, strong shell. They are treated frequently with acid to eat away part of the casing or a notch is filed in them to provide a weak spot and some are even cut into by an emery wheel.

Small seeds are frequently mixed with sand so that they will not be sowed thickly. Some gardeners mix them with radish seeds for the same purpose but with the added advantage that the radishes come up promptly and mark the rows for those seeds which take three or four weeks to germinate. Thus weeds can be kept down between the rows. If you use this method, pull up the radish seedlings when the herbs make their appearance, being careful not to disturb the latter.

Broadcasting, while picturesque at the time, is a poor method for sowing herb seeds because of the difficulty of weeding, particularly if you are not able to recognize the seedlings in their early stages. Seeds sown this way by an amateur are very unevenly distributed, and you cannot help getting clumps of seedlings. The thinning-out process is a great waste, particularly of seedlings which cannot stand transplanting unless they are moved with clumps of earth. It is much better to sow in carefully marked rows which are far enough apart to facilitate weeding and cultivation.

Make a scratch line to mark the row and guide you in placing the seeds. Label each end of the row with the name of the herb and the date of sowing. Then, by help of the germination period, you will know when to expect the appearance of seedlings. If labels are not indelible, slant them to protect the writing so that driving rains will not wash them clear. As a last precaution, make a diagram of the bed and the rows of seeds, marking each row.

As soon as the seedlings show, remove any protective covering. When three or four leaves appear, thin out the row. Pinch off the weaker seedlings at ground level. Remove those to be transplanted, holding down the ground around the others. Some seedlings cannot be transplanted satisfactorily and must be sowed where they are to grow and thinned by pinching off the unwanted plants. Such herbs are anise, chervil, coriander, dill and fennel. The particular requirements of each is given in the tables.

For satisfactory growth, you must discipline the weeds. Do not merely pinch off the tops, but pull them up bodily until each herb plant has a territory of its own. Keep up this weeding at intervals until the plants have grown large enough to touch each other. Then they will keep the weeds down themselves. You will have to be especially diligent at weeding in the beds of slow-growing herbs—anise, caraway, marjoram and parsley.

Those seedlings which will stand transplanting can be handled when the true leaves have appeared—that is, after the fourth leaf has developed. Do the transplanting, if possible, at the end of the day so that the uprooted seedlings, set out in a new location, will have overnight to get adjusted for next day's sun. However, if a cloudy day comes along, use it and gain even more time. It is best to cover newly placed seedlings for three or four days. If you do not have the paper "caps" sold for the purpose, use your ingenuity —strawberry baskets, stiff paper cones, cardboards bent into V-shapes, flower pots and many other possibilities wil present themselves.

The actual transplanting process begins with the preparation of the new bed. Dig the holes for the seedlings, fill them with water; while it is draining away, dig up the seedlings, taking as much soil as possible without disturbing the other seedlings. Place the seedling with its ball of earth into the hole, fill in with soil and firm it strongly into place so as to prevent any air pockets but not so roughly as to break the hairy roots. An hour or so later, water the soil around the transplanted seedlings but do not get water on the leaves. Keep the soil damp until the seedling has taken hold, and the cover is removed permanently. It is a good idea to keep the covers off the plants at night and on cloudy days.

The cultivation of herbs is simple. Loosen the soil every ten days or two weeks, as you weed around the plants, and always after a hard rain as soon as the soil can be worked. Stake the taller plants as soon as they begin to shoot up above a foot high. Tie up clumps of that height by using three or four stakes around the clump and winding the raffia or string around the stakes to form a fence. This will give a better appearing clump than if it is tied to a single stake, and with most herbs, a fence around the one-foot or eighteen-inch mark, will hold the clump during growth. Some of the very tall herbs require stout fences three feet high. Examples are wormwood, tansy, mugwort, elecampane and a few others with heavy foliage which become weighted by the rain.

Do not feel that you must raise all herbs from seed, especially if you are an impatient gardener. Most seeds take from five days to five weeks to germinate but some lie dormant for a year or two, as arnica. It is commonly said that one must not give up hope for seeds until they have been planted two years, and I have found this to be good advice. The best guide, before planting any seed, is to be familiar with its germination period.

In cool geographic sections, lavender and rosemary take from three to five weeks to germinate. If grown from seed they must be started indoors. The plants themselves are normally very slow growing perennials, and will hardly get a start before they are brought indoors again to avoid the chance of frost. If the seed is sown out of doors, the plant is but an inch or two high by frost. Yet, about seventy-five cents buys three small, well rooted plants of either. These will make enough progress the first season so that "slips" or cuttings may be taken, rooted in sand, and a number of much larger and sturdier plants in one season results than could ever be raised from seed.

If and when you buy plants for your garden, be fair to the nursery and kind to your new possessions by treating them intelligently. Do not just drop them in the ground and cover them. Remove them from the pots and examine the tangle of roots wound round and round helplessly. Untangle them so that they can reach out and stretch down into the soil to re-establish themselves. Dip the roots in a pail of lukewarm water and shake them up and down, freeing them of the soil and untangling the mass of roots. Dig the hole for the new plant wide and deep enough to spread the roots out without crowding. Half fill the hole with water and let it drain out. Then, carefully set the plant, spread out the roots, replace the soil, carefully tucking it all around the roots. Firm it down when the hole is two-thirds filled, then fill it up to the crown and press the soil down well, but do not stamp on it or treat it roughly enough to break the roots below. For a day or two, shade the plant from the sun, water the earth about it in the evening and remove the cover until the next morning.

Most perennial herbs need little protection for the winter. Annuals, of course, are all cut down and harvested. As frost approaches, take cuttings from the season's growth to root indoors and pot for the winter. Then cover such plants as may require it. The danger lies in covering the garden too soon. The mice will think you are preparing a winter home for them, and will dig in for the season. The perennials tend to start up a new growth which will be killed when winter really does take hold. Remember that your winter covering is not so much to protect the plants from the cold as it is to preserve an even temperature and to avoid alternate thawing and freezing. Wait until the ground is frozen hard, then cover the plants with straw, salt hay, or any of the purchasable covering materials. Leaves are the most unsatisfactory covering because they bog down in a heavy mass, tend to prevent any circulation of air and cut off all light. Special requirements of individual herbs will be found under the paragraph discussions.

When you think spring has come again, do not be too hasty to remove the winter cover because there is sure to be an unexpected freeze, and this is the time when you stand greatest danger of frost hurting the newly revived plants. Content yourself with lifting up the cover and letting it fall back again lightly. When spring really arrives, take off the cover gradually on cloudy or dark days so that the sun will not burn the new shoots. This is the time when the labels are needed so that you can tell where the perennials are. You may want to transplant or to divide some roots before the late-appearing perennials have shown signs of life, and you may be tempted to put a new plant in what appears to be a bare spot, only to find the roots of a forgotten, unmarked, choice herb.

A variety of labels are important in any good garden and are of the greatest value in maintenance. Besides the small wooden markers for each end of the seed rows, you should have identification labels for mature plants. There are many good commercial labels, none of them perfect, but all with points of value. In England, in the nineties, the Countess of Warwick had made for her garden of sentiment pottery labels in the shape of the two wings of a bird. On one wing was the name of the herb; on the other, the symbolism. For your herb garden, you could have a label giving both the common and the botanical name.

Here at Salt Acres we make our own label, particularly suited to our needs, but much admired and copied in many gardens. The raw materials are what carpenters call "quarter round" and dowel rods. The quarter round is seven-eighths of an inch in size. The cross-section is the same shape as a piece of pie. Two flat sides come to an edge and the third side is rounding. It is cut into five-inch lengths. At the center of the round side, a hole is bored with a three-eighths-inch bit, seven turns after the bit hits the wood. This just brings the point of the bit out at the sharp edge where the two flat sides join. The dowel rods, which are carried by all hardware and lumber dealers, are three-eighths of an inch in diameter, and may be cut twelve inches long for short plants, eighteen for taller ones, up to thirty inches for plants back in the border. They are driven into the bored hole, and when the dowel-rod support goes into the ground, the two flat sides are positioned like the sloping sides of a roof. With drawing ink, black paint or an electric pencil, mark them as you wish. We usually mark both flat sides in bold letters, giving the common name. You might write the common name on one side and the botanical on the other. When, or if, the name becomes blurred, or the label is needed for another plant, plane off the name and a fresh surface is provided for a new one. Soaking the dowel rod in creosote will preserve it for a long period. Even a black pencil printing remains for years if painted over with spar varnish or any of the transparent plastic paints. No hidden crevices provide a place for cocoons, and such labels project well above any winter covering so that they may be seen and not disturbed.

CHAPTER 5

Unusual Herb Plantings

Unusual ways of planting herbs may appeal to you. One is raising several kinds in a strawberry jar. Fill it with a mixture of sandy loam, and in each of the open spaces set in perennial plants or sow seeds of annuals. An advantage of this planting, especially where perennials are used, is that the jar may be brought into the house for the winter and leaves snipped off as they are wanted for culinary dishes, aromatic teas or just for their fragrance. If annuals are used, such as basil, summer savory, chervil, anise or dill, pull up the stalks when they have finished their life cycle, dig up the soil a bit, plant new seeds and have new leaves to pluck. Perennials for the jar might be chives, winter savory, parsley, garden thyme, burnet, apple mint, orange mint, lemon thyme and many others.

An herb barrel is another attractive planting. The ordinary barrel will require a few additional hoops, which may be wire drawn around the barrel and twisted into place. Here and there, just below a hoop, cut through a stave and let it spring out, making a pocket on the side of the barrel. In the bottom of the barrel bore several one-inch holes for drainage. Then, there is a choice of work—either fill the barrel with sandy loam, a layer of stones, broken crockery or sphagnum moss at the bottom, or all three; or provide drainage material at the bottom, and block off the center portion of the barrel by a vertical tube so that you need only soil enough to fill between the tube and the sides of the barrel. The tube may be fashioned from burlap and chicken wire rolled together, or four wide boards nailed together along the edges, or even a smaller barrel, keg or a suitable box. The purpose is to lessen the amount of soil needed and to lighten the barrel. If a keg or box is used as a filler, put the open end down and cover with soil. If earth only is used, insert a pipe, a foot or so in length, for watering, so that the soil

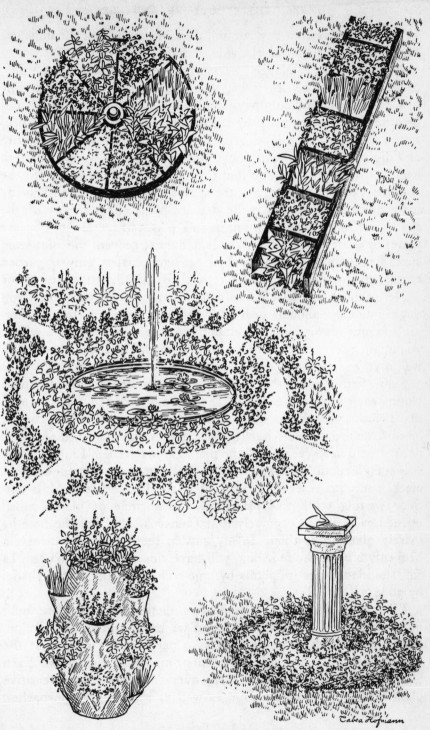

Unusual Herb Plantings

in the center does not dry out and does not absorb all the moisture supplied to the plants in the side pockets.

Another unusual planting is a wheel garden made, preferably, of an old ox-cart or heavy wagon wheel. Plant the wheel with any low growing herbs, but they should not be too bushy or too tall because the divisions made by the spokes will be lost. Choose a protected, sunny spot on level ground, or on a gentle slope. Measure and dig out the circle and prepare the bed, as you would any herb bed. Excavate the center so that the hub sinks in far enough for the rim to set on the ground. Fill the spaces between spokes with sandy loam but let the spokes make definite boundaries. If any of the spaces are to be filled with mints, sink plates of metal—old license plates or sheet iron—around the boundary to prevent the mint from spreading to adjacent beds. You can use parsley, chives, garden thyme, lungwort, dittany of Crete, thrift, dead nettle, orange or apple mint. As the spaces are small enough to dig each year, you might introduce annuals such as dwarf basil, sweet marjoram, chervil, summer savory or any number of others. In place of a wheel, you might prefer an old ladder, or, one made for the purpose, with well marked, tiny beds, easily cared for year after year.

Some herbs, when they flower, are so prompt in opening and closing their blossoms each day, that people in all ages have planted floral clocks, but what is suitable for one country will not, of course, be suitable everywhere. Each gardener embarking on such an enterprise should keep records of the plants in his garden. Linnaeus, the great eighteenth century Swedish botanist, constructed a floral clock, and until recently at least, it was still in existence. His outdoor writing table was placed in a semi-circle of plants which opened each day so regularly that Linnaeus could tell the time by merely glancing at them. In my garden the flowers of chicory, a heavenly blue in the morning, will have closed by half-past ten. In full sun, flax drops its petals by nine o'clock and in partial shade, by noon.

Linnaeus called a group of flowers, meteoric flowers; no doubt many of them are known to us and we have noticed their action. Scarlet pimpernel, for instance, is so persistent in closing at the approach of rain that it is called poor-man's weather glass. Each leaf on the wild senna plant turns over and closes like a sensitive plant when it is going to rain, as well as when night approaches.

The dandelion blossom opens at a definite time in the morning, and the stalks of the downy globe contract in wet weather.

As a hobby, you might try an arrangement of plants that tell time and those that predict the weather. Most of the plants will be herbs, but they lie outside the rigid boundaries of this book for very few of them are now raised for utilitarian purposes.

One of the prettiest beds that can be made with herbs is the gray bed, a garden of green-gray or all gray foliage. It is especially striking on a summer night and, of course, is most effective in the midst of any garden or stretch of lawn. The edging could be beach wormwood and just back of it, dittany of Crete or Roman wormwood. To produce height in the bed, set a plant of great mullein in the center with common wormwood near by. Other plants suitable for this bed are senecio, two and a half feet high with finely cut, branching foliage, gray santolina, spike and true lavender and western mugwort. Then, there are the grayish green plants, such as horehound, houseleek, marsh mallow, garden sage and cardoon, which is quite gray but requires considerable room.

A bed of herbs with blue flowers would be so cool looking that it would be a never-ending delight through the whole season. From spring to autumn some blue herb flowers are in bloom. An edging of bugle-weed with bronzy leaves and blue flowers in spring would be pleasing. The Borage Family have the characteristic that their flowers open a beautiful rose and change to heavenly blue, from the low-growing lungwort, through the anchusas and borage itself to the taller comfrey. The five-foot high chicory has the clearest blue flowers while blue flag, speedwell, cornflower, larkspur and aconite provide many shades of deep blue.

A bee garden would be a novelty for the gardener in search of something new. After you learn the herbs favored by the bees, your imagination and ingenuity will help to form a most delightful garden. A hedge of blue-flowered hyssop might enclose this garden which will swarm with bees from morning to night. In my hedge of hyssop the bees sleep in summer, all tucked down compactly as I stroll through the garden in the late evening. There could be an inner hedge of germander with its deep rose-colored flowers, or the very appropriate bee balm with deep red flower heads or one of winter savory. Near the hives, use some tall-growing plants to set them off, such as fennel, daphne, yellow melilot, and in front of the hives plant lemon balm, sweet cicely and a few low-growing herbs. Other plants beloved of bees are borage, bugloss, marjoram, thyme and lavender.

CHAPTER 6

The Culinary Garden

For delectable dishes you will want to use many culinary herbs or "sweet herbs" as they were called by John Worlidge in his *Art of Gardening,* 1677, and by all the later gardening writers.

These sweet herbs, and I do like the name better than the modern matter-of-fact expression, culinary herbs, include the mints, sage, sweet marjoram, summer and winter savory, sweet fennel, sweet basil and many others.

Besides the sweet herbs which are used mostly for seasoning, there are potherbs such as chicory, white mustard, Good King Henry, which are cooked as vegetables like spinach; and then there are a group of salad herbs such as samphire, nasturtium, lemon balm and others used uncooked in green salads. For each of these groups one could have a special bed, yet many of each group will be found in both the others as you will see by the various tables. It depends on how you wish to use the herbs. If you plan one plot, you might have companion plots for the other two and one for herb teas, to which each of the three other beds contribute. There is no hard and fast line to be drawn between the plots. If you were to make a garden of medicinal herbs used today, as formerly, you would include all four, as well as the fragrant garden and almost all the flower garden.

Have your garden of sweet herbs near the kitchen door, and plan one day to have on the other side an herb tea-garden. The proximity to the kitchen will mean more than you think. When you need but a sprig or two, especially on a rainy day, the temptation will be to go without rather than take a long trip to the vegetable garden, and your cooking will suffer. That sprig or two is necessary to make your dish a masterpiece.

The garden should be in a sunny place or, at least, part sun and must have good drainage, as discussed in a previous chapter. If the

33

culinary herbs cannot be grown near the door, perhaps you can find a small space in the flower border. A half-dozen of each of the plants you choose will take care of the average family's needs. If you wish a larger crop of some one herb, such as basil, fill in some unused space with seeds of that herb. In general, twenty kinds of sweet herbs will give a fine selection, and what beauty and fragrance they will bring to any garden.

For the border, if you plant the herbs two rows deep, put the tall ones—lovage, dill and fennel—back of the lower growing ones. If there is not so much room, the taller herbs may be put in the back of the border, the lower in front.

If you have a small sweet herb garden, arrange the individual plots so as to form a perfect rectangle, and separate the plots by gravel or with an edging of garden thyme, parsley or such thymes as *T. Zygis* or *T. azoricus,* both making soft mounds of vivid green and having a fruity taste. In cool climates these thymes are not likely to be hardy, but they are beautiful for the season and when well protected sometimes come through a winter.

Have one central path through the garden leading to a focal point marked by a sundial, an old-fashioned, straw bee skep, or perhaps a clump of one of the taller perennial herbs which is not cut down when harvested, sweet fennel, for example. If the garden has many plots, you should have cross paths wide enough for convenience in working among the plants.

If the beds are on the ground level, the division between beds and paths can be made by any of the same herbs to separate the plots in the small garden. If the beds are raised, a row of parsley just inside the metal or wood boundary will give a beautiful vivid green line. The paths themselves may be sowed with Roman chamomile, known in recent years as English chamomile. It may be rolled and clipped and is soft as chenille. Stepping stones or brick can be used. At Salt Acres we have used a base of oyster shells well tamped into place and have covered them with a layer of bluestone. This gives a dry path at all times which is a main requirement of garden paths. Chamomile and thyme paths, just as grass paths, must be permitted to dry out before using.

For the boundary of this garden of sweet herbs, there are several delightful possibilities. There might be a wall, a low fence of white pickets, of woven cedar, or of wire lattice, a light rail fence in

A Decorative Herb Garden

An Attractive Kitchen Garden

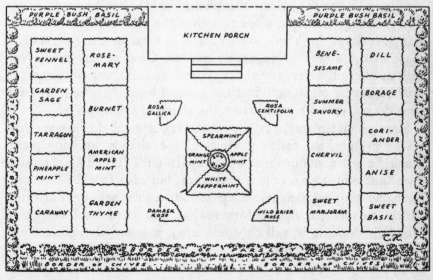

natural color; or you might have a hedge of sweet basil, either the green or purple variety. Pinch out the tops as they come into bud and you will have sturdy bushes which will help thicken the hedge.

After the size of the garden, the layout, and the number of varieties to be planted have been determined, comes the exciting task of collecting seeds or plants. Since French tarragon does not produce seeds, plants will have to be bought but they can be increased by root division in the spring. Commercial growers dig up the plants in the fall after the foliage has been harvested, and cut the roots into short pieces. Each piece potted will produce a plant, and next spring these may be set out to grow into substantial clumps. Any tarragon seed you buy will be the annual Russian variety, considered unpleasant in odor and in taste.

I would not raise chives or mint from seed, unless for the adventure. Clumps of chives are inexpensive and each spring can be divided into many little plants, leaving only three or four bulblets together. As for most varieties of mint, one root set in the ground soon presents the problem of how to keep it from taking possession of the garden. One or two rosemary plants will produce a large number of cuttings before another year, and since the seed germinates so slowly, an initial purchase of plants is advisable. I would raise the other herbs from seed planted in the open ground when there is no further danger of frost. Be sure to label carefully, recording the date of planting so you will know when to expect seedlings to appear. Keep the plants weeded and remember the slow-growing ones need more care than the others. If there are too many seedlings for the space, transfer the excess to any available space in the flower or vegetable garden. Certain herbs, however, such as chervil, anise, coriander, fennel and dill, should simply be thinned out by pinching off at the ground level, for their root systems do not recover easily from the shock of transplanting.

Since annual plants, for the most part, are cut down when harvested in July, successive sowings of the already growing plants should be made, about three weeks apart, until July. This should be done, not only to prevent a bare spot, but also to provide plenty for harvesting, particularly of basil and summer savory. Each time enrich the soil sparingly before sowing, and when much cutting of foliage is done, it is well to mix a small amount of fertilizer into the soil about the roots.

When the flower heads of the chives are past, cut the coarse flower stalks to the ground. Thyme, spreading too far, may be clipped, but mints must be restrained by old license plates or other sheet metal sunk into the ground just inside the boundary lines of the mint beds and they will turn back effectively the underground runners. Each spring harrow the mint beds. For small beds an effective way is to use a sharp edging tool or a sharp spade, and chop down into the mint bed, turning the tool at various angles, so as to cut up the mint roots underground. After thoroughly soaking the bed, cover with a layer of enriched top soil, not manure. At each cut you will get a stalk, and will have a fine, thick bed of mint, instead of a straggly mass of twisted runners clogging up the bed.

Look at the culinary garden diagram; you will find thyme and sweet marjoram in front and opposite each other. They grow but ten inches high and make good companion plants. At the left of the thyme is caraway which forms a beautiful emerald-green rosette of fernlike leaves the first year, then rises to eighteen inches the second year when the seeds are harvested. At the right of sweet marjoram is sweet basil, about a foot high when mature. Be sure to pinch out the budding tops of the basil which not only makes it a bushier, prettier shrub but also gives more foliage to use fresh or dried. Chervil grows to about twelve inches and needs some shade. Instead of planting it in shady ground, it is better grown in the sun, in the shade of taller plants. Anise is rather decumbent in habit but not enough for the delicate white umbels to touch the ground. It is a slow-growing plant but in Southern New England sets seed well before frost. It is a doubtful crop for more northern latitudes. A bed of chives is indicated, and it also makes a colorful border. Mints are "must" plants but do grow more than one variety. Orange mint and the American golden apple mint are wonderfully fragrant and a pleasing change from the usual spearmint or lamb mint.

Two plants of French tarragon are enough for a bed eighteen inches square. Bene, usually called sesame, even in the northern states will develop a seed pod which produces innumerable seeds. This plant is the same as Ali Baba's brother forgot when he had to say the password "Open, sesame," in order to get out of the cave. Coriander is a most evil-smelling plant, but do raise it because the seeds are very fragrant when ripe, and the older they become, the more fragrant they are. Garden sage has gray-green pebbly leaves and, no doubt, you already have had it in your garden and know the virtue of its freshly dried leaves. Burnet is a bushy plant with finely toothed leaves tasting of cucumber, and grows eighteen inches high. Cut the heads off after flowering or it will self-sow in all near-by beds.

Summer savory has half-inch long slender leaves and when it is in bloom looks as though it had been covered with a light fall of pinkish white snow. Borage, with hairy gray-green leaves, has loosely formed clusters of starlike flowers, rose-colored when first open then turning to a clear blue. The flowers are often candied.

For the background of the beds, have all tall plants. Get a plant of sweet bay (*Laurus nobilis*), set it in a tub or pot, and sink it into the bed. It is tender and in cold climates must be taken in for the winter. Each time you move a plant, you may retard its growth, so many good gardeners keep tender plants, such as sweet bay, in pots all year around even though this keeps them from reaching their normal height. On the two opposite outer beds, sweet or wild fennel and dill would make good companion plants, both with yellow-green foliage and large umbels of yellow flowers. In the center of the back, place a few handsome plants of lovage whose leaves taste like celery and when dried and powdered, make an excellent celery salt.

CHAPTER 7

Fragrant Herb Garden

Only in recent years has the cosmetic industry become one of the leading industries of the country but the desire to have sweet odors about us goes back to ancient times. One of the most soul-satisfying of all gardens is that filled with "herbs of a good smell." There are few gardens more pleasing to the senses, and the fragrant garden may be the most profitable, if you desire to make a little pin-money from herbs, either from the sale of plants or from their fragrance packaged in pillows, sachets, sweet bags and potpourri.

You will be greatly enriched by the time you devote learning to discriminate among herb odors. As your interest grows, you will notice differences of which previously you had been unaware. How distinct are the odors of sweet wormwood, pungent santolina, the lavenderish, first whiff of orange mint and camphor plant! You will be amazed how different some of the same herbs smell in separate parts of the garden, in dry soil and moist, in poor soil and rich, in the morning, at noon or at night. Some have one perfume during the day, another at night.

Sick friends will appreciate fragrant tussie-mussies, those tight little nosegays meant to be carried. When made of herbs, they will be doubly acceptable because the heat of the hands in holding them or bruising the leaves releases the volatile oils of the herbs and increases the fragrance. These aromatic bouquets are most refreshing in the sick room, and help to make a room seem cooler on a sultry summer day. They not only last longer than flowers but have proven antiseptic and germicidal qualities, much stronger in the essential oils of leaves than in flowers, for the oils of the latter are released too quickly to have lasting effects. Eucalyptol, recognized as an antiseptic, is found in practically all aromatic leaves. Other oils with antiseptic properties are found in thyme, used from ancient days as a disinfectant, in lemon verbena, lavender, rosemary

39

and rue. In the first World War, herbs were much used to ward off vermin and burned to fumigate hospitals.

Herbs offer great possibilities for beautiful flower arrangements since they have so many shades and tints of color in their flowers, innumerable tones and textures of foliage, and delightful combinations of pleasing odors. Bouquets of aromatic herbs are enjoyed especially in hospitals for the blind. The gay colors of the many-hued flowers cannot be appreciated, but the sense of smell is sharpened and fine qualities of odors missed by many of us are appreciated by them. Odors and textures are Nature's way of writing beauty in Braille.

However you make this fragrant garden, let it be a retreat, distinctly yours, different from any other garden. If area permits, nothing contributes more to this end than a roofed-over summerhouse, covered with climbing roses. Plant the most fragrant herbs near the summerhouse, herbs chosen according to your preferences. Let this be your personality expressed in fragrance. Certain herbs you will want because a whiff of them will take you back through the years to some emotional experience, some scene you love to remember.

In an old town along the New England coast is one of the most restful walled herb-gardens I have seen. On each side of the central path are rectangular beds, faithful to the tradition of ancient gardens. It is a tussie-mussie garden, fragrant with rosemary, lavender, lemon verbena, costmary, meadowsweet, all of these not only herbs in the utilitarian sense but also old-time garden favorites.

The paths through the fragrant herb garden may be of brick or crazy flagstones, the spaces between filled with topsoil and planted perhaps with caraway thyme. It makes a fragrant carpet reminiscent of the custom in Oriental countries where lime, lemon and orange leaves are placed under the mat at the door of a home so that as a visitor steps to the door volatile oils are released and perfume the air.

For an informal edging along the path, you might use perennial winter savory, with long-lasting flowers like a fall of lilac-colored snow, sprawling over the sharp edges of the raised beds. Another choice is calamint with light purple blossoms; a third one is annual dwarf green or purple basil which needs no trimming after the tops have been pinched out. Then there are pennyroyals, the sprawling English variety or the upright American pennyroyal; both kinds have a pungent, minty odor. You might prefer perennial garden thyme or tender sweet marjoram.

Whatever you use along the edging, directly back of it you will want a row of spicy, clovelike, annual sweet basil which may be green or purple leaved, and then the lavenders—the spike, the French and the true lavender. You must have the acrid rue with lacy, blue-green leaves, pungent red yarrow, white yarrow, gray-green sage with pebbly leaves, true French tarragon with odor and taste of anise, salad burnet with a taste and smell of cucumber, pot marjoram, yellow melilot, sweet maudlin and feverfew with its pungent balls of white blossoms. Add to these a plant or two of santolina with flowers of lemon-colored balls a half-inch in diameter, and then the mints—apple, orange, peppermint, all refreshing in odor.

Taller plants will be placed as high spots at intervals to break the level of the garden. You will want bushes of the apothecaries' rose, the cabbage rose, the Kazanlik rose, and here and there the lemony southernwood trimmed vigorously to shape it to your needs. Height will be given by clumps of red bee balm. Other tall herbs are sweet wormwood with feathery foliage and sweet mugwort with tiny white flowers formed in loose panicles. Then there are the tropical looking angelica and lovage, tansy, valerian (garden heliotrope) with panicles of light rosy flowers, and tender pineapple sage with vivid red flowers which appear just before frost.

Among other fragrant plants you must choose warm, piny rosemary, tender lemon verbena, hardy lemon balm and minty costmary often known as Bible leaf. Erect myrtle, tender in cool climates, has a most delicate odor, tiny cream-white blossoms and glossy dark green leaves. Annual dill with its finely cut leaves and yellow umbels is a good foil for tall sweet fennel, which also has yellow umbels and feathery foliage. You will enjoy meadowsweet, Jerusalem oak (ambrosia) and sweet cicely.

Last, but not least in this fragrant garden in some shady spot, you will want sweet woodruff, which is not fragrant in the living plant but smells like new mown hay when dried and used in potpourri. It is an excellent ground cover. We must not forget the bladelike leaves of sweet flag which can be pressed and used in winter bouquets while the root can be dried for your potpourri.

CHAPTER 8

Indoor Herb Gardens

Even if you are an apartment dweller without benefit of an outdoor garden, you can have herbs growing in your windows to use in fragrant teas or culinary dishes. For teas you will want rosemary, lemon verbena, lemon balm, garden and lemon thyme, sage, sweet marjoram, fennel, parsley, dill and peppermint.

With the exception of lemon verbena, lemon balm and peppermint, which you may use in finger bowls as a change from the rose geranium leaf, you can use all of these tea herbs in making delicious culinary dishes. You will also want to grow sweet basil (both the green and purple varieties), chives, chervil, tarragon, summer savory, orange and apple mint.

Your first problem is to decide upon the containers, either window boxes on the sills or pots on shelves in the windows. You may be assured that the useful herbs mentioned are so decorative that you need not confine them to the kitchen. You can, of course, buy window boxes, preferably those with false bottoms arranged for drainage. Any other kind will require a thick layer of stones or pebbles in the bottom to permit surplus moisture to lie below the soil. These standard window boxes may not fit the measurements of your window space, but boxes made to order are inexpensive. They may be arranged to stand on the sills, to hang from them on simple brackets, or an extension shelf may be built out from the window sill. The shelf or brackets will be inconspicuous if painted to match the woodwork. An advantage of made-to-order boxes is that you can have handles attached which makes lifting more convenient. The box can be made smaller—perhaps four inches wide and five inches deep and the length half the window width—and a second box nesting with the first fills the window sill. It is not an easy matter to juggle a full length window box filled with soil and plants, but it is essential now and then to turn the box around to let the sun get directly to the other side.

Another convenient way of housing indoor herbs is in pots, and setting the pots in tin trays. These trays may be the full window width, painted the color of the woodwork, and not less than three inches deep so that the pots can be set on a thick layer of pebbles. Keep water in the tray at all times, but do not let it reach the pots. Evaporation keeps the air around the plants moist and helps to prevent the pots from drying out. Give the pots a thorough soaking once a week by setting them in a pan of water, and water them frequently from the top.

A third way to handle plants indoors is to have glass shelves attached to the sides of the window frame on brackets located so that the window may be opened on mild days. Have the shelves spaced so that the taller herbs will have room, and the top shelf not so high but that it is reached readily. The plants will be in pots set in saucers; several commercial designs are available that permit constant moisture, and yet provide drainage, or they may be deep enough to hold a layer of pebbles.

You will be faced always with the problem that some plants are taller than others, but do not try to place them artistically with the taller plants next to the window. They make a fine background for the smaller plants nearer the room, but they shade the small ones too much. Just as satisfying effects are obtained by grouping the tall plants on one or both sides of the window, or choosing one window for tall plants and others for smaller plants.

A fourth way of taking care of herbs indoors is to use a branching stand, such as is frequently used for pots of ivy or ferns. This is attractive near any window, especially a bay window, supplemented perhaps by pots on glass shelves in the window itself. The more graceful of them may be arranged to give the effect of trees in leaf all winter.

A satisfactory soil is composed of three parts good loam, one part sand, and one part fertilizer or compost. You can have a florist make up the mixture or you can buy his prepared potting soil. In the latter case, have sand added to it because the florist's soil is mixed for flowers which take richer and stiffer soil than that preferred by most herbs. Be sure all the elements are thoroughly mixed. Put a layer of broken pots or small stones in the bottom of the window box or the various pots before filling them.

Four-inch pots are satisfactory for most herbs, unless you have picked out large plants. A few herbs, tarragon, lemon balm, chives and the mints may fit better in a five-inch pot. Some of the herbs, such as rosemary, will do better when young if somewhat pot-bound. While dill normally grows to a height of three feet out of doors and fennel may grow a foot or two higher, as house plants they readily adapt themselves and become dwarfed. You can snip the foliage continually and even pinch back the tops, if you find it desirable. They make a beautiful, lacy border for a window box.

In planting a window box, do not crowd the plants together. Give each one plenty of room to spread. Every few days the boxes should be turned to expose the other side to the sun. Turn the pots, too, or if they are in trays that are not too heavy, it may be convenient to turn the whole tray. Do not over-water the plants, but do not let them dry out, and remember to soak the pots every week or ten days by allowing them to take up water from the bottom. Sprinkle the leaves now and then to clean them because the plants breathe through their leaves, but do not let the sun strike them while they are still wet. Whenever possible give the plants fresh air, but be careful to avoid a cold draft. The air of the room should be freshened every day.

If you are bringing in plants from your garden, do not wait until too late in the fall. An unexpected frost may overtake them. As early as late August in some parts of New England, a sudden cold night has wilted basil. But for most herbs middle or late September is a normal time to pot them. However, they will adjust themselves better if they are potted in advance, and left outdoors in a shady place for a few days before moving them inside. Pot the mints at the same time but leave them outside until after a frost. Then bring them in.

Inside, as outside, tarragon and chervil can stand some shade. Tarragon will stand a heavier soil than any of the other pot plants. The annuals, of course, must not be allowed to flower if they are going to be brought in, but usually it is more satisfactory to sow seeds for a new crop of these plants indoors. I have kept plants of basil brought in from the garden until late January. Sweet marjoram is really a perennial, and will live through the winter if brought into the house. Dill presents a simple problem as it goes to seed early in the season and from these seeds, new seedlings are well advanced by September.

Herbs will take more punishment than what we call flowers, but even they rebel at high temperatures and desert dryness, such as are found in many homes. While sunny windows are preferable, you will have more success in any window where the heat and dryness are a minimum. Frequently, a well lighted entry or an upstairs room has advantages, and for a comparatively small sum, you can buy a window greenhouse whereby your plants are glassed in from the air of the room, except as it circulates through and is moistened from water in the compartment. Such devices are frequently provided with an electric heating cable to take care of freezing nights when the house temperature drops. Since you are not trying to force blooms, it is essential only to keep the herbs from freezing.

CHAPTER 9

Harvesting and Drying

Gathering the crop is one of the most pleasant parts of herb gardening, whether roots, seeds, leaves, flowers or the whole herb. All summer you have enjoyed the herbs fresh and fragrant from the garden. Now you will preserve the flavor and the fragrance for use during the winter. In most sections of the country, August is the big season for the harvest of foliage herbs which constitutes the bulk of your crops—horehound, basil, sage, marjoram, lemon balm, catnip, chervil, tarragon, summer and winter savory, the mints and the thymes.

There is a right time for harvesting the herbs, when they contain the maximum amount of essential oils on which the flavor and fragrance depend. That moment is just when the buds open into full flower. Some plants even increase the amount at that time, though the mints are richest in oils when they come into full flower. If you delay, you not only will have lost much of the essential oils, but will have lost the plant as well. You must finish the cutting process early enough in the season so that the plants will grow up at least a foot or two before frost in order to prevent winter-killing. Some plants such as thyme, sage and catnip after the first year, yield two crops if one is taken in July and the other in September.

On a dry morning, after the dew has gone but before the sun is high enough to take away the oils, cut the perennial plants with their side branches about two-thirds of the way down the stalk, and cut the annuals leaving three or four inches for a second growth. Keep each herb separate from the rest by label and position throughout the drying process, in fact until each herb is in its carefully labeled jar, because when dried the herbs look quite different from the green plants.

Spread out the leafy stalks and branches on a table, pick off the decayed, rusted or yellowed leaves and remove the coarse, heavy base ends. Rinse off any dirt or sand from branches that have lain too close to the ground, but do not soak them.

There are two methods of drying herbs. One is to strip the fresh leaves from the stalks and spread them in a thin layer on drying screens, such as house-window screens covered with cheesecloth and propped up on chairs or legs to permit a good circulation of air all around them. It is important to have air under the drying leaves as well as over them. This process is excellent for short stemmed herbs such as thyme, but in this instance the whole herb may be laid on the screen instead of stripping the tiny fresh leaves from the wiry little stems.

You can dry the leaves out of doors during the day in the shade where there is a gentle current of air, but it is best to cover them with cheesecloth to keep them from blowing away if a strong breeze comes up. The screens should be brought in at night before the dew falls. Turn the leaves once a day so that the air reaches each leaf. The herbs must be dried as quickly as possible in very little sun, in order to retain the volatile oils and the original green color of the leaves. In dry weather about three or four days should be sufficient.

The drying process consists, of course, in removing the moisture from the leaves. One of the best drying spots is an attic with cross-ventilation, little sun and no dust to be stirred up and over the leaves by the breeze. When the attic has become thoroughly heated for the summer, it is likely to stay at an almost even temperature, and there is no bother about bringing in the screens each night nor fear that they may be caught in a sudden summer shower when no one is about to bring them indoors. Label each screen.

Oven drying for most people is a poor method because it is difficult to regulate the temperature so that it will not become too hot and evaporate the oils, scorch and discolor the leaves. If the weather turns damp after the herbs have begun drying, it may be necessary to finish the drying in the oven. In that case, lay the leaves on a baking sheet, keep the oven at a low heat (about 250 degrees) with the door open. In commercial drying a large heated room is often used, with clean, warm air at the desired temperature, often surprisingly low but the air very dry so that it will absorb quickly the moisture of the leaves. Dehydration of the leaves is done commercially by refrigeration, especially of succulent material, such as chives which cannot be dried otherwise.

The second method of drying is tying the leafy stems into small bundles and hanging them on cords stretched across the attic or any room with little sun and a good cross-circulation of air. Again, be sure to label carefully. This is the best method for leafy foliage, and is always the method when the whole herb is to be dried. The drying will take about a week. In using this method, as with screens, the leaves must be thoroughly and crackly dry before the next step is taken, or they will mold and the quality will be poor.

There is an old-fashioned quick and very satisfactory method for drying mints, parsley and the foliage of dill and fennel. Strip the foliage from the stems, dip the leaves into boiling, salted water just long enough to wilt the leaves, and lift them out with a strainer. Shake off the water and spread the leaves on a fine wire-mesh sieve laid on a large pan or baking sheet. Pop them into a medium hot oven with the door open for five or ten minutes, and then rub the crisp dry leaves through a sieve to powder them.

The Italians usually preserve the leaves of their basil, which is the curly basil, by packing them down in a crock, alternating a layer of leaves with a layer of salt. When the cook uses them, she simply shakes the salt off the leaves required. The Italians also preserve the leaves in a crock by pouring pure olive oil over them, but it must be the pure oil.

After the herbs are dried so that the green color and volatile oils are retained, they must be stored carefully. When the leaves dried on a screen are as crisp as fresh corn flakes, they may be rubbed through a sieve to powder them, if they are to be used in cooking, or be left whole if to be used in teas.

If the herbs have been dried in bunches, take them down carefully. It is important to keep the various herbs separate and not to leave any bunches hanging after they are crisply dry. It may be picturesque, but it is unsanitary because of dust and insects, and fragrant oils are lost from prolonged hanging. Lay a sheet on the floor to catch any leaves that fall, and be sure not to mix in scattered leaves that have fallen from bunches of other herbs.

Lay the bunches in a pan or basket, together with the fallen leaves from the sheet. You may, of course, keep the bunches tied up and stored in a large tightly closed container, stripping the leaves only as you use them. I prefer, however, to strip them before storing, holding the stem in one hand and stripping off the leaves with the other, which should be covered with a glove. Then, as before, rub the culinary herbs through a coarse sieve, but keep whole those leaves to be used in teas. Do not store the dried leaves in paper bags or cardboard boxes because dampness will get in and the oils will be lost, partly by escape and partly by being absorbed by the paper. If the herb is woody or has tiny leaves, such as thyme, summer and winter savory, you need not strip them but put them, not only the leaves but also the stems (which contain much oil), through a meat grinder, using the coarsest wheel.

You can express yourself in the attractive inexpensive jars in which you store your crop and in the labels, perhaps your own design, maybe a drawing of your favorite herb. Although the herbs are in their containers, watch them for about a week, and if you see any signs of moisture on the inside of the jars, it means that the leaves are not thoroughly dry and that they will mold unless steps are promptly taken. Pour them out and dry them for three or four more days, depending on the weather, and turn frequently until the leaves are crackly dry. Then return them to the jars and cover tightly.

If your herb shelf is sunny, your crop must be stored in opaque jars or the sun's rays will fade the leaves. If the shelf is in the shade or dark, glass jars will be just the right containers to show the beautiful greens that only carefully home dried herbs have. However, with all herbs, most of the oils will evaporate within two or three years, so do not go on using the herbs of one harvest indefinitely. It is better to share your crop with others, retaining enough to carry you over a poor harvest year if one should come.

Perhaps you will want to dry the roots of some herbs, such as lovage, angelica, comfrey, sweet flag and Florentine iris (orris root). The drying of roots requires more time and care than other plant parts because they are so fleshy. The roots should be dug in the fall when the growing season is over or early in the spring while they are still dormant. At these times the root cells are filled completely with plant food. If roots are dug at other times they will shrink greatly.

Spade up roots and wash them thoroughly, by placing them on a wire screen and hosing them. Scrape them if necessary to remove any dirt. Large roots are sliced or split, spread in thin layers on wire screens so that air can pass over and under them, and the slices must be turned two or three times a week so that they dry evenly. The screens may be set out of doors during the day and brought in at night. After the roots are partly dry, combine the contents of several screens and the drying may be hastened by putting the screen in the oven at a very low heat. Keep the door open to let the moisture escape. If you use a coal stove, the screens may be kept on the back of it. The drying takes from three to six weeks; the test of complete dryness is for a root slice to break with a snap when it is bent. Store in containers that can be tightly closed because most roots are attacked readily by insects.

The seed harvest takes about two weeks. The herbs grown for their savory seeds are dill, anise, caraway, coriander, fennel, cumin, bene (sesame), poppy and sometimes mustard. All are harvested and dried the same way. When the seeds are brown and the stalks dried-looking, cut off the seed heads. Do not wait too long or the seeds will drop, particularly coriander seeds which are so heavy that they drop quickly. The best method of collecting them is to spread paper in a basket and cut the umbels or seed pods directly into the basket. Then spread them in a thin layer on a heavy cloth or canvas laid on the floor of a well-ventilated, warm room for five or six days, or use your drying screens covered with cheesecloth. Thresh gently to remove the seeds from pods or stems, being careful not to bruise the seeds. This process is best done out of doors where there is a good breeze to carry off the chaff. If the crop is small, rub the umbels or pods between the palms of your hands. Put the seeds in a sieve fine enough to hold them but coarse enough to pass the fine particles of stems. Spread the seeds on the cloth-covered, drying screen for a week or ten days longer, turning them frequently. Store the seeds in jars but watch for signs of moisture within the jars for a week or two.

A harvest of herb flowers, such as chamomile, lavender, calendula and safflower, may be made. Chamomile flower heads are gathered when in full bloom. Cut off the heads and spread them thinly on a drying screen covered with cheesecloth. Only the yellow part of the flower contains the essential oils, although commercially the whole flower is powdered and sold. After the heads are well dried, they may be rubbed through a sieve until the green part of the calyx begins to show.

Harvest the flower heads of lavender when the blossoms are opened to the middle of it and the top shows color. Cut them in the morning just after the dew is off, and spread them on a cloth-covered screen in a shady room with cross-ventilation. Keep moist heat away from them, and when dry, strip the stalks.

The orange floret rays of calendula are the parts used for coloring matter or flavoring. Remove the florets, spread on a covered drying screen so that they do not touch, and dry in the shade since it is necessary to keep the color. The florets of safflower and the stigmas of saffron are the essential parts and they are treated as calendula florets. All of these flower parts, when dried, are stored in tightly closed containers, but keep watch for signs of moisture.

CHAPTER 10

Herb Dyes

Many herbs produce such fine colors that they are used for coloring and dyeing. *Anemone Pulsatilla,* pasque flower, temporarily imparts a green color to paper and linen, and in early days was used in Russia to color Paschal or Easter eggs. Hollyhock blossoms are used in volumetric analyses. Alkannin or anchusin paper for acid-alkaline tests is made by impregnating white paper with a one per cent alcoholic tincture of alkanet root and drying it. The paper is then red, but will turn blue or green when put in an alkaline solution. Acids will turn it red again. We know also that solutions of alkanet root, because of its red color, are used to color leather, marble, wood, pomades and wax in dentistry. The roots of madder and lady's bedstraw supply a red vegetable coloring for home use. Although madder is used commercially as a dye, the roots of bedstraw are so small that the plant is not practical for large-scale use.

Safflower with its yellow and red stamens is used as an adulterant of saffron, coloring matter for candy and cosmetics, such as rouge and lipstick. Flowers of calendula and lady's bedstraw supply a yellow color for butter and cheese. The brilliantly yellow saffron buns, famous in England, owe their name and color to that herb. Many wines and liqueurs are colored with the juice of vegetables such as beets and with herbs such as parsley, violet petals, saffron, alkanet root and elderberries.

Most of us have made a magenta-colored ink by pressing ripe pokeberries through a sieve and straining the juice through cheesecloth. The ink can be kept from spoiling by adding one teaspoon carbolic acid to a pint of the juice, or two tablespoons vinegar and two teaspoons salt to the same amount. To give the ink an agreeable odor, add a decoction of bergamot, lemon verbena or any other strong-smelling herb, two tablespoons to a pint of ink. The expressed juice of blue cornflower is used with alum water for making a water color drawing dye. The root of yellow flag has so much tannin in it that it has often been used instead of galls in making ink.

Many herbs give satisfactory coloring matter for dyeing, although most of them are not of commercial importance; yet it would be an amusing experiment to see what colors could be obtained.

A fixative (or mordant as it is technically called) is essential in the dyeing process not only to hold the colors fast so they will not fade or wash out, but in some cases to bring out the color. Alum is the mordant generally used with cream of tartar added to brighten the color, since alum alone does not affect it. Copperas (iron sulphate) is much used as a mordant for wool and cotton, and often it is added to the dye-bath after the material has been boiled for a time; the boiling is continued for fifteen to twenty minutes longer. Stannous chloride is rarely used alone but with other mordants. It has a tendency to harden wool but brightens the colors and makes them more permanent than do other mordants. Potassium chromate leaves the wool very soft, but the procedure is difficult since the dye-bath containing the material must not be exposed to the air during the process. With cream of tartar, copper is sometimes used to mordant the material before dyeing.

Wool yarn is the easiest kind of material for your experiments. Silk is dyed by about the same method as wool, but the mordant and dye-baths are kept at a lower temperature. Often the silk is simply soaked in a strong cold solution of the mordant. Cotton and linen are quite difficult to dye because the fibers do not absorb the dyestuff without quite a complicated preparation. Certain dye material, barberry bark and safflower, will give a fast color to cotton without the use of mordants. Otherwise, cottons and linens are first boiled in an astringent solution such as tannic acid. When the mordant is added the acid helps the fibers of the material to take in the coloring matter, and makes the color more brilliant.

Herb dyes are prepared by making a strong decoction of the part of the herb to be used—seeds, flowers, berries or leaves bruised, or stems, bark or roots cut up finely. Be sure to have enough liquid so that the material is completely immersed, simmer for about two or three hours or until all the color has been extracted from the herb. The utensils must be non-corroding, such as unchipped enamel kettles and spoons.

There are four methods of dyeing wool. The simplest way is to boil the wool in the mordant and then in the dye-bath, or add the mordant to the dye-bath after the material has been saturated with the coloring matter. Another way is to add the mordant to the dye-bath at the beginning and boil the wool in the mixture, and although the color is not so fast, the color in some cases is brighter. To obtain a very fast color, the wool is mordanted, then dyed, then mordanted again, not using as much the second time.

The following is a routine that can be followed at home with wool. For one pound of wool, put one-quarter pound alum and one ounce cream of tartar in an unchipped enamel kettle, add enough water so that the wool is completely immersed in it. Put the kettle over a slow fire and when the water is fairly warm, add the wool, stir it in so that it is below the level of the solution, gradually raise the temperature to the boiling point, and boil very gently for an hour. The mordant is precipitated on the wool which then is ready to take up the dye stuff. The wool must be left in the mordant solution long enough for the chemicals to get through every fiber. Otherwise the material will dye unevenly, the color will not be so bright and will fade. The longer it stays in the solution the better the results will be.

At the end of an hour remove the kettle from the fire and set aside to cool overnight. Take out the wool and drain through an enamel sieve, pressing the material lightly to remove excess solution. Put the wool in a piece of clean linen for four or five days, rinse in water and immerse in the slightly warm dye-bath. Bring to the boiling point and boil gently for about two hours, more or less according to the intensity of the color desired, remembering that the material will be lighter when dried. About one-half hour before the end of the boiling, if you want the color brighter, remove the wool, add one-half ounce stannous chloride and two ounces cream of tartar, stir to dissolve thoroughly, put the wool back in the kettle and boil for one-half hour. If you want the color darker, remove the wool, stir into the dye-bath until dissolved one-half ounce copperas and one ounce cream of tartar. Put the wool back into the dye-bath and boil for another half-hour. Remove the kettle from the fire, set aside to cool overnight, rinse in water until no dye colors the water, wash in soapy water to soften the wool and dry.

Many factors affect the shade or tint of the dye—the kind of material, whether wool, silk, cotton or linen; the length of time left in the dye bath; the kind of mordant or combination of mordants. The colors also depend on the part of the herb used for dyeing, whether seeds, roots, berries, flowers, leaves, stems or bark, and the season of the year when the dye material is gathered.

Two dye plants seem worthy of special attention. One is madder, the dye stuff taken from the roots of *Rubia tinctorum,* because the various mordants used will produce several colors, red, pink, lilac, purple, brown, orange and black. Madder roots are also used with other dye stuffs to give compound colors. The dye-bath has to be heated very gradually to bring out all the color of the root, taking about an hour to raise the solution to the boiling point. If boiled too long with the material, the color will be dulled—about ten or fifteen minutes is sufficient. Water containing lime makes the color brighter and if that mineral is lacking, two per cent chalk may be added and a handful of bran.

Woad (*Isatis tinctoria*) furnished a dyestuff on which the British dye industry was founded centuries ago. Woad was the only blue dye material in that part of the world until indigo was brought from India. Although woad was long used as a dye, it is now used in making indigo dye and is a mordant for black dye. However, it produces a faster color than indigo. The preparation of woad leaves for extracting the color is quite a long process. The leaves are dried, bruised into a paste, piled into heaps, exposed to the air and allowed to ferment for about two weeks. Then this mass is made into cakes, dried, broken up and allowed to ferment for nine weeks longer. The color is brought out by mixing the woad preparation with water in which lime has been deposited.

A more simple way of preparing an indigo-bath is to pour boiling water over woad leaves in a kettle, put a weight on them and let the kettle set in a warm place for an hour. Pour off the water, add potassium hydroxide and later hydrochloric acid. If leaves are left in the solution longer, green and brown colors will be obtained.

Some of the herbs are most interesting to note because of the varying shades and tints of colors they give, according to the mordant and material used. I have grouped a number of herbs according to the colors they can produce.

RED

Garden Sorrel roots.

Lady's Bedstraw young roots, formerly much used in the Hebrides to dye wool. The material becomes deep red when stannous chloride is added, and terra cotta when boiled for some time.

Madder root.

Pokeweed flower (crimson).

BLUE

Elderberries.

Chicory leaves.

Elecampane root, mixed with ashes and whortleberries.

Woad leaves.

Yellow flag flowers.

Indigo plant.

YELLOW

Agrimony whole herb, gathered in September, pale brownish yellow. If gathered later, dyes wool a deep yellow.

Lady's Bedstraw stem and leaves.

Dyer's Broom (Dyer's Greenwood) gathered in June and July, for wool with alum and cream of tartar, bright yellow. Called *greening weed* because it is used to turn blue wool green.

Fumitory flowers, for wool.

Yarrow flowers, with alum.

Toadflax flowers.

St.-John's-wort flowers, with alum.

Calendula flowers, boiled.

Cardoon bottoms.

Daphne seed, for woolens.

Goldenrod flowers with alum, lemon yellow. Bright yellow when stannous chloride added.

BROWN

Hops stalks, brownish red.

Teasel flowers.

Wild marjoram flowering tops for linen, brownish red.

Goldenrod with copperas.

GREEN

Elder leaves, with alum.

Hyssop leaves, greenish gray with copperas.

Tansy young shoots, greenish gray with alum.

Scotch broom plant.

Dyer's broom combined with woad, alum, cream of tartar, sulphate of lime.

Lily-of-the-valley leaves.

Parsley leaves.
Yarrow leaves.

PURPLE

Pokewood berries, reddish purple, magenta.
Elderberries with alum, violet; with alum and salt, lilac.
St.-John's-wort flowers with tannic acid, pinkish purple.
Wild marjoram flowering tops, wool.

BLACK

Yellow flag roots with sulphate of iron.
Elder root and bark of older branches.

CHAPTER 11

Potpourri

In summer we harvest culinary herbs to use all winter for delectable dishes. We can also collect the color and fragrance of our herb garden for potpourri jars to set on a table or mantel in the living room. If you have many roses, you might gather a few of each variety and put them into a rose bowl or jar, or add other flowers for a true potpourri.

Since roses have always been the basis of most of the sweet-smelling mixtures, you must take stock of your rose bushes. Certain varieties are preferable—the old-fashioned cabbage rose, which is the original Provence pink; the damask rose with about eighteen wonderfully fragrant petals, and the Kazanlik, also a pink rose, grown for centuries in the Balkans for the attar or otto of roses. Then there is the apothecaries' rose, a rosy-red single rose also called *rose de Provins,* from a city near Paris where the flowers were grown for making sirups and cordials. These petals do not release all their odor until they are dried. Many of the hybrid perpetuals such as George Dickson or Ulrich Brunner, or the hybrid teas such as Gruss au Teplitz, Etoile de Hollande, Chateau de Clos Vougeot and E. G. Hill are delightful for potpourri.

Our great-grandmothers made their fragrance jars by the one method then known, now called the moist method. They put a layer of partially dried petals in a wide-mouthed crock, a layer of salt and alternated layers of salt and petals until the crock was filled. The mixture was allowed to "cure," really to rot. From the process came the name "potpourri," from the French verb *pourrir,* to rot. The word is pronounced "po-poor-ree" with accent on the last syllable. Nowadays we use what has come to be known as the dry method, which will preserve the color as well as the fragrance of the flowers.

You will find the roses most fragrant in the sunniest, most protected spot in the garden for there they develop their essential oils to the highest degree. Collect the flowers, before the sun is high, on a dry day after two or three days of dry weather. Never use inferior, rain-soaked blossoms or those that have been open for several days. Do not expect fragrant oils to be present in those that have been in the house for a week. If for sentimental reasons you wish to preserve roses that are not fresh, they will hold artificial oils and spices added to them when dry.

Keep the colors of the various kinds of flowers separate through the collecting, drying and storing processes because you may not want to finish making the potpourri until months later, and by then you may have several ideas for color combinations. Remove the petals, separate and place them in thin layers on drying racks made, for instance, by window screens elevated on the backs of chairs and covered with cheese-cloth to hold the small fragments of petals. If the screens are large, a more elaborate rack can be made with several screens, one above the other, with uprights nailed at each corner to act as legs and to keep the screens spaced a foot or so apart, horizontally.

Set the drying rack in a warm place where air will reach each petal. By drying them on a screen, rather than on paper spread on table or floor, the air will pass under as well as over them. If the drying space is limited, do not gather more flowers for each drying than your racks can hold in thin layers.

In the moist method the petals are left on the screens for about twenty-four hours, enough to wilt them so that they will have lost about half their original bulk. Place a half-inch layer of wilted petals on the bottom of a wide-mouthed crock and add a layer of common salt, not iodized. Continue the process each day until the crock is two-thirds filled or until you have all the petals you wish. A crock with straight sides is best so that you can easily stir the petals and salt. Each day stir the mixture with a wooden spoon, add more layers of petals and salt, press the mass down with a wooden potato masher and put a weight on the top, such as a flat iron on a plate. If a sort of broth or fermentation rises, stir the mixture thoroughly, and let it stay in the crock for ten days. By then a cake will have formed which may be taken out, broken into small pieces and mixed with other ingredients—fixatives, oils and spices—such as used in the dry method.

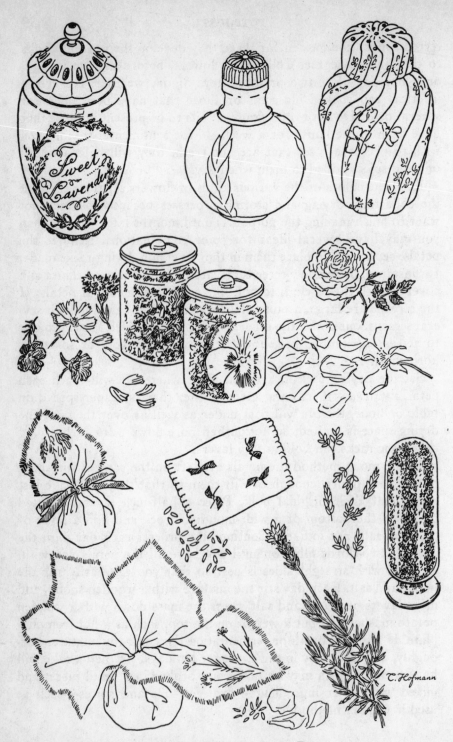

Fragrance Jars and Sweet Bags

In following the dry method, set the rack in a room where little sun strikes the petals to fade the color, but where there is cross-ventilation. Be sure not to gather more than your racks will hold in thin layers. If there is much of a breeze, cover the petals with cheesecloth. Leave the petals on the rack until they are chip dry, like fresh corn flakes; stir now and then so that the air will reach all the petals and all will dry thoroughly. Store the petals, each color separately, in large opaque containers or in glass ones, if you keep them away from the light. Either type should close tightly. Add petals to this stock all summer, for it may be fall before you have either time or enough petals to make the potpourri.

To mix the potpourri, put the petals in a large pan or bowl and add a fixative. This must be done not only to blend the fragrances of all the ingredients, but also to help retard the evaporation of oils. Without a fixative, the fragrance of the potpourri will soon disappear, but with a fixative and proper blending, the fragrance will last for many years.

Fixatives may be of animal origin or of a vegetable nature. Of the first type there is ambergris, a substance resembling wax of varying colors—white, ash gray to yellow, black or even variegated like marble. It is a secretion from the alimentary canal of the sperm whale. Then there is civet, a butterlike substance of a yellow-brown color found in a sac in the body of the civet cat. Undiluted it has an offensive, musky odor, but when minute portions are diluted with other substances the result is an odor pleasing to many. Castoreum is a bitter, orange-brown substance, with a strong odor, found in the body of the beaver. All these fixatives of animal nature are difficult to obtain and are quite expensive.

The most commonly used fixatives of vegetable nature are gum benzoin, storax and crushed roots of calamus and orris. Benzoin is a resin from a tree (*Styrax benzoin*) found in Malacca, Java and Sumatra. Storax, a brown, honeylike balsam is obtained from the bark of a tree called *Liquidambar orientalis* and hardens as it stands. Calamus is the root of the sweet flag (*Acorus Calamus*); orris is the root of Florentine iris. Whichever of these substances is used, it should be crushed, not powdered, before adding it to the petals, if you are using the dry method. You may put the potpourri into crystal containers and they will be clouded by a powdered fixative. About one tablespoonful of fixative to one quart of petals is the amount commonly used. If the moist method is followed, the same proportion is correct, but it does not make any difference whether it is powdered or crushed because such potpourri is put in opaque jars.

The next step is to stir in thoroughly a mixture of crushed spices such as cinnamon, nutmeg, allspice and mace. The proportion is a tablespoonful of spices to a quart of potpourri. Bits of other fragrant substances which may be added, the amounts according to your preferences, are angelica and vetiver roots, fragrant roots long used in the deep South for scenting clothes. You may wish to add crushed seeds of anise, caraway, coriander or cardamon, bits of tonka and vanilla beans. Do try the peels of orange, lemon and tangerine, scraped of the pith, stuck with cloves, cut into small bits with a pair of shears and then dried twenty-four hours.

A few drops of fragrant oils may also be added and thoroughly stirred into the mixture, but the one great caution is not to have too many different oils, or the result will be decidedly unpleasant because some of the pleasant odors may counteract each other. The following oils are pleasant when used sparingly: patchouli, rose geranium, eucalyptus, rosemary, rhodium, lemon verbena, bergamot (not from bee balm but from *Citrus Bergamia*), a drop or two of peppermint. Avoid letting one oil dominate but let them all blend. I suggest making up small portions of potpourri, experimenting with two or three oils and four or five fragrant substances besides the crushed spices. Vary the combination to see which you prefer. The fixatives and oils may be bought at a drugstore.

After the potpourri is thoroughly mixed, put it into a large crock, filling it about two-thirds full, thus leaving room for the mixture to be stirred. Close tightly for six weeks to blend, but two or three times a week turn or rock the crock. Then turn the mixture into a large pan, mix thoroughly and fill small containers. Even after the six weeks, the potpourri may be a little "raw," but in the containers, it will take on a smooth mellowness, increasing with the years.

It is essential in filling the small containers that some of the fixative and spices go into each one. If the moist method has been followed, you will want pottery jars such as the old-fashioned potpourri jars with two covers, one solid and the other perforated. When you wish to release the scent, the solid cover is removed and the perforated one lets the odor out gradually. If the dry method has been used, you will want to show the color of the flowers and the containers should be of glass, perhaps with a pressed pansy or hollyhock fixed on the inside of the glass with white of egg used as a colorless glue. The jar must be wide and shallow enough so that your fingers can reach well inside for this operation.

It must be remembered that lavender flowers and roses are about the only common flowers that keep their fragrance when dried. You can, however, gather the whole season's colors into the potpourri by drying thoroughly the petals and leaves of other plants by the same method used for rose petals. These you can add to roses, or make a potpourri of them alone.

Many special potpourri may be made, such as a patriotic mixture of bee balm, cardinal flower and Paul's scarlet which dry a pure red without the purple cast characteristic of most dried, red rose petals. For the white, use any white petals such as daisies but do not use white roses because they dry a brownish yellow. For the blue, use blue cornflower, delphinium, larkspur and aconite.

A spectrum potpourri may be made of *red* bergamot (bee balm), Paul's scarlet, cardinal flower; *orange* calendula, elecampane, nasturtium; *yellow* primrose, woad, nasturtium; *green* leaves; *blue* cornflower, aconite, delphinium, larkspur; *violet* peppermint flowers, violets.

An aromatic and distinctly herbal potpourri can be made with herbs chosen from Table P Chapter 18.

Three favorite recipes of mine and another that I like are:

1. One quart of mixed red and deep pink rose petals; 1 pint of lemon-scented leaves, preferably mixed lemon verbena and lemon balm; 1 pint of rose geranium leaves or rose and skeleton leaves mixed; a generous handful of rosemary leaves; a heaping tablespoonful of small bits of dried orange peel stuck with cloves (these may be ground up in a mortar) ; 6 drops each of the oils of bergamot, rosemary, lemon verbena, and rhodium; 1½ heaping table-spoonfuls of crushed spice mixture, preferably cinnamon stick, cloves, mace, nutmeg, allspice, cardamon seeds, ginger root, all crushed together in a mortar; 2 tablespoonfuls of fixative, preferably gum benzoin sumatra and orris root mixed and crushed; 1 tablespoonful of finely cut vetiver root.

2. One quart rose petals; 1 heaping tablespoonful of crushed spice mixture containing nutmeg, cinnamon stick, allspice, mace and cloves crushed together in a mortar but not ground fine; 1 heaping tablespoonful of crushed orange peel; 3 drops of eucalyptus oil; 5 drops of peppermint oil; 1 tablespoonful lavender flowers.

3. One quart rose petals; ½ pint of lavender flowers; 1 teaspoonful of anise seed mixed with 1 tablespoonful of mixed cloves, nutmeg and cinnamon stick, all crushed together in a mortar; 1 tablespoonful of fixative, preferably gum benzoin crushed; 5 drops each of oils of jasmin, rose geranium, patchouli, rosemary.

4. A sixteenth-century pungent and refreshing mixture which comprises 1 pint each of leaves of peppermint, thyme, and lavender flowers; 1 tablespoonful of crushed spice mixture (cloves, coriander and nutmeg) to which is added 2 tablespoonfuls of caraway seed also well crushed; and the most satisfactory fixative is 1 tablespoonful of crushed gum benzoin.

CHAPTER 12

Herb Products

Herbs fresh and herbs dried, in many combinations and for innumerable uses, may be assembled for your own use in the home, for gifts or for selling, either commercially or for a little pin-money. You can make up packages of seeds, pots of seedlings or full-grown plants, window boxes, household preparations, culinary products, sweet bags and fragrancies. Attractiveness is increased by having a label which carries your own insignia, name and address, besides the name of the product. In the imaginative person's mind the following suggestions will inspire many other ideas for herb products.

FRESH SEEDS

Seeds to Grow. Many people with small planting space do not want full-sized packets of seeds, and the disadvantages of buying a packet of mixed seed have already been discussed. Therefore, package about one-fourth teaspoon of each of several kinds of herb seed, depending on size, in separate containers. These containers may be:

1. Small glassine or cellophane envelopes, sealed and the name of the herb carefully written on a plain label or on one of your own design. Accompany each by a slip of paper on which is typed or neatly written a jingle or line or two, giving its height, cultural directions, use or other information.

2. Small manila envelopes on which may be sketched or painted a picture of the herb, accompanied by directions.

3. For Valentine's Day, Easter or Mother's Day, choose appropriate cards with double fold. On the right-hand side of the fold, or third page, staple or paste a few packets of seeds, labeled, and on the left side of the fold give information about planting or uses. If many packets are used, a separate sheet with jingles or brief information may be inserted.

4. A two-page booklet, with a half-dozen labeled cellophane packets pasted or stapled on one side, on the other side sketched or painted pictures of the herbs and accompanying information, either written on the page or on colored strips of paper pasted underneath the picture.

FRESH HERBS

Potted Plants. These are always welcome as gifts or items for sale. Culinary herbs will be the most popular but other fragrant plants will be appreciated. They can be potted in paper pots, but for Valentine's Day, Easter, Mother's Day and Christmas, clay pots trimmed with crepe paper suitably decorated would be especially appropriate. You can offer seedlings or mature plants potted; window boxes planted with culinary or fragrant herbs or a general mixture. (See Chapter 8 for planting window boxes.)

Wreaths and Bouquets. At Christmas it is always a joy to have herbs still fresh and green. What delightful winter bouquets and unusual wreaths you can fashion from these almost evergreen herbs! (See Table O, Chapter 18.) Herbs lend themselves admirably to graceful vase or low bowl arrangements, from the low carpet bugle-weed, calamint, dead nettle, santolina and thymes, to the taller sage, hyssop, rue, burnet and southernwood.

Wreaths can be made by covering a wire construction with a scanty background of hemlock, balsam and holly. Then, fill in with sprigs of gray sage, santolina and horehound, blue-green rue, deep green hyssop and winter savory. Bugle-weed and the creeping thymes woven through and around the wreath give a softening effect. In more severe climates, where the garden is covered before Christmas, these plants will be fresh as ever underneath the winter protection.

Tussie-mussies. These old-fashioned, tightly-made nosegays, surrounded by a crisp paper frill and meant to be carried in the hand, are again popular and are particularly suitable for Valentine's Day. They expressed the "Language of the Flowers," the principal sentiment being given center position in the bouquet, with other suitable emotions surrounding this. In the middle might be heliotrope for eternal love or rose for love, surrounded by burnet (merry heart), marjoram (happiness), southernwood (constancy), blue violet (loyalty). Tiny tussie-mussies would be pretty novelties for favors and place names at a luncheon. Buy the smallest size paper doilies, either in white or perhaps to match the luncheon color schemes. The place name can be written on a card and tied to the little nosegay and set so that it can be read while the guests are finding their places.

Place Cards and Favors. Besides the tussie-mussies, attractive place cards are made by pressing tiny sprays of herbs and lightly pasting them on the card. Interest is increased by having a guessing contest of identification. Unusual favors that can be taken home are cuttings of herbs. Wrap the cut part of the stem in a piece of moist paper toweling and with waxed paper. If desired, this could be covered with crepe paper to match the table decorations. Around each slip tie a card identifying the herb.

HOUSEHOLD PREPARATIONS

Aromatic Bath. Several herbs have been used for centuries and are still used in the bath not only for relaxing tired muscles of perfectly healthy people, but for relieving nervous ailments, skin diseases and poor circulation. A simple method of preparing herbs for use in the bath is to tie a handful of the leaves or leafy tips in a three- or four-inch square of cheesecloth. The bag may be dropped into the bath water or into a quart of boiling water fifteen minutes before the bath is drawn, and the infusion poured into the tub.

An acceptable gift box is a dozen herb-bath bags of various combinations or of single herbs. Most popular are those of the mints or thymes, sage, rosemary, pennyroyal, flower heads of chamomile, lavender, lemon verbena and lemon balm. Pleasant combinations are equal parts of pennyroyal, sage, rosemary and angelica; or equal parts of lavender, rosemary and pennyroyal; or equal parts of lemon balm and peppermint; or equal parts of thyme, elder flowers and flower heads of chamomile.

Fragrant Rubbing Lotions. These are made easily by infusing herbs in alcohol. Leaves of thyme, lavender, mint, marjoram, lemon verbena, lemon balm and rosemary, besides being refreshing and invigorating, are very pleasant scents and impart a beautiful green color to the liquid. Use wide-mouthed jars, fill about one-quarter full with each of the herbs, crushed with a wooden potato masher, and pour over them unscented rubbing alcohol that may be bought from a drugstore. Fill within an inch or two from the top, cover tightly and let stand for two weeks, with an occasional vigorous shaking. Strain the liquid through fine muslin or cheesecloth, and pour into small lotion bottles that can be bought at cosmetic counters.

Skin Tonics and Fresheners. These are made by the same method as the rubbing lotions, but use rose petals, elder flowers or calendulas, since they have astringent qualities.

Herb Teas. In Chapter 15 soothing teas are discussed. Packages of several of these herbs in a box would be a welcome gift for those who suffer from insomnia. Suitable herbs are lemon verbena, aniseseed, peppermint, catnip, celery or lovage leaves, rosemary, sage, sweet marjoram, mugwort, flower heads of chamomile and lemon balm.

Perfumed Ink. This has long been a commercial product and it is delightful to write with an aromatic, herb-scented ink. Make a very strong decoction of an herb with a distinctive odor, such as bee balm, lemon verbena, rosemary or lavender, and add one teaspoonful to a bottle of ordinary ink.

Hair Rinses. Simmer rosemary tips or lemon verbena leaves for half an hour in rain or artificially softened water, strain off the liquid and bottle for use. These rinses give a refreshing fragrance to the hair. In most beauty parlors, here and abroad, chamomile rinses are used to preserve golden tints of the hair. The liquid is obtained in the same way as for rosemary and verbena but use only flower heads of chamomile.

Catnip Pads. Take material with a good firm weave, unbleached cotton or figured cotton with dye-fast color, and cut the cloth to make a finished envelope about three by four inches. Sew up three sides on a machine so that the seams will be strong. Fill with catnip but do not crowd the envelope, finish sewing by hand with strong thread. The catnip should be loose enough in the pad so that it can be crushed to bring out the oils that your cat loves so well. The pad should be small enough so that he can pick it up in his claws and rub it over his head or carry it from one place to another.

Catnip Mice. These can be made from gray outing flannel, with gray yarn for tail and whiskers, black beads tightly sewed in the material for eyes and a black pencil mark for a mouth. Your cat will not quibble at the lack of resemblance to a live mouse as long as it is filled with catnip.

Herbal Incense. Aromatic herbs when dried and burned act as a purifying incense since the oils are not only fragrant but also antiseptic, and can be used to dispel tobacco, kitchen or sickroom odors. They make a pleasing accent when burned at tea-time by the open fire, and will freshen the air in the living-room just before company arrives. The leafy tops of lavender, rosemary, sage, lemon balm or southernwood may be dried, rubbed through a fine sieve and the powder stored in small, wide-mouthed containers. To go with each set make a tiny cone-shaped tweezer of metal which can be plunged into the jars of powder, squeezed tightly and opened carefully on an incense burner. The little mound of powdered fragrance readily lights and is most delightful.

Moth Preventives. Many combinations of moth preventive mixtures can be made and inclosed in small pads or bags about three by four inches. These should be placed among winter clothes when they are put away for summer or hung over garment-hangers inside the garments all winter to impart a permanent fragrance to them. The following are very effective mixtures:

A handful each of dried and crumbled (not powdered) thyme, tansy, southernwood; one tablespoon crushed cloves.

Two handfuls each of dried lavender flowers, rosemary; one tablespoon each crushed cloves and small pieces of dried lemon peel.

One tablespoon crushed cinnamon; one handful each of dried and crumbled santolina, tansy, mint, wormwood.

CULINARY PRODUCTS

Culinary Seasonings. For these, foliage herbs may be powdered, crushed or the leaves left on the stems and packaged in carefully labeled glassine or cellophane envelopes, small glass or crockery jars. From six to a dozen of these containers may be put in attractive boxes or baskets. The foliage herbs most popular and commonly used are sweet basil, sweet marjoram, summer savory, thyme, tarragon, lovage or celery leaves, chervil, parsley, apple mint, orange mint, rosemary and sage. Combinations of herbs, packaged as above, are also much used. In Chapter 14, seven herb combinations for the following uses are given and may be so labeled: ground beef mixture, vegetables, pork, lamb and veal; egg and chicken, poultry stuffing, vegetable cocktails.

Herb Bouquet. Preparation of bags and mixtures are given in Chapter 14, and may be packaged as above for fish, soups and stews. Single bags may also be pasted or stapled to a gift card; or a plain folder which the artistic person can adorn with suitable picture and verse, or a line or two describing the use of the bag.

Savory Seeds. These are particularly attractive packaged in transparent containers because of the variety of sizes and shapes. The most commonly used savory seeds are anise, bene, caraway, coriander, dill, fennel and white mustard.

Vinegars and Pickles. The recipes for these are to be found in Chapters 13 and 14 respectively, and they may be packaged very attractively in small glass bottles and containers. Popular items are: herb vinegars, such as tarragon, mint, burnet, marjoram, dill, rose, violet, clove pinks and lavender; dill pickles; pickled nasturtium seeds; fresh cucumber slices.

Jellies and Sweets. (See Chapter 14 for recipes.) The following are always popular: herb jellies; candied angelica stalks, mint or sage leaves and flowers; candied roots of lovage; of sweet flag; quince-mint meat relish; mint-flowered citrus fruit peel; horehound drops; peppermint wafers; sesame (bene) bars; honey of roses; seed cookies; Halloween apples.

Herb Teas. Crushed foliage or whole seeds of several of the tea herbs may be packaged in the same way as the culinary seasonings. Herb teas are discussed in Chapter 15.

SWEET BAGS AND FRAGRANCIES

Herb Pillows. These may be made as small as boudoir pillows. They serve many purposes—to lay on bed pillows, on a chaise longue, to induce sleep to those suffering from insomnia, to soothe aching heads and as large sachets for bureau drawers. The covers of the pillows may be of old-fashioned printed muslin or cotton, sewed up on three sides, filled with an herb mixture and then sewed on the fourth side.

More elaborate covers are two matching handkerchiefs, either white or pastel shades, of sheer material and a hemstitched inner square, about six and one-half inches. An inner envelope contains the herb mixture, and is slipped within the handkerchief square which has been sewed up on three sides. The material of this envelope may be of sateen or percale in white or deeper colors to show through the fine material of the handkerchiefs. If pastel colors are used, attractive combinations can be made, such as a lavender envelope inside a yellow handkerchief, blue within pink. In sewing up the handkerchief square, stitch on the outside of the hemstitching so that a fine line of the color of the inside envelope shows.

The fillings for these pillows are of many combinations. One type can be of potpourri mixtures. Decide what accent you want—sweet, pungent or lemon, and then combine the herbs that emphasize these types. (See Chapter 11 for a complete discussion of potpourri.)

For relieving headaches, a mixture of several of the mints and bee balm, with orris root as a fixative, is suitable. Print material with predominating color of green, a green envelope in a white handkerchief or in a green handkerchief are particularly appropriate to hold the mint mixture. This mixture is especially invigorating because of the traces of camphor in bee balm and of menthol in peppermint. Lavender flowers in a lavender envelope within a white handkerchief covering makes a most attractive pillow. For those suffering from insomnia a lemony accent is good, lemon balm, costmary and lemon verbena predominating, or a mixture of rose petals, mint and cloves. Pillows of dried hops are good, not only for those suffering from insomnia but for those subject to asthma. The hop flowers are sprinkled with alcohol to remove the crackling of the little dried conelike flowers.

Sweet Bags and Sachets. These small bags are used in many ways —to lay among lingerie, to hang over bedposts or over the arms or back of a boudoir or wing chair and over dress-hangers. They will impart a delicate fragrance to the air about them or to the garments they touch. The material should be of very fine silk, either white, plain colors or old-fashioned prints. Make the bags about three by four inches, fill with a fragrant herb mixture and lightly gather in the top of the bag, leaving an inch heading. Around the gathers, tie a length of one and one-half inch ribbon, matching or contrasting in color.

If the mixture is to scent linen, pads instead of bags are more satisfactory since the piles will lie flatter. Simply sew up the fourth side without gathering. These pads, put under the pillows in the guestroom, offer a fragrant gesture. Have different mixtures so that your guests may choose their favorite fragrances. Clean-smelling mixtures are lavender, lemon verbena, lemon balm, skeleton-leaved pelargonium (sweet-leaved geranium), rose petals and mint leaves. These herbs are so lasting in scent that it is not essential to add a fixative though it is better to do so. A spice mixture of your own preferred combination may be added. Any of the herbs with stronger scents—lavender, mint, rose geranium or lemon verbena —may be used alone.

These mixtures may be tied into small chiffon handkerchiefs, and if you are artistic, an herb spray painted in one corner. Let the mixture determine the color of the handkerchief—for mint or lemon mixtures use green; for lavender use lavender handkerchief, or white tied with lavender ribbon; for rose accent a pink handkerchief or white tied with pink ribbon.

Little sachets may be in the form of flower baskets and filled with any of the above herbs or mixtures. One way is to make a small pad about one and one-half by two inches, and crochet a basket with frilly top in different colors for the flowers and also a slender handle. Keep the top open and slip in the pad. Another way is to cut thin silk, printed muslin or ribbon into the form of a basket, about two by three inches. Embroider a spray on one side, perhaps, and sew up three sides, fill with fragrant mixtures, sew up the fourth, twist a length of narrow ribbon and attach to each side of the top for a handle. To conceal the sewing on the fourth side, sew on tiny rosebuds that you make or buy in a dress-trimming department.

Padded Coat Hangers. Wrap padding cotton evenly about the hanger, sprinkle it with one of the fragrant herb mixtures, cover with silk and tuft with narrow ribbon. Hang a sweet bag from the center of the hanger for an extra touch.

Fragrant Foundation for Bureau Drawers. A fragrant foundation for bureau drawers may be made by cutting two pieces of cheesecloth or fine net a half-inch larger than the size of the drawer. Cut two pieces of thin cotton padding a bit smaller than the drawer. Lay one piece of cotton flat on a table, sprinkle over it a generous layer of a scented mixture of herbs, cover with the other piece of cotton, baste the cheesecloth around the edges and make tackings of threads through the pad. Of the net, make a bag open at one end and carefully place the scented padding in it. Sew up the other end, and tuft with contrasting or harmonizing ribbon in several places to hold the pad firmly. The edges may be featherstitched or bound with ribbon to match the tufts.

Christmas Cards. Buy note paper with a Christmas design on the first page but no writing, and write a personal greeting. On the third page make two diagonal slits in the middle, and slip in a sprig of lavender, rosemary or lemon verbena that has been pressed and dried. Buy plain Christmas cards and either paste or slip through two slits made in the card a pressed sprig of a fragrant herb. Make tiny sachets, not much larger than the size of a postage stamp, and mail with your Christmas cards.

Fragrant Confetti. Instead of throwing rice at the bride and groom, use dry rose petals. Tie them up in tissue paper, the size of packages of confetti, and distribute them among the guests to give a fragrant send-off to the couple.

Articles Made from Lavender. Flat pads are more satisfactory to lay between piles of linen, because fat little bags make a high pile a bit precarious. Make envelopes of organdy, about four by five inches in size, fill with just enough herb mixture to make a plump pad, but not over-stuffed, then tuft in four places with narrow contrasting or harmonizing ribbon. With matching silk feather-stitch the ends, primarily to cover the sewing on the end left open for filling. Pads of lavender flowers and leaves in lavender organdy envelopes, tufted with a deeper shade of ribbon, are most attractive. Other herbs for the pads are mixtures of rose geranium and a small amount of lavender or sometimes of rosemary; lemon verbena and finger-bowl pelargoniums; lemon thyme and lemon verbena; costmary and skeleton-leaf pelargonium.

Lavender Fans. Cut stalks of true lavender or spike lavender when in full bloom, cut them the length of the sticks in old-fashioned fans and lay them out flat to dry. Cut two pieces of lavender organdy or muslin the shape of an open fan. Lay the stalks on one piece of the material and weave lavender colored ribbon three-eighths of an inch wide, from the center back and forth toward the wide part for about four inches. Turn in both pieces of the material evenly at the edges about one-quarter of an inch, lay them with the turned in edges together and baste around the whole fan and between each two stalks. Then with lavender silk, featherstitch around the fan and between the stalks.

Lavender Bottle. Cut about one hundred stalks of spike lavender when in full bloom, lay the heads together and cut the ends off evenly. About six inches from the flower ends of the stalks, tie a cord firmly about the bunch. Bend the stalks back over the flower heads and weave three-eighths inch ribbon through the stalks, picking up five or six the first time around, and continuing five or six turns. Tie a ribbon around the outside and fasten with a bow.

CHAPTER 13

Herb Vinegars

Herb vinegars can be used as a pleasant means to flavor iced beverages and culinary dishes, and to revive flagging spirits. Mint vinegar not only sharpens up a fruit punch but when patted on the forehead will relieve an aching head. Almost all fragrant culinary herbs are grist for the mill of the herb vinegar enthusiast, from the fragrant, delicate flower infusions and the heavier foliage vinegars to the strong savory seed vinegars. Vinegars can be made of so many herbs, one alone or several in combination, that to name them all would result in much too long a list of seasoning herbs, savory seeds and flowers. Experiment with small amounts of many different kinds to determine which you prefer.

The most commonly used vinegars of a single kind of foliage herb or savory seed are tarragon, mint, burnet, basil, marjoram, dill and caraway. Several others are made from combinations of herbs. A revival of the use of vinegars made with flowers is growing. In the old days and until the middle of the nineteenth century, flower vinegars such as rose, violet, spicy pink, elder flower, lavender and rosemary were very popular, not only for toilet preparations but also for salads and iced beverages.

The process of making vinegars is very simple and the methods are similar whether flowers, leaves or seeds are used, although there are slight differences. To get the full flavor it is best to use fresh plants. To make vinegars of foliage, cut the leafy tips just before the plant flowers, and pack them loosely into a wide-mouthed jar, and bruise the foliage with a wooden potato masher or pestle. Bring either cider or white wine vinegar to the boiling point and pour it over the leaves, filling the jar to within two inches of the top. Cover tightly. Let the mixture infuse for ten days in a warm place, shaking the jar about once a day. Taste the vinegar, and if it is not strong enough, strain the herbs through a sieve, and add another charge of well bruised herbs to the same liquid without boiling and infuse ten days more. When the vinegar is strong enough, strain the herbs through a sieve, and filter the vinegar through muslin, flannel or French filter paper. Store the vinegar in glass bottles. Some cooks put the used herb leaves back in the original jars for use in winter salads.

In making flower vinegars, collect a cupful of petals, cut off the white bases, put the petals into a wide-mouthed jar, add a pint of boiling white vinegar and proceed as above. In making vinegar of seeds, measure two heaping tablespoonfuls of seeds, crush them to facilitate the release of oils, put them into a wide-mouthed bottle, add a quart of boiling vinegar, and follow the general directions.

Though it is quite unusual, vinegars can be made also from fresh roots, such as lovage with odor and taste of celery. Wash and scrape the roots, rub them over a coarse grater or grind through the fine cutter of the meat chopper to facilitate the release of flavor when boiling vinegar is added. Use one-half cup grated root to one quart of vinegar. Proceed as with the other types of herb vinegars. Root vinegars may seem strange but, as a matter of fact, prepared horseradish is grated horseradish root with a little vinegar added.

It is simple enough to make a vinegar from one herb but when a combination of herbs is used, a great deal of artistry is required, and caution must be observed in regard to the amount and choice of herbs. Basil, tarragon, chives and mint, for instance, are each so strong that they stand out above much milder herbs such as chervil or marjoram. Even a little of the strong herb and much of the mild herb result in a vinegar taste of the strong herb. The following combinations make delicious blends:

1. Equal parts tarragon and lemon balm.
2. One part tarragon; two parts each of lemon thyme, basil, chives, burnet.
3. Equal parts basil, burnet, young borage leaves.
4. Equal parts garden thyme, basil, chives, lovage leaves.
5. Equal parts crushed seeds of dill, celery, caraway, anise, cumin, coriander.

Sometimes instead of one flower alone, a combination or bouquet vinegar is made for toilet use, such as these:

1. One part lavender flower petals; four parts fragrant red rose petals.
2. Equal parts clove pinks, rose petals, rosemary and elder flowers.

The uses of these pleasant vinegars are limited only by the imagination, but a few details may be mentioned here. Tarragon vinegar has long been on grocers' shelves and its uses are well known. Mint vinegar is served with lamb when fresh mint leaves cannot be obtained. It is one of the vinegars favored in iced drinks, gives character to cole slaw, and is pleasing in French dressing for any kind of salad. Vinegar of burnet leaves or seeds has such a flavor of cucumber that, mixed with salad oil for French dressing, it adds a cucumberish taste to tomato or green salad without producing the after effect that many people experience from the cucumber.

All the vinegars of herb leaves, seeds and roots are excellent with salad oil for French dressing to be served with vegetable or green salad:

Three tablespoons salad oil; one tablespoon herb vinegar; pinch of pepper; one half teaspoon salt; one half teaspoon sugar.

Any of these vinegars is good to be used for the brine or pickle in which beef is soaked in making sauerbraten. Flower vinegars give a deliciously different flavor to fruit salads or to green salads, but are most comforting when used to bathe an aching head.

CHAPTER 14

The Uses of Herbs in Cooking

Treat culinary herbs as additional seasonings to the usual ones of salt, vinegar, mustard and pepper. Experiment with a pinch of an herb, that is, less than ¼ teaspoonful, until you and your family are familiar with various flavors.

Seeds of anise and of fennel taste distinctly like licorice; caraway is reminiscent of licorice but more pungent and warm. Seeds and foliage of dill are similar, and have a stronger herb taste. Coriander seeds are warm and spicy. Sesame seeds have a delightful taste and are substituted for nuts in confections. Lemon balm has a definite odor and taste that suggests its name. Basil has a clovelike flavor and is often used in place of pepper in tomato and cheese dishes. The young leaves of burnet and of borage taste like cucumbers. On biting and chewing the foliage of lovage you could not distinguish between that and celery. Chives are similar to mild onions, while chervil resembles parsley. Thyme has a strongly herbal, pungent taste; marjoram is slightly bitter and aromatic. Rosemary is rather piny and resinous on the tongue, while tarragon has its own peculiar sweet taste recalling anise. Summer savory has an aromatic fragrance and taste somewhat like thyme but milder.

Seasoning should bring out the flavor of the food, and the taste of herbs should not stand out so prominently that it is recognized as any definite herb.

In each herb there is an essential volatile oil which characterizes the flavor of the herb, and upon those oils depend the flavor and fragrance which are given to food. The longer the herb is in food the more the oils will be released, heat acting upon them more quickly than cold. It takes a little time to start the oils, so do not put in more herbs than the recipe calls for but give them a chance. If you put in too much, by the time the dish is to be served it will

78

taste as bitter as the spring herb tonic your grandmother gave you when you were very young.

Add herbs to soup or stew about three-fourths of an hour before the end of cooking. To cold food, vegetable cocktails and soft cheese, herbs should be added several hours or overnight before serving. Savory seeds should be crushed and soaked in the liquid called for in the recipe an hour before making up the recipe. Foliage herbs for food that is to be cooked, no matter how short a time, do not need to be soaked because the oils are released so readily, and they may be added directly to meat mixtures or stuffing or sprinkled over roasts. This applies to small amounts of herbs. Where the flavor of the herb is emphasized as in herb jellies, the herb is not only boiled in the required liquid for several minutes but bruised beforehand.

Fresh herbs contain more oils than dried ones, but for most uses, it is immaterial whether they are fresh or dried. Since the oils are volatile, they gradually evaporate. Even if herbs are kept carefully in containers with tightly fitting covers, they do not retain their oils more than a year.

WHAT HERB TODAY?

BREADS, CAKES, PASTRIES: Caraway, coriander, sesame, anise, cumin.

CHEESE, HOT DISHES: Basil, sweet marjoram, thyme, tarragon.

CREAM OR COTTAGE CHEESE: Chives, mint, dill, sage, basil, caraway.

COCKTAIL (TOMATO): Combination of basil, sweet marjoram, thyme, summer savory, tarragon.

CONFECTIONERY: Mint, sesame, caraway, coriander, borage flowers.

EGG DISHES: Chives, tarragon, basil, sweet marjoram, chervil, thyme.

DESSERTS: Mint, sweet marjoram, caraway, anise.

FISH: Fennel, sage, thyme, basil, chives, chervil, parsley.

FRUIT CUP AND COLD BEVERAGES: Mint, borage, lemon balm, burnet, rosemary, thyme, anise.

GARNISHES: Parsley, thyme, rosemary, sweet marjoram, lemon balm, basil, chervil, summer savory.

JAMS AND JELLIES: Mint, rosemary, lemon verbena.

MEATS:
  BEEF: Basil, sweet marjoram, summer savory, thyme, rosemary.
  PORK: Sage, basil, rosemary, sweet marjoram, chives.
  LAMB: Sweet marjoram, summer savory, rosemary, dill.
  VEAL: Rosemary, summer savory, thyme, sage.

PICKLES AND CONDIMENTS: Dill, tarragon, borage, sage, rosemary, fennel, anise.

POULTRY: Summer savory, tarragon, thyme, sweet marjoram, sage.

SALADS: Burnet, mint, chives, dill, basil, borage, fennel, tarragon, chervil, summer savory, thyme, anise, lemon balm, caraway, chicory (witloof), white mustard.

SALAD DRESSINGS: Dill, tarragon, chervil, parsley.

SAUCES:
  MEAT AND POULTRY: Dill, mint, tarragon, thyme, chervil, marjoram.
  FISH: Fennel, parsley, chervil, dill, thyme, mint, tarragon (tartare).
  SOUPS AND STEWS: Basil, sweet marjoram, summer savory, parsley, thyme, mint, tarragon, chives, chervil.

TEAS: Mint, sage, anise, lemon balm, sweet marjoram, thyme, chamomile, lemon verbena.

VEGETABLES:
  BEETS: Basil, summer savory, fennel, caraway, coriander.
  CABBAGE: Mint, caraway, fennel.
  CARROTS: Summer savory, mint, basil, parsley, thyme.
  ONIONS: Tarragon, thyme.
  PEAS: Mint, summer savory, basil, rosemary.
  POTATOES: Mint, parsley, basil, chives.
  SPINACH: Sweet marjoram, mint.
  STRING BEANS: Summer savory, sweet marjoram, sage.
  TOMATOES: Basil, sweet marjoram, sage.

VINEGARS: Tarragon, burnet, dill, basil, mint, lemon balm, sweet marjoram.

A FEW SUGGESTIONS

Sprinkle chopped young dill foliage on broiling lamb chops five minutes before the end of cooking.

Use other herbs besides parsley as a garnish for meats; foliage of anise, basil, caraway, chervil, sweet marjoram, mint, winter savory, thyme, burnet; as garnish for salads, flowers of borage, violets or larkspur, petals of red roses or calendulas.

Use parsley, rich in vitamins, more frequently in foods and not simply as a garnish.

Add a sprig of apple mint or orange mint to peas or to carrots ten minutes before the end of cooking.

In serving iced tea, arrange a variety of mints in a bowl—orange mint, American apple mint, spearmint, anise-flavored mint, American (white) peppermint, English (black) peppermint.

Marinate cooked beets one hour before serving in any of the herb vinegars (see Chapter 13), or vinegar to which a teaspoonful of caraway seeds has been added.

While canned soup is heating, add a pinch of basil, savory or thyme to improve the flavor.

Add a teaspoonful of crushed coriander seeds to the other spices in making apple pie.

Add a teaspoonful of sieved summer savory to boiling fresh string beans or to canned string beans as they are heating.

Add one teaspoonful finely chopped or powdered rosemary to the regular recipe for baking powder biscuits.

For coloring sauces and puddings yellow, instead of the expensive saffron, use a strong infusion of calendula petals.

Try a few dill seeds among the apples for pie to strike a "different" note.

Leaves of lovage can be substituted for those of celery.

For a delicious canape, work into cottage cheese, one tablespoonful of dried and sieved or chopped parsley, make up tiny balls of the mixture and roll them in poppy seeds.

For another delicious canape, spread fingers of toast with salmon (mixed with mayonnaise and salted to taste) and sprinkle with dill seeds.

For a tasty unusual canape, choose potato chips with curled edges, fill the hollow with softened cream cheese or cottage cheese into which freshly chopped apple mint has been worked and let stand for a few hours. This mixture is also good on salted crackers.

For another canape, work into softened cream cheese or cottage cheese, one-half teaspoonful salt and one tablespoonful of any desired sieved foliage herb such as basil.

Cranberry juice cocktail is improved by adding the juice of an orange and one tablespoonful apple mint or orange mint, let it stand two hours, and strain before serving.

For a light luncheon dish, heat fillets of sardines, lay them on fingers of toast and pour over them hot tomato sauce to which a pinch or so of basil and summer savory have been added.

Make a roast of lamb delicious by sticking a dozen whole cloves in the top of the raw meat and by sprinkling it evenly with a mixture of three tablespoonfuls brown sugar and one tablespoonful sweet marjoram.

For serving with salads, butter crisp crackers, sift celery salt over them and shake off the excess, place on a metal cookie sheet in a medium hot oven until the butter is melted. (Celery salt is a mixture of ground celery and salt.)

Drop a few crushed cumin seeds into canned soup when it is heating and notice the spicy flavor, and try a pinch of finely crushed seeds in part of a batch of sugar cookies for a pleasing variety.

HERB COMBINATIONS

Herbs should be mixed according to individual preferences—there is no set rule. In the various recipes there are about as many combinations as mathematics allow. Novelty in dishes is obtained by varying the herb accent. There are some splendid combinations which may be relied upon to produce delicious results. No matter what other herbs may be in the mixture, some foods seem to call loudly for certain herbs; pork for sage; tomato and cheese for basil; fish for fennel; lamb for marjoram; string beans for summer savory; clam chowder for thyme; eggs for tarragon. Avoid sameness in herb combinations by adding to or subtracting from a given mixture. After you become acquainted with individual flavors you will enjoy experimenting. Until then try the following combinations which have been used with success. These may be made up in large quantities of dried and sieved herbs. Follow the proportions given and use the amount called for by the recipe. Some mixtures will be added directly to the food, others will be tied up in little bags and added to liquids.

Aux fines herbes means that finely chopped fresh or dried and sieved herbs are added directly to the food so that they will be scattered throughout the mixture.

An *herb bouquet,* or according to the French *bouquet garni,* is a bouquet of fresh herbs tied together, immersed in a liquid, such as soup or stew, and removed before the dish is served. Since we use herbs so much we put the same herbs, dried and sieved, into cheese-cloth bags, about two and one-half inches square, and use them as we do the fresh bouquet. By this method of using herbs in soups or stews, the specks of foliage do not show, but the full flavor will be obtained.

FINE HERB MIXTURES

1. *For ground beef mixture:* 1 tablespoonful each of summer savory, basil, sweet marjoram, thyme, parsley, lovage or celery leaves.
2. *For vegetables:* 1 tablespoonful each of summer savory, sweet marjoram, chervil, basil.
3. *For pork dishes:* 1 tablespoonful each of sage, basil, summer savory.
4. *For lamb and veal dishes:* 1 tablespoonful each of sweet marjoram, summer savory, rosemary.
5. *For egg and chicken dishes:* 1 tablespoonful each of summer savory, tarragon, chervil, basil, chives.
6. *For poultry stuffing:* 1 tablespoonful each of summer savory, sweet marjoram, basil, thyme, parsley, celery or lovage leaves; 1 teaspoonful of ground dried lemon peel; 1 teaspoonful sage may be added.
7. *For vegetable cocktails* (for 1 pint of liquid) : ½ teaspoonful each of sweet marjoram, basil, tarragon, thyme, summer savory; 1 tablespoonful chopped chives.
8. *For fish* (2 cups of liquid) : ¼ teaspoonful each of sweet marjoram, thyme, basil and sage, crushed seeds of fennel.
9. *For soups and stews* (2 quarts of liquid) : 1 teaspoonful each of parsley or chervil, thyme or summer savory, basil, sweet mar-

joram, celery or lovage leaves; ½ teaspoonful each of sage, rosemary, dried ground lemon peel.

RECIPES

APPETIZERS

Tangerine Mint Cup

Tangerines   ¾ cup water
⅛ cup apple mint   Granulated sugar
⅛ cup orange mint

Allow 1 tangerine to a cup. Remove outside peel and scrape off thready fibers. Separate into sections. Remove seeds at the inner edge of each section and lay the sections in a bowl. Make a strong infusion of ¼ cup of equal parts apple mint and orange mint in ¾ cup of water in a porcelain saucepan, boil for 5 minutes, crush leaves frequently. Strain out the leaves, cool the tea, pour over the tangerines. Sprinkle with sugar (not too much since an appetizer should be tart) and set the bowl in the icebox for at least 1 hour, longer if possible. When ready to serve, arrange the tangerine sections in individual glasses, pour over each a little of the tea, and sprinkle on finely sieved dried mint or chopped fresh mint, ¼ teaspoonful to each cup.

Ham or Beef Canapes

1 cream cheese or   1 heaping tablespoonful dried
½ lb. of cottage cheese   and sieved or chopped fresh
                      sweet marjoram or basil or
1 tablespoonful cream   summer savory or freshly
                      chopped chives
                      Thinly sliced boiled ham or
                      dried beef

Put cheese into a small bowl and soften with cream. Add and mix thoroughly with the selected herb; a heaping tablespoonful of a mixture of these herbs may be preferred to a single one. Let this stand for an hour or so to bring out the essential oils. Spread the mixture on the ham or dried beef which has been cut into slices about 3 by 2 inches. Roll up the slices from the short end and fasten with toothpicks.

Fruit Cup

1 cantaloupe
1 honeydew melon
1 thick slice watermelon
1 cup diced fresh pineapple
1 cup granulated sugar

2 tablespoonfuls finely chopped apple mint, orange mint, garden mint, peppermint
1 tablespoonful shaved candied angelica

With a small scoop make tiny balls of cantaloupe, honeydew melon, watermelon, and add diced fresh pineapple. Put the fruit into a bowl and pour over it a cup of sugar, according to taste but the mixture should be tart. Add equal proportions of finely chopped mints, about a tablespoonful to a quart of fruit. Leave some of the mint to be used later. Let the mixture stand 2 or 3 hours in the refrigerator. Just before serving, pile the fruit into serving glasses and scatter over the top a bit of the mint and a few shavings of candied angelica.

Tomato Juice Cocktail

1 pint plain tomato juice, canned or fresh
#6 herb mixture

½ teaspoonful salt
1 teaspoonful sugar
Juice of 1 lemon and 1 orange

Put tomato juice into a bowl; add herb mixture, salt and sugar and let infuse overnight, if possible, or at least 4 or 5 hours. When about to serve add the lemon and orange juices and strain into glasses.

SOUP

Next Day Soup

Chicken stock from bones of roast chicken
Chicken stuffing (see recipe under Stuffings)
Left-over glazed carrots (see recipe under Vegetables)

Left-over creamed onions and boiled potatoes
1 tablespoonful salt
¼ teaspoonful pepper
¼ teaspoonful celery salt

Boil bones with a little more than enough water to cover them. Strain the broth into a soup kettle, add any meat to the broth. Soften a cup of stuffing in a cup of hot water and mash with a fork. Add to the kettle; also add carrots, diced potatoes, onions, salt, pepper, celery salt. Add enough water to make one serving per person but do not "over-thin" the soup. Since the ingredients are already cooked, simply a blending is needed; let the soup simmer for about ½ hour.

FISH

Baked Fish Steaks

1½ pounds slices of halibut, salmon or swordfish	Butter
	Flour
3 cups water	#7 herb mixture
Salt and pepper	2 tablespoonfuls orange juice

Remove skin and as much bone as possible without destroying the shape of the steaks. Boil these trimmings in water about 15 minutes. Strain into a bowl and save stock. Put the steaks into a buttered baking dish; season with salt and pepper, and dot well with butter. Dust evenly with flour; add fish stock, and drop in a bag #7 herb mixture. Bake in a moderate oven (350 degrees F.) about ¾ hour, or until tender. Remove bag; lay fish on a hot platter. Add orange juice to stock, heat and pour over fish. This makes a rich, tart sauce.

EGGS

Indian River Eggs

1 cup flaked crab meat	1 tablespoonful mixed herbs (equal parts of basil, parsley, sweet marjoram, summer savory)
1 tablespoonful butter	
1 tablespoonful flour	
1 cup cream	
½ teaspoonful salt	6 eggs
⅛ teaspoonful pepper	Grated Parmesan or American cheese

Line the bottom of a buttered casserole with flaked crab meat. Melt butter in a saucepan; stir in flour, add cream gradually, stirring to make a smooth paste, and cook until slightly thickened. Add salt, pepper, herbs, and mix thoroughly. Poach the eggs, allowing one to a serving. Pour the cream sauce over the crab meat, arrange poached eggs very carefully on top, sprinkle with cheese and brown in a moderately hot oven (375 degrees F.) until a crisp crust has formed. Serve immediately.

Scandinavian Eggs

Hard boiled eggs
Mayonnaise
Cooked beets

Salt and pepper
Caraway seeds *or* basil and parsley

Cut hard boiled eggs in half lengthwise; remove yolks and mash with enough mayonnaise to make a thick paste. Add finely chopped cooked beets equal in amount to the paste. Season with salt and pepper to taste. Mix thoroughly and fill the egg whites to a rounding heap. Sprinkle with caraway seeds or finely chopped basil and parsley. This makes a delicious base for salad, is useful for picnics or light supper on a hot day.

Stuffed eggs aux fines herbes

4 hard boiled eggs
1 teaspoonful prepared mustard
1 teaspoonful mayonnaise
Salt and pepper

1 tablespoonful #5 herb mixture
Parsley
Paprika

Cut hard boiled eggs in half lengthwise. Remove yolks, mash and mix with mustard, mayonnaise, salt and pepper, herb mixture. Instead of pepper you may add a ¼ teaspoonful more basil. Fill the whites heaping full and sprinkle powdered parsley and paprika over the yolks. This makes a hearty luncheon dish if a cream sauce is poured over the eggs and served with bacon curls.

Omelet aux fines herbes

4 eggs
4 tablespoonfuls warm water
½ teaspoonful salt
Pepper

1 tablespoonful #5 herb mixture
Butter

Beat yolks and whites separately. To the yolks add water, salt, a dash of pepper and #5 herb mixture. Fold the whites into the yolks. Pour into a smoking well buttered pan. Turn fire down low and cook the eggs slowly. When the omelet has risen and is a golden brown next to the pan, set it in a slow oven (300 degrees F.) till it has finished cooking. Then crease through the middle and fold over. Serve immediately.

Breakfast Eggs

Catering to individual taste is very pleasantly and easily done in serving the morning eggs. Porcelain egg cups with screw tops may be bought singly or in sets, with a metal rack and wire handle. In sets each cup may be a different color; each member of the family may choose a color and have his egg boiled with any herb accent preferred and for the time he wishes. Grease the inside of the cup with butter, add a pinch of the desired herb or herb mixture, break the egg into the cup and stir the white very carefully from the bottom so the herbs will be scattered through the egg instead of settling at the bottom. Screw on the top and place in the rack. When all are ready, lower the rack into the hot water, boil and leave each for the required time. When the covers are taken off, the most delightful aroma arises.

CHEESE

Savory Cheese

1 tablespoonful flour	or tomato relish chopped fine
1 tablespoonful butter	
¾ cup milk	½ pound American cheese finely cut up
¼ teaspoonful salt	
¾ teaspoonful basil	1 cup cooked vegetables such as peas, string beans or spinach
¾ teaspoonful summer savory	
2 tablespoonfuls chili sauce	

Blend flour and butter in a saucepan over a low flame, smooth out with milk, add salt, herbs, chili sauce or relish. Add cheese and stir until it is melted and smooth. Add the cup of vegetables, stir them in, and serve on toast with a dash of paprika over each serving. This makes a delicious luncheon dish when a slice of tomato and strip of crisp bacon is placed on the cheese.

POULTRY STUFFINGS

Plymouth Colony Stuffing

(For a 12-pound bird. Divide recipe for smaller fowl.)

2 teaspoonfuls salt
9 cups toasted bread crumbs
¼ teaspoonful pepper
1 teaspoonful each of summer savory, sweet marjoram, thyme, celery leaves and parsley, powdered or chopped

½ teaspoonful grated orange or lemon peel
2 large onions minced
2 tablespoonfuls butter
1 egg
¾ cup hot water or milk (optional)

Clean the fowl, rub the inside with 1 teaspoonful salt and leave it while the stuffing is being made. Toast day old bread made of whole or cracked wheat and break into crumbs. Toasting not only prevents the bread from becoming soggy, but gives a delightful nutty flavor, especially to cracked or whole wheat bread. Mix the dry seasonings and crumbs well. Fry the minced onion in the butter until a golden brown and mix with the other ingredients. Stir in the egg slightly beaten. If a moist stuffing is desired, add about ¾ cup of hot water or milk. When the mixture is cold, fill the bird but do not cram the stuffing in, but leave room for the bread to swell. If possible, the fowl should be stuffed the night before roasting so the flavor will infuse through the whole bird. This same stuffing is excellent with pork chops.

Chestnut Stuffing

Use the above recipe, substituting for the onion, 4 cups of finely chopped boiled chestnuts and use 5 cups bread crumbs instead of 9.

MEATS

Stuffed Pork Chops

Pork chops

Small portion of Plymouth Colony Stuffing

Have the butcher slit each chop to make a side pocket. Fill this
with the stuffing and fasten with small skewers. Arrange the chops
in a shallow baking dish, add about ½ cup water, cover and bake
in a moderate oven for ½ hour; uncover and bake ¾ hour longer
or until tender, basting frequently.

Pork Chops with Scalloped Potatoes

Pork chops	2 teaspoonfuls salt
Sliced raw potatoes	¼ teaspoonful pepper
Sliced raw onions	2 teaspoonfuls #3 herb mix-
2 cups heated milk	ture
½ cup flour	Butter

Trim off most of the fat from the chops and heat in saucepan to
remove the grease. Peel and slice raw potatoes and as many onions
as your taste dictates. Heat milk over a low flame. Discard the
pieces of fat, pour a tablespoonful of the melted fat into a baking
dish and oil the bottom thoroughly. Arrange the chops in the dish,
then a layer of potatoes, then a layer of onions. In a small bowl
mix flour, salt and pepper and #3 herb mixture; sprinkle over the
onion layer. Repeat the layers of potatoes, onions and dry mixture
to within an inch of the top with the dry the last layer. Add the rest
of the melted pork fat and enough heated milk to reach the top of
the last onion layer. Dot with butter. Set the dish in a hot oven for
10 minutes, and cook at moderate heat for about an hour. Allow
plenty of time because pork should be very well cooked before it is
eaten.

Chicken Fricassee

Chicken cut into pieces	2 cups water
Butter for frying	12 small white onions
2 tablespoonfuls flour	#9 herb mixture
2 tablespoonfuls butter	Boiled rice

Roll pieces of chicken in flour and brown in butter. Blend butter
with flour and make a sauce with 2 cups water. Lay chicken in deep
skillet, add sauce, onions and herb bag, #9 mixture, into the liquid.
Cook until chicken is tender, adding hot water to make about 2 cups

liquid for gravy at the end of cooking. Remove chicken to hot platter. Make a delicious gravy by heating 3 tablespoonfuls of the liquid in the kettle with the yolk of an egg, stirring back into the remaining liquid and boiling 5 minutes. Remove herb bag. Pile on hot platter a mound of flaky boiled rice and arrange the chicken around it. Serve gravy in a bowl with rosemary biscuits.

Luncheon Chicken

3½ tablespoonfuls butter	1 egg
1½ tablespoonfuls flour	1 tablespoonful minced onion
1½ cups milk	1½ cups cooked chicken diced
1 teaspoonful salt	1½ cups steam rice
¼ teaspoonful pepper	Grated cheese
#5 herb mixture	

Blend 1½ tablespoonfuls butter with flour; smooth out with the milk and add seasonings. Set aside to cool for 5 minutes and stir in the egg slightly beaten. Fry the minced onion to a golden brown in 2 tablespoonfuls of butter and mix with chicken and rice. Pour white sauce over and mix thoroughly, and sprinkle with grated cheese, dot with butter and set the dish in a pan of hot water in a moderate oven for about 50 minutes.

Veal Cutlets aux fines herbes

1½ pounds veal	½ teaspoonful salt
2 teaspoonfuls #4 herb mixture	1 egg
¾ cup cracker crumbs	1 teaspoonful water
	2 tablespoonfuls butter

Cut 1½ pounds veal into individual servings. Mix #4 herb mixture with cracker meal or fine crumbs and salt. Spread on a paper and roll the cutlets in this mixture. Dip them into a mixture of slightly beaten egg and water; dip again into the herb-crumb mixture. Melt butter in skillet and brown cutlets on both sides; lay them in a buttered baking dish. Pour 1 cup hot water into the skillet and bring to a boil. This will make a rich stock to pour over the veal. Bake in a moderate oven ¾ hour or until veal is tender.

Veal Birds

Small portion of Plymouth Col-   Flour
ony Stuffing   Salt and pepper
Veal steaks 2 inches by 4 inches

Spread stuffing on each steak, roll and fasten with toothpicks. Roll in flour mixed with salt and pepper, and fry in bacon drippings or butter until brown. Place in a baking dish, partly cover with water and cook in oven 350 degrees F. until tender, probably about ¾ hour.

Hamburger Cakes de luxe

1 pound chopped beef   1 large onion minced
1 egg slightly beaten   2 tablespoonfuls butter
1 teaspoonful salt   Bacon
2 teaspoonfuls #1 herb mixture Parsley
   Bread crumbs

Mix beef, egg, seasonings and add enough bread crumbs to hold ingredients together. Fry onion in butter and stir into mixture thoroughly. Form into balls, flatten slightly, wrap a strip of bacon around each cake and fasten with a tiny skewer or toothpick. Place in baking dish with ½ cup hot water and bake in a moderate over ½ hour, adding water if necessary to keep the meat from burning. To crisp the bacon, set under boiler for a few minutes. Serve with a sprig of parsley on each cake.

Royal Meat Cakes

    Meat cakes   1 teaspoonful burnt onion juice
1½ tablespoonfuls flour   1 teaspoonful Worcestershire
1½ tablespoonfuls bacon drip-   sauce
    pings   1 tablespoonful #1 herb mix-
 1 cup tomato juice   ture

Make meat cakes according to recipe for hamburger cakes de luxe. Arrange in baking dish, add basting sauce made by blending flour with bacon drippings and smoothing out with water. Add tomato juice, burnt onion juice, Worcestershire sauce, enough water to make 3 cups of sauce and add #1 herb mixture. You may prefer to tie the herb in a little square of cheesecloth, drop the bag in the sauce, simmer for 5 minutes, remove the bag to the baking dish until just before serving. Pour sauce over meat cakes, set dish in a hot oven for 10 minutes, cook at moderate heat for 30 minutes more, basting frequently with the sauce in the pan.

Preferably, when arranging the balls in the baking dish, place over each ½ strip of bacon and allow them to cook as above described. Just before serving, set the dish under the broiler to crisp the bacon.

Plate Steak

2 teaspoonfuls salt	2 tablespoonfuls bacon drippings
¼ teaspoonful pepper	
1 teaspoonful celery salt	1 can tomatoes
1 heaping tablespoonful mixed herbs (basil, summer savory, thyme, chervil, sweet marjoram)	1 teaspoonful Worcestershire sauce
	12 small sweet pickled onions with two tablespoonfuls of the juice
½ cup flour	
A slice of round steak 1¼ inches thick	Potatoes
	Carrots
	1 cup fresh green peas

Combine all dry seasonings with flour, mix thoroughly. Spread 2 tablespoonfuls on a clean metal tabletop or other firm surface, lay the steak on flour and sprinkle the top with as much more flour. Turn it over, pour more flour on top and pound again. Repeat until as much of the flour as possible is worked into the steak. Put bacon drippings into heavy skillet, lay steak on it and over a hot fire sear both sides, lay steak in a large baking dish. Blend the flour that did not work into the steak with fat still in the skillet. Smooth out with tomato juice in which the tomatoes have been well mashed, add Worcestershire sauce. Distribute onions over and around the steak and pour the pickle juice over it. Clean and slice potatoes and carrots and arrange them over the meat, carrots on top. Leave at least 1½ inches from top of dish. Pour liquid from the skillet over all. Spread green peas over the top. Cover and bake in a moderate oven from 1½ to 2 hours. The green of the peas next to the orange carrots makes a colorful dish. Pounding the steak with the edge of plate, an old country custom, made such an impression on the household the first time the dish was "heard," that it has ever since been known as Plate Steak.

Kentucky Loaf

1 large onion, minced	corn
3 tablespoonfuls melted bacon fat	1 small green pepper, diced
1 pound round steak ground	1 cup bread crumbs
1 egg, slightly beaten	3 teaspoonfuls #1 herb mixture
1½ teaspoonfuls salt	1 can condensed vegetable soup
¼ teaspoonful pepper	
1 cup cream style canned	½ teaspoonful kitchen bouquet

Fry onion in 1 tablespoonful of the bacon fat. Mix remaining ingredients except the soup. Form into a loaf and place in a baking dish in which the remaining fat has been melted; add 1 cup hot water. Bake in a moderate oven (350 degrees F.) for ½ hour. Pour vegetable soup into a skillet; thin with equal amount hot water, and add kitchen bouquet. Bring to a boil, and use to baste the loaf frequently during cooking. This makes a delicious rich gravy. Serve in a baking dish. Sufficient for 10 servings.

The King's Meat Loaf

LOAF

1 large onion, minced	sweet marjoram, thyme, parsley and celery leaves
3 tablespoonfuls bacon fat	
2 cups toasted whole wheat bread crumbs	1 egg, slightly beaten
	1 pound round steak ground
½ teaspoonful grated orange or lemon peel	1 #1 can cream style corn
	1 small green pepper, diced
1½ teaspoonfuls salt	¼ teaspoonful prepared mustard
¼ teaspoonful pepper	
½ teaspoonful each of dried and sieved summer savory,	½ teaspoonful Worcestershire sauce

Fry onion in bacon fat. Add bread crumbs and remaining ingredients. Mix well, and shape into a loaf in middle of a greased baking dish, leaving a good 1 inch space all around.

SAUCE

1 can condensed vegetable soup	1 teaspoonful salt
½ can water	1 teaspoonful burnt onion juice (optional)
1 teaspoonful Worcestershire sauce	

Mix ingredients in order given and heat. Pour 1 cup of sauce around loaf, and bake in a hot oven (400 degrees F.) for 10 minutes to sear the top. Add another cup of sauce and continue baking in a moderate oven (350 degrees F.) for about ¾ hour, basting with the sauce which, at the end of the cooking, will be a thick gravy. Serve in a baking dish. Sufficient for 8 servings.

Corned Beef Loaf

1 (No. 2) can corned beef	2 teaspoonfuls Worcestershire sauce
2 cups Plymouth Colony stuffing	1 egg
2 onions	Hot water
1 small pepper, diced	1 can condensed vegetable soup
¼ teaspoonful prepared mustard	1 teaspoonful burnt onion juice
	1 teaspoonful salt

Grind the corned beef; make the stuffing using 2 onions instead of one, and mix with the meat. Add diced pepper, mustard, 1 teaspoonful Worcestershire, 1 egg and enough hot water to make a moist loaf. Pour into small greased baking pan and shape into a loaf, leaving 1 inch space all around.

Heat the soup, diluting sufficiently for a basting sauce to which add 1 teaspoonful Worcestershire sauce, 1 teaspoonful burnt onion juice and 1 teaspoonful salt. Pour a cup of soup around the loaf, set in a hot oven (400 degrees F.) for 10 minutes, and bake in a moderate oven (350 degrees F.) for 30 minutes more, basting with the rest of the soup which finally cooks down to a thick gravy.

Rolled Round Steak

1 pound round steak	Plymouth Colony stuffing
1 tablespoonful flour	Basting sauce for Royal Meat Cakes
½ teaspoonful salt	

Have steak cut into one or two strips about ¾ inch thick or a little less. Dip each piece into flour mixed with salt. Spread thickly, fairly moist poultry stuffing on each piece of steak, roll up tightly like a jelly roll, tie with a string and lay rolls in a baking dish. Bake meat with the sauce poured over it, in a hot oven (400 degrees F.) for 10 minutes, then cook in a moderate oven (350 degrees F.) for 1 hour or until done, basting frequently to keep the meat from getting dry. Serve in the dish with the basting sauce.

Beef a la mode with Rosemary Biscuits

½ cup flour
1½ teaspoonfuls salt
¼ teaspoonful pepper
1 pound stewing beef, cut in 2-inch cubes
1½ tablespoonfuls bacon fat

4 carrots, sliced
1 large onion, sliced
6 potatoes, quartered
1 (No. 2½) can tomatoes
1 tablespoonful #1 herb mixture

Mix flour, salt, pepper; roll meat cubes in it and brown in bacon fat. Arrange in the bottom of a large deep baking dish. Add carrots, onions, potatoes and pulp drained from canned tomatoes.

Stir remainder of flour mixture into the bacon fat; add gradually juice from canned tomatoes. Cook until slightly thickened. Add #1 herb mixture. If you do not care for flecks of herbs in the liquid, tie this mixture in a little square of cheesecloth and tuck it down in the middle of one side of the baking dish. Pour the liquid over meat and vegetables adding, if necessary, enough water to come 1 inch from top of the dish. Cover, and bake in a moderately slow oven (325 degrees F.) for 1½ to 2 hours. The longer the cooking, the better this dish will be.

Serve with Rosemary Biscuits. (Page 81)

VEGETABLES

Glazed Carrots aux fines herbes

Carrots
2 tablespoonfuls #2 herb mixture
Butter

1 tablespoonful granulated sugar
½ cup water

Split carrots in half lengthwise; parboil. Butter a shallow casserole, or a glass pie plate, which makes a very pretty dish to serve at table. Spread 1 tablespoonful of #2 herb mixture evenly over the bottom of the plate, lay carrots flat side down. Sprinkle the rest of the herb mixture evenly over the top of the carrots. Dot generously with butter and sprinkle sugar over all. Pour ½ cup of water into the dish carefully and cook in a moderate oven (350 degrees F.) about 15 minutes or until carrots are tender.

Savory Beets

1½ cups cider vinegar	1 teaspoonful basil
½ cup water	1 teaspoonful winter savory
1 (No. 2) can of beets or 1 bunch (usually 6) fresh beets	1 tablespoonful butter

Dilute strong cider vinegar ⅓ with water, making enough liquid to cover beets completely. Tie up herbs in cheesecloth bag and drop into the vinegar. Simmer gently in a porcelain saucepan for 10 minutes. Press the bag thoroughly, remove and squeeze it above the pan and discard it. Add beets to this vinegar with a tablespoonful of butter. Spiced vinegar may be used instead of cider.

Creamed Mushrooms

1 cupful (¼ pound) mushrooms	2 tablespoonfuls flour
1 tablespoonful #2 herb mixture	½ teaspoonful salt
2 thick slices lemon	Cream
2 tablespoonfuls butter	4 slices of toast

Wipe mushroom caps and stems, if they are tender. Put into a kettle with enough water to a little more than cover them, add bag of #2 herb mixture and lemon. Cook until mushrooms are tender and the liquid reduces to about a half cupful. Remove soup bag and lemon, strain and save liquid. Blend in a skillet, butter, flour and salt. Add the mushroom stock and enough cream, gradually stirring to make a medium thick sauce. Stir in mushrooms, cook 5 minutes and serve on toast.

Baked Potato

6 tablespoonfuls butter   3 large or 6 small baked pota-
1 teaspoonful salt   toes
6 teaspoonfuls powdered basil

Cook butter, salt and basil gently over a low flame for 5 minutes. Just before serving, split freshly baked potatoes in half lengthwise, scoop a tiny bit of potato out of the middle and criss-cross the length and breadth 2 or 3 times with a knife spreading cuts. Carefully pour over herb butter mixture letting it soak down the cuts. Serve immediately.

Stuffed Peppers

1 cup left-over chicken   1 teaspoonful salt
1 cup left-over stuffing   2 cups chicken stock
1 large onion, minced   3 green peppers
2 tablespoonfuls butter   3 slices bacon
1 egg, slightly beaten

Instead of the usual minced beef and rice stuffing, use the rest of the poultry stuffing and the odds and ends of meat on the bones of the bird. Stew bones in enough water to cover. Put meat and stuffing through the meat grinder and turn into mixing bowl. Fry onion brown in butter and add to the mixture; add egg and salt. Strain chicken stock and add enough to make a very moist mixture. Stuff the peppers; lay a half slice of bacon on each one; arrange in baking dish; add a cup more of the chicken stock, and bake in moderate oven (350 degrees F.). Use remaining stock for frequent bastings until peppers are done, about ½ hour.

Stuffed Onions

6 large Spanish onions   1 tablespoonful butter
½ pound sausage meat   1 tablespoonful flour
½ teaspoonful salt   ¾ cup milk
1 tablespoonful #3 herb mix-
    ture

Parboil onions for 15 minutes. Scoop out the centers of the onions being careful not to pierce the bottom. Stuff with sausage meat. Add salt and herbs, mixed thoroughly. Arrange onions in a baking dish. Melt butter in saucepan; stir in flour; add milk gradually, stirring to make a smooth paste, and cook until slightly thickened, and pour sauce around onions. Bake in a moderate oven (350 degrees F.) for about ¾ hour or until done. Baste a few times during the baking with the sauce.

Stuffed Tomatoes

4 large tomatoes	1 heaping tablespoonful #2
1 cup cooked vegetables, diced	herb mixture
	1 egg, slightly beaten
4 tablespoonfuls bread crumbs	2 tablespoonfuls grated cheese
	2 tablespoonfuls melted butter
1 teaspoonful salt	1 can condensed vegetable soup
¼ teaspoonful pepper	

Scoop out tomatoes carefully. Put pulp in a bowl, add 1 cup cooked string beans, peas or asparagus, or a mixture of vegetables and bread crumbs. (You can also add a cup of leftover meat, minced. The amount of stuffing will be gauged by the size and number of hollowed out tomatoes.)

Add to mixture in the bowl all seasonings, stir in egg; fill tomatoes heaping full with the mixture. Sprinkle with grated cheese and add butter. Arrange tomatoes in a buttered baking dish. Baste frequently with soup until it is all used. Bake in a moderate oven (350 degrees F.) for ½ to ¾ hour.

Broiled Tomatoes

3 tomatoes	1 tablespoonful #2 herb mixture
5 tablespoonfuls bread crumbs	½ teaspoonful grated cheese
½ teaspoonful salt	Butter

Cut large, firm tomatoes into thick slices. Mix bread crumbs, salt and herbs. Cover each slice with a heaping teaspoonful of the mixture, sprinkle with grated cheese and dot liberally with butter. Arrange slices on a shallow pan or cookie sheet, set under the broiler at medium heat, watching carefully until done, about 10 minutes.

Scalloped String Beans

4 tablespoonfuls butter	1 tablespoonful #2 herb mixture
2 tablespoonfuls flour	
1 cup top milk	4 cups cooked string beans
½ teaspoonful salt	2 tablespoonfuls bread crumbs
	2 tablespoonfuls grated cheese

Melt 2 tablespoonfuls butter in a spider, stir in flour, add milk gradually, stirring to make a smooth paste and cook until it is a medium thick sauce. Add salt, herbs and string beans and heat thoroughly. Pour into a buttered baking dish, sprinkle with bread crumbs, then grated cheese, dot generously with butter. Bake in a moderate oven (350 degrees F.) for 25 minutes.

SALADS

Chicken Salad

2 cups chicken meat	Salt
Lettuce	½ teaspoonful celery salt
4 hard boiled eggs	1 heaping tablespoonful #5
Mayonnaise or old-fashioned	herb mixture
boiled dressing	1 (No. 2) can asparagus tips
3 tomatoes	or 1 bunch fresh
	Paprika

Chicken salad is capable of practically limitless elasticity if you unexpectedly find yourself with 8 to serve instead of 3. You probably will not have on hand the amount of chicken you would have served for a portion, but you can "stretch" with vegetables and still have a most delicious salad.

In our family we prefer shredded lettuce to celery so I mix about equal parts lettuce and cut up cooked chicken. Slice eggs with a commercial slicer, if possible, so as to have some thin even slices, and from each egg save 2 or 3 of the best slices for a garnish. Chop up finely the rest of the eggs and add to the chicken. Add salad dressing to make a moist mixture but thick enough to stay heaped up. Peel and slice tomatoes, again saving out a slice or two of each. Chop up the rest and stir into the mixture. Salt to taste. Add celery salt, #5 herb mixture (either dried or finely chopped fresh herbs). Stir mixture thoroughly and pile in the middle of a large platter. Garnish with tomato and egg slices, cooked asparagus tips and a dash of paprika. This makes 1½ quarts.

Pear Salad

3 fresh or 1 (No. 2) can pears
1 package cream cheese
1 teaspoonful cream
¾ teaspoonful powdered rosemary and sweet marjoram

Chopped nuts
3 teaspoonfuls apple mint or orange mint

If fresh pears are used, peel, cut in half and scoop out the fibrous center. Soften cream cheese with cream; add rosemary and sweet marjoram, and stir thoroughly. Make little balls of the cheese mixture, roll in finely chopped nuts and place in the center of the pears. Sprinkle over each half ½ teaspoonful of chopped fresh or dried and sieved apple mint or orange mint or a mixture of both. Serve with the (b) dressing for fruit salad given on page 103.

Potato Salad

1 tablespoonful equal parts basil, summer savory, marjoram
1 cup mayonnaise or boiled dressing
2 onions
Cider vinegar

2 hard boiled eggs
4 cold boiled potatoes
Salt and pepper
½ teaspoonful celery salt or celery seed

Two or 3 hours before you make the salad, stir herb mixture into salad dressing and let infuse. Slice the onions and let them soak in cider vinegar to take out some of the sharpness. Slice the eggs leaving a few of the best for decoration. Into a large bowl, slice the potatoes, add onions, eggs and salad dressing. Salt and pepper to taste; add celery salt or seed. Mix thoroughly when arranging salad on platter, decorate with the egg slices, shake paprika over and if in the spring cut up over it the leaves of a few dill seedlings. This makes 1 quart.

Green Salad

The picture of the housewife complete with garden hat, basket and shears clipping here and there among her herbs for the makings of a green salad is a pretty picture, but may result in a pretty terrible salad. If you do not know your herbs, their odors and tastes, you are likely to snip off some never meant for salads. The leaves of hyssop have an odor of skunk, while those of coriander smell and taste horribly, although the dried seeds are most fragrant. Table R, page 210, gives practical suggestions.

For the bulk of the salad use leaves of young lettuce, white mustard, chicory, dandelion and lovage. Add leaves of fresh young chives and of basil, sweet marjoram, caraway, fennel and dill seedlings. To garnish, you might use sliced radishes, olives, tomato and hard-boiled eggs. For the dressings see the recipe for French dressing *aux fines herbes*.

SALAD DRESSINGS

French Dressing aux fines herbes

3 tablespoonfuls salad oil   Salt and pepper to taste
1 tablespoonful burnet vine-   1 teaspoonful mixture of mar-
   gar (see Chapter 13)   joram, basil, summer savory

Put all ingredients in a cruet and shake well before serving.

Salad Dressing for Those Who Are Not So Slim

6 tablespoonfuls mineral oil   Pinch of salt
1 tablespoonful mixture of   2 tablespoonfuls lemon juice
   parsley, basil, summer sa-
   vory, marjoram

Put all ingredients in a cruet and shake well before serving.

Two Dressings for Fruit Salad

(a) Mash two tablespoonfuls of mint jelly, add the juice of a lemon, a pinch of salt and 4 tablespoonfuls of mayonnaise. Mix thoroughly and combine with 4 tablespoonfuls of whipped cream.

(b) 3 tablespoonfuls salad oil   Sugar to taste if juice is from
    1 tablespoonful any kind   citrus fruit
      of fruit juice

Put ingredients in cruet and shake well before serving.

SAUCES

Mint Sauce

¼ cup vinegar   ¼ cup water
1 teaspoonful granulated   1 heaping tablespoonful
  sugar   orange mint and apple
                                     mint

Boil all ingredients gently for 10 minutes and cool before serving. Instead of sugar, 1 heaping teaspoonful of orange marmalade
may be used.

Vinaigrette Sauce

8 tablespoonfuls salad oil   ¼ teaspoon salt; pinch of
5 tablespoonfuls herb vinegar   pepper
  (see Chapter 13)   Hard boiled yolk of egg,
1 medium sized dill pickle,   mashed
  minced   1 teaspoonful mixed herbs,
                                     chervil, chives, tarragon,
                                     basil

Mix and beat thoroughly before serving.

Fish Sauces

(a) *Herb Butter Sauce*—Mix thoroughly 1 level tablespoonful
of flour and 1 of butter; smooth out with top milk or thin cream
to the consistency you wish. Add ¼ teaspoonful of salt, a pinch of
pepper and 1½ teaspoonfuls of mixed herbs—equal parts of basil,
sweet marjoram and finely powdered fennel. From time to time
vary the combination of herbs and thus avoid monotonous sameness.

(b) *Cream Sauce*—In broiling mackerel or steaks of halibut or
salmon, you will enjoy the delicious taste resulting from the addition of an herb mixture to the butter spread over the fish before

putting it under the fire. Take ¼ cup soft butter, add ½ teaspoonful salt, ⅛ teaspoonful pepper, 1½ tablespoonfuls mixed herbs—basil, chervil, thyme, marjoram and finely powdered fennel seeds. Mix these ingredients thoroughly. Spread half on the fish, and after turning it over, spread the other side with the remaining mixture.

DESSERTS

Indian Pudding

1 quart milk	½ teaspoonful ginger
5 tablespoonfuls yellow corn meal	2 eggs
	1 cup dark molasses
1 teaspoonful salt	2 tablespoonfuls butter
¾ teaspoonful cinnamon	1 extra cup rich milk

Scald 1 quart milk in the upper part of a double boiler. Add corn meal slowly, stirring constantly. When the meal has been well stirred in, cook in the double boiler for ½ hour. Beat seasonings with eggs and add molasses and butter to the corn meal mixture. Stir thoroughly and pour into a buttered baking dish. Add cup of rich milk and bake in a moderate oven (350 degrees F.) for 1 hour. Serve with cream or with homemade vanilla or lemon ice cream.

A fine addition to the above is made by crushing a tablespoonful of coriander seeds and putting them in the milk before scalding.

Ambrosial Delight

3 oranges	1 tablespoonful shredded coconut
1 can small pineapple slices	
1 teaspoonful granulated sugar	1 teaspoonful chopped orange and apple mints
	Maraschino cherries

Arrange in dessert dishes, slices of pineapple with orange slices on top. Sprinkle with sugar, coconut, and mints. Top each dish with a maraschino cherry and a teaspoonful of the juice. Chill thoroughly before serving.

CAKES AND COOKIES

Applesauce Cake

1 tablespoonful coriander seeds	1½ cups flour
¾ cup raisins	4 teaspoonfuls baking powder
¾ cup hot water	1 teaspoonful cinnamon
1 cup sugar	½ teaspoonful nutmeg
½ cup butter	¼ teaspoonful allspice
1 cup thick applesauce	¼ teaspoonful cloves
1 egg, well beaten	½ cup chopped nutmeats
	1 teaspoonful salt

Put crushed coriander seeds in a bowl with raisins and add hot water. Let stand for 15 minutes, stirring frequently so they will be thoroughly soaked. Cream sugar and butter, add applesauce and egg. Sift dry ingredients into a bowl and mix thoroughly. Add coriander seed and raisin mixture to the applesauce mixture, and gradually add dry ingredients, stirring well after each addition. The batter may be baked in a loaf or in layers. An amusing way is to bake in 3 square layer cake pans, graduated in size. I put the layers together in pyramid form with uncooked icing.

Icing

1 tablespoonful butter	Top milk
Confectioner's sugar	Orange coloring (optional)
1 teaspoonful vanilla	

Melt butter, add sugar, vanilla and blend with top milk. Alternate sugar and milk until the desired amount and a spreading consistency are reached. When I first made this layer cake, it happened to be Halloween; I added orange coloring of a reliable commercial brand, mixing thoroughly until an even color was achieved. After icing the cake, I placed at each of the 12 corners a tiny chocolate pumpkin, and in the center of the top layer a larger pumpkin filled with "kernels of corn." This cake lends itself beautifully to any holiday decoration.

Gingerbread

1 teaspoonful coriander seed	1 teaspoonful cinnamon
¼ cup warm water	⅔ cup shortening
2 cups flour	½ cup brown sugar
1¼ teaspoonfuls baking soda	2 eggs, well beaten
½ teaspoonful salt	¾ cup molasses
3 teaspoonfuls ginger	¾ cup boiling water

To bring out the flavors, that is, the essential oils of herbs that are to be used in fairly dry mixtures, soak the required amount of the leaf or seed in some of the liquid for ½ hour before using. Crush coriander seed and soak in ¼ cup warm water. Add this mixture when the boiling water is added.

Sift the flour twice with soda, salt, ginger and cinnamon. Cream the shortening with brown sugar until light and fluffy. Add eggs and beat well. Add ¼ of flour mixture and blend; add molasses and beat until smooth. Add remaining flour mixture, beating well. Add boiling water (and spice water) gradually and beat until smooth. Turn into greased square loaf pan and bake in moderate oven (350 degrees F.) 50 minutes.

Seed Cookies

Use a good basic recipe for a sugar cookie, and add whatever variety of seed you choose.

Aniseed Cookies

½ cup butter	1½ teaspoonfuls salt
1½ cups sugar	Grated rind of lemon or orange
2 eggs, well beaten	
3 cups flour	¼ cup milk or orange juice
2 teaspoonfuls baking powder	1 tablespoonful of aniseed

Cream butter and sugar, add eggs and mix thoroughly. Sift flour, baking powder, salt and grated rind. Add this to the first mixture gradually, alternating with milk or orange juice. Then add aniseed, crushed or whole. If you wish a blended flavor of anise, crush the seed, but if you prefer to bite through the seed to get the entire flavor, add them whole. After the ingredients are mixed thoroughly, chill the dough, roll out thinly on a slightly floured board, cut with cutter which has been dipped into flour, and bake about 10 minutes in a moderately hot oven (350 degrees F.). The length of time for baking depends on the thickness of the cookie. If you prefer drop cookies, add more liquid to the dough, drop from a teaspoon, about 1 inch apart, and let stand for a few hours in a cool place. Instead of aniseed you may add 1 tablespoonful caraway seed or sesame seed, slightly toasted to bring out the nutty flavor; or after cutting the dough into forms for sesame cookies, press down ½ teaspoonful poppy seeds on each shape.

Filled Savory Seed Cookies

A filled cookie may be made by rolling out thinly the dough of the basic recipe for sugar cookies, cutting into small oblongs and spreading each one with a mixture of the seeds of sesame and poppy, ground nutmeats and enough strained honey to hold the mixture together. Roll the dough into a cylinder. You might cut the thinly rolled dough into squares with a little of the seed mixture in the center and fold up the corners.

SANDWICH SPREADS

In the following recipes always salt to taste; use about 2 table-spoonfuls herbs to a cup of cheese, mayonnaise or other mixture. Let the herbs infuse in the mixture for 3 or 4 hours before spreading on bread. Herb butter may be used to spread any of the sandwiches before the mixtures are spread or the herb butter alone may be spread on bread to serve with salads. To ½ pound of butter that has been softened add ½ cup herbs, such as tarragon, chives, basil and summer savory, and mix thoroughly. Let the mixture stand and chill before using.

Mix equal parts of orange mint, apple mint and parsley, and enough mayonnaise to hold the herbs together. Spread on slices of white bread, and cover with whole wheat bread.

Cream cheese softened with cream and chopped chives or chopped fresh or dried and sieved basil, summer savory and sweet marjoram added.

Fresh grated cheese with prepared mustard mashed to a paste by adding vinegar. Add and mix thoroughly chopped chives, any herb you wish—basil, summer savory, parsley or a combination of herbs.

Hard boiled eggs with prepared mustard mashed to a paste by adding vinegar. Add and mix thoroughly tarragon or basil and summer savory.

Lay lettuce leaves or one slice of bread spread with herb butter. Spread another slice with mayonnaise in which chopped chives have been mixed.

Mash hard-boiled eggs and cooked mushrooms. Add enough mayonnaise to make a consistency for spreading. Add and mix thoroughly tarragon.

A pretty accompaniment for a fruit salad or for afternoon tea is a rose petal sandwich. The night before place a thick layer of fragrant red rose petals in a glass or earthen jar; lay on top a slab of butter, then another layer of petals, and cover the jar until ready for use. Cut bread into rectangles 2 inches by 3 inches, spread with the butter and place on it several petals. Then either roll up the bread with the petals showing a little, or top the slice with another piece of bread and serve as a flat sandwich.

SWEETS

Apple Jelly Flavored with Herbs

Just before the liquid comes to a rolling boil, add a handful of apple mint, orange mint, lemon verbena, lemon balm or skeleton leaf geranium. Boil 3 minutes, strain into glasses, seal at once with paraffin.

Another way of imparting the herb flavor is to pour the jelly into glasses, float a few leaves of the smaller foliage and one leaf or part of one of the sweet-leaved geranium on top of the jelly; seal with paraffin at once. When this cover is removed the leaves will come out with the paraffin, and the jelly has been permeated with the herb flavor.

Candied Angelica

Cut stalks of angelica the desired length. Put into boiling water to which green coloring has been added. To prevent stalks from losing their shape, put the smaller inside the larger ones. Cook until just tender, drain and place stalks in a jar (not glass), and pour over them a hot, thin sirup (25 degrees density if you have a saccharimeter). After 20 minutes drain and again bring the sirup to the boiling point, and pour it over the angelica. Let stand from 12 to 14 hours. Drain again and you will find the sirup has lost part of its density. Add sugar to bring it up to 25 degrees, boil and skim. Pour again over the angelica. Let it remain 2 days and repeat until the angelica is transparent and jewellike and the density is 35 instead of 25. Keep in glass jars until wanted. Then drain and crystallize. Add about 1 cup of karo or glucose to prevent crystals from forming.

Herb Jellies

Herb	Cups Water	Juice	Herb	Cups Sugar	Color
Savory	½	1 cup grapefruit	2 tbl.	3½	green
Marjoram	1	½ cup lemon	2 tbl.	3½	red
Thyme	½	1 cup grapejuice	1 tbl.	3	
Sage	½	1 cup cider	2 tbl.	3½	yellow
Rosemary	¾	½ cup orange and ¼ cup lemon	2 tbl.	3½	orange
Mint	1	½ cup cider vinegar	1 cup	3½	green

The above chart gives proportions for ½ bottle of commercial pectin. Wash herbs, leaves and stems, put into a skillet and mash thoroughly. Add liquids and sugar, set over a medium fire and boil for 7 or 8 minutes very gently to bring out the oils of herbs. Add vegetable coloring matter to the desired intensity, turn up the fire, bring to a boil, add the liquid pectin, beat rapidly ½ minute, skim off herbs, sieve through a fine cloth into glasses. Pour melted paraffin over jelly at once.

Halloween Apples

6 red apples
6 wooden meat skewers

½ cup granulated sugar
½ cup corn sirup

Stick the skewers firmly into apples after stems have been taken out. Into a small deep kettle put sugar and sirup and cook slowly until sugar is dissolved. Boil until sirup hardens when a little is dropped into cold water. Take from the fire and set in a pan of hot water. Holding the end of the meat skewer, turn the apple around in the sirup until completely covered. Set each apple well separated from one another on waxed paper to cool.

Sesame Bars

1 cup sesame seeds
½ cup granulated sugar
½ cup brown sugar
1 tablespoon strained honey

½ cup water
Pinch of salt
Pinch of soda

Brown seeds to a golden color in the oven. Put the sugar, honey and water in a saucepan and dissolve the sugar over a slow fire, and turn to a medium fire; boil the sirup until it hardens when dropped from a spoon into cold water. Remove from fire; add salt and soda; stir in sesame seeds and pour on buttered pan. As soon as the candy begins to cool, mark into small bars or squares. Roll the pieces in wax paper and keep in air-tight jar to keep moisture from candy.

Horehound Candy

1 cup horehound leaves
1 teaspoonful crushed aniseed
1 quart water

1½ pounds granulated sugar
1½ pounds brown sugar

Boil horehound leaves and aniseed in the water for 20 minutes and strain through cheesecloth. To the liquid add sugar, cook over a slow fire until sugar is dissolved, then boil over a moderate fire until sirup hardens when dropped from a spoon into cold water. Remove from fire, pour into a buttered pan and when cool, mark into small squares.

Peppermint Wafers

⅜ cup English or ½ cup American peppermint leaves
1½ cups water

2 cups sugar
¼ teaspoonful cream of tartar

Boil peppermint leaves in water gently for 10 minutes and strain through cheesecloth. To the liquid add sugar and dissolve over a slow fire; boil over a medium fire until, dropped from a spoon into cold water, the sirup will form a soft ball. Remove from fire, add cream of tartar and set the kettle into a pan of hot water and beat until creamy. Drop mixture from end of spoon on waxed paper. If it becomes too thick add a spoonful of boiling water.

Honey of Roses

Cut off the white heels of ½ pound of sweet-scented roses. Mash them with a wooden masher; boil for 15 minutes in 1 pint of water; add 2 pounds of strained honey and boil down to a thick sirup. Pour into scalded glass jars and seal.

Mint-flavored Candied Citrus Fruit Peel

6 oranges or 4 grapefruit or 8 lemons	3 cups granulated sugar
	2 cups water
1 cup equal parts orange mint and apple mint	2 cups additional sugar

Scrape the white membrane from inner side of fruit. Cut into ¼ inch strips 3 inches long with scissors. Put into kettle, cover well with cold water, bring to a boil and drain off liquid. Pour more cold water over the peel and again bring to a boil. In the meantime, make a strong infusion of mints with 2 cups of water. Boil for 10 minutes and strain. For peel of 6 oranges take 3 cups of granulated sugar. Dissolve this in strained mint infusion. Put peel into liquid and boil until strips are tender and clear. Strain sirup off, roll peel in granulated sugar and, until cool and dry, keep separate on a platter. Store in a tin box that can be tightly covered.

Candied Flowers or Leaves

There are two methods, cold and hot. One is to brush the petals or leaves with white of egg mixed with a little water. Sprinkle them thoroughly with granulated sugar and lay on wax paper to dry. The other method is to dip petals or leaves in rose water in which gum arabic has been steeped, sprinkle sugar over them and dry in an oven at low temperature. Store in a tin box that can be tightly covered. Arrange petals or leaves on wax paper so that they do not touch and between each two layers put a layer of wax paper.

Candied Roots of Lovage and Sweet Flag

Dig roots at the end of the growing season in the autumn, when they will shrink less than at any other time. Wash them by letting water run full force from faucet or hose on them. Scrape roots, slice thin and boil for 1 hour; change the water and boil for another hour. When slices are tender drain off water and boil in a sirup previously prepared of 2 cups sugar and ½ cup water, until the slices are clear. Lay them so that they do not touch, on wax paper to dry. Store in a tin box between double layers of wax paper and cover tightly.

RELISHES AND PICKLES

Dill Pickles

(A 3 gallon crock holds about 10 quarts of cucumbers)
Cucumbers   ½ pint vinegar
Grape leaves   1 gallon water
½ pound salt

Cover bottom of a good sized crock with a layer of well scrubbed cucumbers of a fairly even size. Continue this process to within a few inches of the top of crock. Grape leaves, placed on the very bottom and over the top layer, will help to keep the pickles green. Make up as much brine mixture as will cover top layer, using this proportion of material: ½ pound salt, ½ pint vinegar, 1 gallon water. Pour this mixture (the Agricultural Bureau says it should be 86 degrees, and not hot since hot brine will prevent the desired fermentation) into the crock and cover with a weight which will keep the cucumbers submerged. In about 2 weeks they should be dark green in color and well-flavored. When this state is reached, transfer the pickles to jars, add a little dill and spice. Make a new brine, or use old one, bring to a boil, cool just a bit, fill jars to overflowing, seal and keep in a cool place. The Department of Agriculture Bulletin "Making Fermented Pickles" (5¢) is helpful. Ask for Farmer's Bulletin No. 1438.

Fresh Cucumber Slices

To avoid the disturbing effects of cucumbers, slice them into a bowl, cover with salt and let stand for 2 hours; put them in a colander and run cold water on them for several minutes, to remove the salt. Squeeze out the water; arrange in a dish, sprinkle dill seeds between each two layers.

Quints-Mint Meat Relish

1 grapefruit	2 lemons
4 tangerines	1 cup of equal parts apple mint, orange mint, spear-mint, packed down
3 oranges	
2 large limes or	
3 small	4 cups water
	Sugar

Cut grapefruit in half, remove seeds, scoop out the pulp without the membrane into a porcelain kettle. Turn skins inside out and scrape out the rest of the pulpy part and put into a second porcelain kettle. Set aside the peel. Let tangerines soak ½ hour in hot water. Then the peel is removed easily and sections come apart readily. Remove fibers from the skin and set skin aside. Remove fibers from the sections, cut them in half, squeeze out seeds and put the broken halves in the first kettle with the grapefruit pulp. Squeeze the juice from oranges, limes and lemons and put in the first kettle. Turn peels inside out, scoop clean, putting the pulp and membrane into the second kettle.

Grind peels with medium coarse chopper of the meat grinder. Put them immediately into a third porcelain kettle and cover with water to keep them from darkening. Set over a medium fire and boil ¾ hour or until tender. Put mints into a porcelain saucepan, add 2 cups water, boil quietly for 5 minutes, strain through a fine sieve into a bowl. Add 2 cups of water to the pulpy membrane in the second kettle and boil over a medium fire for 15 minutes and strain into the bowl with the mint tea. When the ground up peel is tender, combine with the liquid and pour into the first kettle and add sugar equal to half the amount of the mixture. Put over a moderate fire and boil as for jelly and as the old books say, "scum" frequently. Boil until the jelly stage is almost reached, turn into glasses (about 10 or 11) and pour melted paraffin on top. A delicious breakfast marmalade can be made by continuing the boiling to the jelly stage.

Pickled Nasturtium Seeds

1 pound nasturtium seeds	1 quart white wine vinegar
4 whole cloves	1 teaspoonful salt
2 blades mace	

Put seeds, cloves and mace in an earthenware crock. Bring vinegar and salt to the boiling point and pour over seeds. Cover the crock tightly. Let stand 1 month before using.

CHAPTER 15

Herb Teas and Beverages

Nothing equals a nice "dish o' tea" on a wintry afternoon before crackling logs in the fireplace, not just ordinary China or India tea, but the pleasant teas of herbs used for thousands of years and definitely a part of our own heritage. The aroma will remind you of the past summer days when you pressed those same fragrant leaves in your hot moist hands as you strolled down the garden paths. You will also enjoy these refreshing teas when you feel exhausted from the summer's heat. They will be drunk gratefully when you feel shivery with a cold coming on, or when you are ready to scream from frayed nerves. In early days herbs were taken, for the most part, in the form of teas for all degrees and kinds of illnesses. Today most of us have doctors diagnose and prescribe for serious troubles of the body, yet some seventy-five or more herbal teas, some taken hot and some taken cold, still are administered as simple home remedies for common ailments. Many people prefer these teas on account of their flavor and fragrance to any other beverage. Our most popular soft drinks are herbal preparations, as are some beers, many wines and almost all liqueurs.

For afternoon tea, a few leafy tips or a small handful of herbs may be added to a brew of ordinary tea—herbs such as lemon thyme, lemon balm, peppermint, spearmint, apple mint, lemon verbena, costmary, chamomile, wintergreen or any one of these brewed by itself makes a deliciously different tea. The French make a fragrant tea of the leaves and flowers of agrimony to be served with meals. Speedwell tastes similar to Chinese green tea and is commonly used on the Continent under the name of *Thé de l'Europe*.

Some combinations of herbs are pleasant for afternoon tea, such as equal parts of peppermint and elder flowers; equal parts costmary and orange mint; two parts rosemary leaves and one part lavender flowers. Those combinations are old favorites to take very

115

hot in tea form before going to bed in order to induce perspiration in the case of feverish colds. All of these herbs have long been used for colds as have teas made from catnip, feverfew, boneset, yarrow, lemon balm, sage or queen of the meadow. Stimulating teas for anyone exhausted from fatigue are made from sweet woodruff, golden rod, boneset, mugwort and sweet marjoram.

Many different kinds of herb teas are taken to relieve nervous headache or hysteria, and act as a sedative or a "night cap" drink. These are teas made from the flower heads of chamomile or from the leaves of catnip, peppermint, aniseed (seed used), lemon balm, celery or lovage (which tastes like celery), rosemary, mugwort, sage, sweet marjoram, lemon verbena. For the relief of indigestion we may turn to the teas of beebalm, boneset, sage, aniseed, fennel seed, caraway seed, peppermint or basil, the latter two for overcoming nausea.

Asthma sufferers turn to the teas of mullein or sweet marjoram and often to a tea made of a combination of one ounce each of the leaves of vervain and horehound and the roots of elecampane, all simmered for twenty minutes in three pints of water, strained and cooled. Take a wine glass full three times a day. For persistent coughs and bronchial troubles, favorite teas are those of horehound, coltsfoot, ground ivy and angelica, very bitter when hot and usually taken cold because of their taste. Horehound tea, somewhat on the road to fermentation, is essentially the famous "bitters" or bitter beer of the lower class in England.

For heat exhaustion herb teas are greatly flavored, either a mucilaginous drink made from simmering one tablespoonful of clary sage seeds in one-half pint of water for twenty minutes, or peppermint tea taken hot, or a beverage made by simmering a handful of hop leaves, stalks and blossoms in a pint of water, taken cold. Teas of calendula or saffron are given to "bring out" the measles, while teas of coltsfoot leaves mixed with ordinary tea are given as spring tonics. Infusions of wintergreen leaves (because of salicylic acid in the herb), of boneset or of celery often are taken for rheumatism. Some herbs used in teas as blood purifiers are sage, equal parts red clover and elder blossoms, celandine, gill-over-the-ground (ground ivy), hop leaves, chamomile.

The general process of making any herb tea is the same, the amounts and treatment varying slightly according to the ease or difficulty with which the oils are released. Teas may be infusions or decoctions. To make an infusion, pour boiling water over the herb and let the tea stand until sufficiently strong. In a decoction, the water with the herb is boiled to bring out the fragrant oils. Infusions are made from parts of the herb containing oils easily released, such as flowers and most leaves. If they were boiled, the oils would evaporate. Leaves of a few herbs, such as beebalm, horehound, lemon balm, all roots and all seeds (which should always be crushed), must be boiled to extract the full flavor.

Whether the teas are made by infusion or decoction, use a porcelain or glass container—any kind but metal. Measure out and put into a pot a tablespoonful of the dried and sieved herb or a handful of fresh leaves, or leafy tips of dried foliage that has not been stripped from the stems. Let the herb infuse for ten or fifteen minutes, but for a decoction boil for fifteen or twenty minutes. Strain the liquid into another non-metal teapot which has been heated, or strain directly into warmed teacups. Honey may be added for sweetening, and if you wish, a slice of lemon, but do not cloud the tea or destroy its flavor by adding milk or cream.

When making horehound tea for coughs or for bronchial disturbances, the following recipe is good:

1 good handful horehound leaves	2 tablespoonfuls granulated sugar or rock candy
1 quart boiling water	Juice of 1 lemon

Put leaves into an unchipped enamel kettle, add water and simmer for 20 minutes. Remove from the fire, strain, press the leaves to get all the liquid, add sugar and lemon juice and cool. If desired, 1 teaspoonful crushed aniseed may be boiled with the leaves. Aniseed has a soothing effect on the throat.

Some herbs make most refreshing cold beverages and give a piquant flavor to rather mild drinks. For example:

Mintale

1 cup equal parts orange mint, apple mint, spearmint	Juice of 1 orange and 1 lemon
1 pint water	1 large bottle ginger ale
2 tablespoonfuls sugar	Sprigs of apple mint

Steep herbs in water for 15 minutes. Strain, add sugar and set aside to cool. Add juice of orange and lemon. Just before serving, add ginger ale with a sprig of apple mint in each glass.

A few hints about the use of herbs in iced beverages will no doubt whet your imagination for other combinations of herbs and beverages. Young borage flowers, sprigs of burnet or lemon thyme floated on claret cup give a delicious flavor. For a pleasing change add leafy sprays of sweet woodruff to champagne or white wine, the main ingredients of the German Maybowl. When serving tea, have sprigs of different kinds of mint, orange mint, apple mint, spearmint, in a bowl, and let your family or guests choose the mint they wish for their glasses of iced tea.

You will enjoy the delicate and different flavors of the herb teas and cold beverages mentioned here and in Table T, and no doubt you will want a special garden plot for these fragrant plants—your own herb tea garden.

CHAPTER 16

Marketing of Herbs

Raising herbs for profit requires not only space for growing plants, labor and harvesting; a place for properly drying and preparing the harvest; but also time and energy for selling them. Growing, harvesting and preparing herbs are routines which anyone can learn from study and experience, but marketing herbs at a profit is like marketing any other product—it requires a special sort of genius. There are no established channels, no place where you can simply ship the herbs and expect a check in the return mail. For the most part you will have to make your own market by correspondence or by advertising. The small grower has one type of problem and the large grower has just as acute a problem but of a different sort.

Marketing of medicinal herbs is a field in itself. The outlet for this harvest is limited to the various crude drug houses and crude drug importers who for a generation or two have been buying the dried herbs abroad at prices so low as to be beyond the reach of ordinary competition. They have built up certain requirements in this industry, not only as to the organic composition of the herbs (which is affected by the soil and climate), but as to method of preparation and of shipment. For the most part they require a minimum consignment of about one hundred pounds of any one herb, after samples have been tested and approved. The grower who is interested in the medicinal phase of herb growing and marketing should get in touch with his state agricultural bureau to determine for which crops, if any, his soil and climate are suitable. He should become familiar with the surveys made by the National Farm Chemurgic Council or published from time to time in their bulletins, showing which sections of the country are best suited for medicinal herb crops. Correspondence is also advised with the large crude drug houses located in Boston, Philadelphia, New

York and Chicago. These addresses may be secured from any drug-store and from almost any physician. Such correspondence, how-ever, will be a waste of time unless you have several acres available and time and money for a period of experimentation and trial, as well as a stout heart to fortify yourself against many disappoint-ments.

Another large outlet for herbs is found among manufacturers of liquors, liqueurs, many soft drinks, condiments, toilet preparations and cosmetics. These firms must be located, however, and it must be remembered that they have some established source of supply at the present time. Many have their own herb farms. One and all they are interested, not in an occasional shipment, but in an assured and constant supply tempered to their needs year in, year out.

The market for culinary herbs is also a hidden quantity. For the most part they, too, are imported by the crude drug importers, and are packaged or processed by the condiment, seasoning and spice wholesalers. At your grocery store you will find boxes of pepper and of mustard, packaged by some firm whose name appears on the label. That firm also packages other herbs and spices, and requires a constant supply.

These suggestions are for those who wish to raise herbs in a large way and to market them wholesale wherever there may be an opportunity. There are, however, other methods of marketing herbs which have been found profitable by an increasing number of people particularly during the last decade. These people have approached the public directly, usually starting in a small way with a limited line of products—sometimes through door to door can-vassing, often through roadside stands, in conjunction with refresh-ment places, restaurants and tea rooms, and frequently through gardens arranged to attract visitors and tourists.

You must decide who your customers will be; no one can buy from you until they hear of you. Your customers must want the things you have for sale and must be attracted to your particular products instead of others. In general, your customers can be divided into two classes, those who come to you and those to whom you will go in person or by mail. In the first class are those attracted to your garden, your little shop or booth or roadside stand or tea room. In the second group are those in professional offices, in grocery and drugstores, in hotels, restaurants, gift shops, markets, church fairs, flower shows and many other places.

You will spend hours conjuring up ways and means of making attractive the articles you have for sale—pots of living plants, packages of dried herbs, products containing herbs or having an herb flavor (see Chapter 12). You will want your herbs for sale at the psychological time, which you will learn from observation and experience. "Lots of people" do not always mean sales. Fifty thousand on the way to a ball game would not take a potted plant as a gift, but a dozen people on the way to visit relatives might buy you out.

In short, you will always be on the alert to win customers and to keep them. It is most important to have them come back or to write, for only by adding old customers to new can you increase your business. Then, too, those who do not buy today may buy tomorrow, if your courtesy, helpfulness and welcome are remembered.

The attractiveness and appeal of your package are your ultimate selling arguments. Containers that are distinctive, such as those identified with the state or the locality, often have a maximum appeal. Have a distinctive name for your place or product and an insignia. Be sure your address is on everything so that it is found easily. Be sure that everyone, whether they buy or not, carries away something that identifies you—a card, a list of products, a map, a tiny scent bag or gift package.

You must advertise your wares and not depend solely on passersby. Posters or cards in stores and public places are helpful. Effective, also, are circulars to friends who will speak for you. Possibly the local paper will take weekly notes on herbs, gardening or cookery. Mailed cards inviting people to a display of herbs or a demonstration of herb-cooked foods will help. The local bridge club, women's club, garden club, or some prominent resident might agree to sponsor an herb tea or afternoon demonstration, if you furnish the food and decorations. Through such an event many successful ventures have been launched quickly. Anything you can do to associate your name with high quality, home-grown herbs and herb products in the minds of friends and neighbors, is bound to reach many others in a gradually widening circle.

Still another phase of herb marketing falls somewhere between the sale of your crop as a whole to some manufacturer who uses herbs and the sale of your herb products direct to the consumer. It may take one of two forms. If you have or can get from others, a plentiful supply of culinary herbs, you can package them yourself under a trade name, and distribute them through a middleman or "jobber" who, in turn, sells them to retail dealers. Another form of this same method is to devise some specialty, such as a condiment, a ketchup or relish; or a complete line of products, such as a variety of herb vinegars, jellies, mustards or pickles. Arrange with a distributor to handle your entire output, either as a jobber who buys from you and sells to the retailer or as a commission merchant, sometimes called a "factor," who takes your products and retains a commission or percentage from whatever he sells. These methods require some initial capital investment and usual business risks. You are, in fact, becoming a manufacturer in competition with all the others in your field, dependent for your success on public acceptance and preferment of your particular products.

CHAPTER 17

Tabular Paragraphs on 101 Useful Herbs

ACONITE—Monkshood (*Aconitum Napellus*). *Propagation:* by division of roots in autumn; by fresh seed, germination period 20 days. *Nature of plant:* tall; used for back of border and cut for flower arrangements. *Spacing of mature plants:* 18 inches. *Cultural requirements:* rich, fairly moist soil; cool, half shady spot. Should be left undisturbed for several years. Spray with Bordeaux mixture every 2 weeks to prevent mildew. To increase at end of third or fourth year, dig up roots before bud for next year begins to grow. Although a perennial, each main root lasts only a year but the daughter roots formed at each side reach maturity as plant dies down and carry on. Enrich soil with rotted manure before replanting. Stake plants when 15 to 18 inches high.

    Uses: poisonous; all parts of the plant in medicine; roots more often than other parts; heart sedative; in dentistry with tincture of iodine; various preparations applied locally for neuralgic pains, lumbago, rheumatism.

AGRIMONY—Church Steeples, Cockleburr (*Agrimonia Eupatoria*). *Propagation:* by seed; pod is a bristly burr designed to catch in fur of animals or clothes of passers-

by and is thus distributed. *Nature of plant:* 3-foot stalk almost without branches but with small yellow flowers along the tall spike. Good for rock garden or wildflower border. Rich green, deeply cut leaves 6 inches long, arising from rootstalk, keep the stem from a bare appearance; should be planted in clumps. *Spacing of mature plants:* about 7 inches. *Cultural requirements:* dry spot with some shade.

Uses: (household) yellow dye from leaves; (culinary) leaves in tonic tea; (medicinal) astringent properties of leaves for gargles.

ALKANET—see BUGLOSS

AMBROSIA—see JERUSALEM OAK

ANEMONE—see PASQUE FLOWER

ANGELICA—Garden Angelica (*Angelica Archangelica*). *Propagation:* by division of old roots; by transplanting offshoots of a 2-year-old plant; by fresh seed as soon as ripe. *Nature of plant:* tall, tropical looking; good for back of shady border. *Spacing of mature plants:* from 2½ to 3 feet. *Cultural requirements:* moist, light, well drained, medium rich soil; cool spot in part shade; cultivate frequently. Plant will be perennial if flower heads are cut off before they set seed. If flower heads go to seed, plant dies at end of second year. If seed is gathered, sow immediately for more plants.

Uses: Seed—(culinary) oil and custards; (industrial) oil for chypre and fern type of perfume, flavor for wines (muscatel), Chartreuse, Vermouth, Benedictine, substitute for juniper berries in making

gin, blender in dental preparations. Root
—medicinal tea for bronchial colds and
indigestion; (culinary) oil in creams and
custards, and bread; (industrial) blender
in dental preparations. Leaf—(culinary)
boiling with fish, midrib blanched and
eaten like celery, a flavoring for rhubarb
jam; (medicinal) tonic tea; poultices for
lung and chest diseases; (industrial) preparation of hop bitters. Stalk—(culinary)
stems and stalk candied and sold as French
rhubarb, stewed alone or with rhubarb.
Whole Herb—(culinary) flavoring for
cooking fish; (medicinal) tea.

ANISE—(*Pimpinella Anisum*). *Propagation:* seed not more than 2 years old, germination best from fresh seed. *Nature of
plant:* very slow-growing, decumbent
habits; requires continual weeding. *Spacing
of mature plants:* 8 inches. *Cultural requirements:* fairly dry, light, sandy, well
drained, moderately rich soil; warm, sunny
spot. Thin out seedlings or pinch off at
the ground but do not transplant because
the delicate root is liable to break and
plant does not recover readily from shock.

Uses: Leaf—fresh ones in salad and as
a garnish. Seed—(culinary) in bread,
cake, apple sauce, stew, soup, confectionery; (medicinal) tea; (industrial) liniment, sachet, soap, perfume, dental preparations, flavoring horehound drops and
other cough medicine and licorice preparations, and many liqueurs, base of anisette,
bait for mice and drag hunts, hair preparations, antiseptic with oils of peppermint or
wintergreen; (household) vermifuge with
oil of sassafras and carbolic acid, ointment

(mixed with lard) for lice and itching from insect bites. Flower—flavoring muscatel wine (powdered and infused with vermouth).

ARTICHOKE—see CARDOON

BACHELOR'S BUTTON—see CORN-FLOWER

BALM—Lemon Balm, Sweet Balm (*Melissa officinalis*). *Propagation:* by root division; by cuttings in spring or fall; by seed, very slow germination, perhaps a year; seeds viable even after 3 or 4 years. *Nature of plant:* spreading; very hardy; intensely fragrant leaves; good for flower border. *Spacing of mature plants:* 18 inches. *Cultural requirements:* medium dry, poor, light, sandy soil is best for plants get weedy in fertile soil; prefer part shade; pinch tops back to increase foliage, for continuous bloom during summer and to keep flowers from going to seed; keep weeded.

Uses: Leaf — (culinary) tea, soup, sauce, stew, salad, flavoring summer drinks, with Swiss chard, in egg dishes, added to tarragon vinegar; (medicinal) induces perspiration; (industrial) in perfumes and toilet water, in Chartreuse, Benedictine and other liqueurs, furniture polish oil, salve.

BASIL—Any one of five varieties of basil may be used in cooking: Sweet basil (*Ocimum Basilicum*) with inch-long, dark green leaves and a clove-pepperish odor and taste; a variety of sweet basil with purplish red leaves; a green leaf dwarf variety; a purple leaf dwarf variety; Italian or curly basil (*O. crispum*) with large, crinkly, light green leaves and a stronger odor and taste than the sweet basil. All have the same cultural requirements. *Propagation:* by seed, in spring, outdoors; germinates easily in 4 or 5 days. *Nature of plant:* if tops are pinched out, plants will grow into little bushes, the dwarf varieties into beautiful compact ones; makes attractive annual border plants; culinary importance. *Spacing of mature plants:* Italian 15 inches, sweeet 12 inches, dwarf varieties 6 inches. *Cultural requirements:* dry, light, well drained, medium rich soil, in sunny sheltered spot; after severe cutting dig a little fertilizer into soil about roots; in harvesting, if cut but part way to the ground, a second crop can be had later.

Uses: Leaf — (culinary) in vinegar, soup, stew, salad, with cream or cottage cheese, in egg or tomato dishes, chopped meat, sausage, in butter sauce for fish, sprinkled over peas or boiled potato, in vegetable juice cocktails; (household) plants in house said to drive away flies, dried powdered leaves are used as snuff; (industrial) perfumes; (medicinal) stimulant, nervine.

BEACH WORMWOOD—see Wormwood

BEDSTRAW—Yellow Bedstraw (*Galium verum*), also called Our Lady's Bedstraw or Cheese Rennet; White Bedstraw (*G. Mollugo*), also called False Baby's Breath or Wild Madder. Both very decorative garden plants. *Propagation:* by fresh seed in autumn; by root division in spring into small clumps because plant spreads readily by underground running roots; by layering.

Nature of plant: yellow variety especially beautiful for borders or rock gardens, rises to 3 feet topped by butter-yellow panicles of flowers; white variety 2½ feet, blooms 2 weeks earlier than yellow, has wider, softer leaves and more brittle stems than yellow; both useful for softening effects in flower arrangements; dried stems resemble straw; formerly used for mattresses. *Spacing of mature plants:* 2 feet. *Cultural requirements:* dry, sandy soil in sunny spot; both varieties have weak stems and start to shoot up the second year and must be staked in a clump as soon as they are a foot high; use several stakes and a cord or raffia hoop to avoid spoiling the graceful effect of the clump; a higher hoop will be required when the growth reaches 3 feet.

Uses: (both varieties) Root—(industrial) as a red dye. Stem and Leaf—(household) curdling milk for cheese, decoction for soothing foot bath; (medicinal) in epilepsy, skin diseases, gentle laxative. Flower—(household) for coloring cheese and butter yellow.

BEE BALM—see BERGAMOT

BENE — Sesame (*Sesamum orientale*). *Propagation:* by seed. *Nature of plant:* sturdy, erect, unbranching annual with lavender-colored flowers like foxglove; rather decorative in gardens which have a long growing season; a culinary herb. *Spacing of mature plants:* 8 inches. *Cultural requirements:* mellow, well drained soil in sunny spot.

Uses: Seed—(culinary) oil in cooking, seeds in bread, and pastries; (industrial) in manufacture of soap, oleomargarine, drawing ink, cosmetics and adulterant of other oils; (medicinal) oil for laxative, liniment, ointment. Leaf—from gummy matter is made a mucilaginous drink for diarrhea, dysentery, catarrh and for making emollient poultices.

BERGAMOT (RED)—Oswego tea, Bee Balm (*Monarda didyma*). *Propagation:* by seed; by root division in spring, if divided later is apt to winterkill. *Nature of plant:* good in large clumps for a shady border, but will grow in sunny, moist soil; useful for flower arrangements; fragrant leaves. *Spacing of mature plants:* 18 inches. *Cultural requirements:* prefers moist soil in open spaces; plants spread so quickly that they should be taken up every 3 years, divided and reset, or they are apt to die out; roots are woody and fibrous and can be pulled apart by hand; replant only outside newer roots and discard exhausted center. To increase the size of blooms, do not let plants flower the first summer; thereafter cut back the whole plant after the first blooming and it will flower again in early autumn; late in autumn cut down stalks and cover completely with enriched soil; leaf mold on shallow, creeping roots is beneficial.

    Uses: Whole Herb—(industrial) oil in perfume, hair tonic and pomade, to mask odor of iodoform, naphthalene and other evil smelling chemicals, yields an oil similar to thymol; (medicinal) stimulant, carminative, rubefacient.

BIBLE LEAF—see COSTMARY

BLESSED THISTLE—Holy Thistle (*Cnicus benedictus*). *Propagation:* by seed, easy germination. *Nature of plant:* branching thistlelike plant; suitable for rock gardens. *Spacing of mature plants:* 2 feet. *Cultural requirements:* dry, sandy soil.

Uses: Herb and Seed—(culinary) bitter tea; (medicinal) fever, dyspepsia, tonic, emetic, induces perspiration; (industrial) in vermouth. Flower—(industrial) substitute for hops.

BONESET—Thoroughwort, Purple Boneset (*Eupatorium perfoliatum*). Joe-Pye Weed (*E. purpureum*). *Propagation:* by seed sown as soon as ripe in early autumn; by root division in spring. *Nature of plant:* the 4-foot-high perennial boneset with white, fluffy flower heads is a striking contrast with colorful flowers in borders; useful for flower arrangements. Fragrant, purple boneset is effective in flower arrangements and in borders. The leaf arrangement of both plants is interesting. *Spacing of mature plants:* 12 inches. *Cultural requirements:* both like light, moist, rich, well drained soil in a sunny spot for luxuriant growth and beautiful terminal clusters of flowers, but either will grow well in almost any soil or location; protect with a straw mulch.

Uses: Both varieties have same uses. Leaf and flowering top—(medicinal) gentle laxative, emetic and purgative in large doses, used in catarrh and feverish colds.

BORAGE—Bee Bread, Star flower (*Borago officinalis*). *Propagation:* by seed, germinates easily; self-sows freely and result-

ing plants are sturdier and more luxuriant than those from first sowing; seeds are said to be viable for 8 years. *Nature of plant:* good for bee gardens; since the pure blue flower clusters droop, the beauty of the plant is best seen from below and it should be planted at the top of a slope, such as a height in a rock garden. *Spacing of mature plants:* 12 inches. *Cultural requirements:* dry, poor, light soil in sunny spots; because of delicate root systems seedlings should not be transplanted but weaker ones should be thinned out or pinched off at ground level.

Uses: Leaf — (culinary) cucumber flavor of steeped young leaves provides a cooling summer iced drink, young leaves cooked as greens, in salads and pickles; (medicinal) gentle laxative, in catarrh, rheumatism, skin diseases. Flower—candied for confectionery.

BUGBANE—see SNAKEROOT

BUGLE-WEED — Carpet   Bugle - Weed (*Ajuga reptans*). *Propagation:* by seed, easy germination; by root division in spring or fall. *Nature of plant:* spreads rapidly by creeping runners; makes a beautiful ground cover for shady spot, rock gardens, edging for flower borders. *Spacing of mature plants:* 12 inches; eventually they will run together. *Cultural requirements:* grows in sun or shade, in moist or dry soil.

Uses: Whole Herb—(medicinal) tonic tea for coughs, helps circulation, mild narcotic, resembles digitalis in its action.

BUGLOSS—Four interesting plants of the Borage family, with characteristic hairy leaves and stems and with flowers that are

rose colored at first and later turn a beautiful light or purplish blue are Dyer's Bugloss or real alkanet (*Alkanna tinctoria*); Common Alkanet (*Anchusa officinalis*) which is not real alkanet; Italian Bugloss (*Anchusa azurea*) variety Dropmore; Viper's Bugloss or Blue-weed (*Echium vulgare*). *Propagation*: by seed, quite easy germination, self-sows freely; by root division in the spring. *Nature of plant*: Italian Bugloss grows to 5 feet, the flowers ¾ inch across, are in purplish blue clusters; a vivid high spot in the garden and splendid for flower arrangements. Common Alkanet grows to 18 inches, flowers ¼ inch across, bright blue and useful for masses in flower border. Dyer's Bugloss is much cultivated in southern Europe, flowers are purplish blue, the root very large in proportion to the rest of the plant, height of plant 20 inches. Viper's Bugloss, an erect bristly plant, 2½ feet tall, found on roadsides, in meadows and dry, waste places, stems and leaves sometimes spotted red, flowers a vivid blue, grows best in chalky, gravelly soil. In rich soil plant grows coarse, flowers scanty and not so colorful. *Spacing of mature plants*: from 12 to 18 inches. *Cultural requirements*: in light, sandy, well drained soil in sunny spot, except Italian Bugloss which prefers part shade and some moisture; in dividing plants in spring, be careful not to break the long, branching, brittle roots. Any roots left in the ground will develop a new plant.

Uses: Plant — (medicinal) Italian Bugloss, removes inflammation, cooling infusion induces perspiration; Common Alkanet, expectorant, aperient, induces perspiration. Root—(industrial) Dyer's Bugloss, red dye for staining wood imitation mahogany and rosewood, to color oil, furniture polish, spurious port wine, dental wax, pomade, leather, as acid-alkaline indicator by impregnating white paper called alkannin paper; (medicinal) Viper's Bugloss, astringent, blood purifier.

BURNET — Salad Burnet (*Sanguisorba minor*). *Propagation:* by seed, self-sows freely and resulting plants are hardier and more luxuriant than those of first sowing; by root division in the spring. *Nature of plant:* bushy plant with lacy leaves, beautiful in flower border, almost evergreen, culinary importance. *Spacing of mature plants:* 15 inches. *Cultural requirements:* moderately dry, poor, limy or sandy soil in sunny spot; do not transplant but pinch off weaker seedlings at the ground, delicate root system until established; grows in same spot for many years, to prevent self-sowing and to keep plant blooming all summer, cut off flower heads; for constant supply of young leaves for salad, cut back when 4 or 5 inches high.

Uses: Leaf—(culinary) in salads, vinegar, iced beverages; (medicinal) astringent properties, used in controlling hemorrhages.

BUTTERFLY WEED—Pleurisy Root, Orange Swallow-wort (*Asclepias tuberosa*). *Propagation:* by seed. *Nature of plant:* brilliant orange-colored, flat flower heads topping a 3-foot stem, for borders and for flower arrangements, dried seed pods are ornamental. *Spacing of mature plants:*

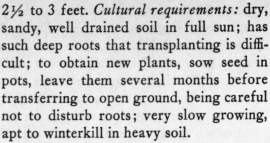

2½ to 3 feet. *Cultural requirements:* dry, sandy, well drained soil in full sun; has such deep roots that transplanting is difficult; to obtain new plants, sow seed in pots, leave them several months before transferring to open ground, being careful not to disturb roots; very slow growing, apt to winterkill in heavy soil.

Uses: Root—(medicinal) emetic, used in bronchitis, rheumatism, induces perspiration.

CALAMINT—Alpine calamint (*Satureja alpina*). *Propagation:* by seed; by division of roots; by cuttings. *Nature of plant:* makes a lustrous green, aromatic mat, about 6 inches high, with whorls of purplish flowers on delicate stems, very aromatic foliage. *Spacing of mature plants:* 8 inches. *Cultural requirements:* dry, sandy soil in full sun.

Uses: Leaf—(culinary) a cordial tea; (medicinal) in fevers, induces perspiration.

CALENDULA—Pot Marigold (*Calendula officinalis*). *Propagation:* by seed, germination about 10 days, self-sows. *Nature of plant:* its light green leaves and orange flower heads are brilliant additions to the garden and to flower arrangements. *Spacing of mature plants:* 12 inches. *Cultural requirements:* light, sandy, moderately rich soil in full sun; do not transplant seedlings because of rather large succulent leaves; to increase length of stem remove side buds; size of bloom also will be increased; keep flowers cut for bloom all summer.

Uses: Flower petal—(culinary) in soup and stew, gives color to pudding; (household) yellow dye; (medicinal) tincture for cuts, burns, bruises, sprains and wounds, used to prevent gangrene, internally for fever, tea to hasten eruption of measles, to prevent formation of scar tissue, taken after accident to bring out bruises and prevent internal complications; (industrial) adulterant for saffron, colors butter.

CARAWAY—(*Carum Carvi*). *Propagation:* by seed; germinates easily; self-sows year after year; do not transplant because of long tapering root and tiny fibers; thin out seedlings or pinch off at ground. *Nature of plant:* grown for its savory seeds, feathery foliage and delicate, creamy white umbels of flowers, resembles Queen Anne's lace; if not wanted for seed, the 2-foot flowering stems lend themselves to graceful flower arrangements. *Spacing of mature plants:* 12 inches. *Cultural requirements:* sow seed thinly in dry, light soil in full sun; since it is a biennial, it will not produce a crop the first season if sown in spring, but will grow to 8 inches, the bright green cluster of carrotlike leaves forming a beautiful rosette; if seeds are sown in autumn, a harvest can be made in early summer and spillage of seed will produce another crop the following year.

Uses: Leaf—(culinary) in salads and boiled in soup. Seed—(culinary) in rye bread, cake, cheese, German sauerkraut, apple pie, baked apples, German and Hungarian cabbage soups, goulash, in spiced beets, and sugar-coated for confectionery, munched after meals as preventive of indigestion; (industrial) in oil for mouth wash, in perfume, Kümmel and other liqueurs, perfuming soap, in confectionery; (medicinal) in oil for colic, to disguise flavor of medicine, to correct nauseating and griping effects, for scabies, to stimulate digestion. Root—boiled as vegetables.

CARDOON — Cardoon Artichoke (*Cynara Cardunculus*). *Propagation:* by seed, quite easily; by suckers; by root division in spring. *Nature of plant:* handsome tropical plant, 5 or 6 feet high, spiny leaves rising from the root, not very practical for ordinary vegetable garden but a novelty for a gray garden with ample room. *Spacing of mature plants:* 3 feet. *Cultural requirements:* rich soil and plenty of moisture; sow a few seeds in a deep pot since the roots become so long; if seed is sown in April, the seedling will become potbound by July; dig a deep hole, fertilize well and transplant; if wanted for table by September, fasten up stalks by tying a band around them a foot or so from the top, and pile the dirt up around them on a good dry day to blanch them; as plants grow, add earth but do not cover leaves; if plant is grown for ornament, blanching is not desirable.

Uses: Root—(culinary) blanched and eaten like celery; (industrial) in Europe the fuzzy down of plant is used as rennet in making cheese; (household) yellow dye; (medicinal) gentle laxative. Stalk—(culinary) stalks of leaves when blanched are stewed as vegetable, used in soups and salads.

CATNIP—Catmint (*Nepeta Cataria*). *Propagation:* by seed, easy germination, seeds viable for 4 or 5 years; by root division in spring. *Nature of plant:* 3 feet high; downy, heart-shaped leaves make it suitable for a gray bed; because of its mauve blossoms in dense spikes, the plant gives a softening effect to a bright flower border. *Spacing of mature plants:* 15 inches. *Cultural requirements:* sow seed in spring or fall where plant is to grow; dry, sandy soil in full sun makes plants more fragrant; fall sowing gives better germination; cut plants back in July and a second crop may be had in fall, early enough to permit good recovery before frost; plants need little attention except weeding.

Uses: Leaf—(medicinal) in hot infusions as a sedative and for feverish colds; fresh or dried leaves are good for cats.

CHAMOMILE—Both German (*Matricaria Chamomilla*) and Roman (now called English) (*Anthemis nobilis*) chamomiles have the same characteristic thready, lacy leaves, small daisylike blossoms, and similar properties but different habits of growth; Roman (English) chamomile is called ground apple; German chamomile is the wild or bitter. *Propagation:* Roman—seed, easy germination; by root division; by layering of runners; German—seed, easy germination; self-sows freely; fragrant plant. *Nature of plant:* Roman variety is excellent for ground cover and paths, if mowed and rolled; German variety rises to 15 inches; its self-sowing propensities make it poor for the garden but prolific in production of flower heads. *Spacing of mature plants:* 6 inches.

Cultural requirements: dry, light, sandy soil in full sun.

Uses: Flower head—(medicinal) in infusions for sedative and for feverish colds, anthelmintic, tincture mixed with water and applied to exposed parts of the body will keep off insects; (household) as a rinse to keep golden tints of the hair; (industrial) Roman—oil used in perfume, shampoo powder, hair rinse, flavoring for tobacco; German—oil is solvent for platinum chloride and because of that property is used in process of coating glass and porcelain with platinum, in perfumery process for blending compounds, combined with oils of patchouli, lavender and oak moss in perfumes.

CHERVIL — (*Anthriscus Cerefolium*). *Propagation:* by seed, easy germination, seeds viable for 3 years; sow where plants are to grow as root system does not stand transplanting well; thin out seedlings by pinching off at ground. *Nature of plant:* culinary importance; resembles a mild parsley. *Spacing of mature plants:* 9 inches. *Cultural requirements:* light, well drained soil, moderately rich; needs shade or part shade but preferably that of taller plants.

Uses: Leaf—(culinary) in sorrel or spinach soup, egg dishes, salads, French dressing, fish, bearnaise and ravigote sauces, butter sauce for chicken, with wine and butter over cutlets; (medicinal) applied to bruises.

CHICORY—Succory (*Cichorium Intybus*). *Propagation:* by seed, easy germination; by underground runners. *Nature of plant:* beautiful clear blue flowers which close by

noon; larger leaves are near the ground and make a good filler for plants with bare stems in midsummer; leaves resemble those of dandelion and plant sometimes called blue dandelion. *Spacing of mature plants:* 12 inches. *Cultural requirements:* dry, light, sandy soil in full sun; if the plant is used for decorative gardens, runners must be severely restrained by slicing down all around plant with a spade and removing the cut-off pieces of root.

Uses: Root—(industrial) roasted and ground-up roots are used to adulterate coffee, gives it a bitter taste; (medicinal) in jaundice. Leaf—(culinary) blanched for salads, sometimes sold under the name of witloof.

CHIVES—(*Allium Schoenoprasum*). *Propagation:* by seed, slow germination; by division into clumps of 3 or 4 bulblets in spring and reset clumps in rich soil. *Nature of plant:* resembles fine leaved onions; pompoms of lavender flower heads; makes an attractive edging for vegetable, herb or flower bed or border. *Spacing of mature plants:* 5 inches. *Cultural requirements:* average, light, medium rich soil in sunny place; clumps increase so rapidly that they should be divided every third spring or they will grow too thickly; cut flower stalks to the ground after blooming; leaves may be cut close but severe cutting requires enrichment of the soil afterward.

Uses: Leaf—(culinary) in soup, soft cheese, salad, vegetable cocktail and omelet, chopped very finely and added to mashed potatoes, mild flavor of onions.

Bulb—pickled as small onions but more delicate, in sausage.

CICELY, SWEET—Sweet Chevril (*Myrrhis odorata*). *Propagation:* by seed, slow to germinate, about 8 months, plant seed in fall; by division of roots. *Nature of plant:* grows about 2 feet high, with fernlike, downy leaves, the first ones triangular in shape; taste is similar to anise with sweet accent; lacy foliage makes it a most decorative plant for flower border. *Spacing of mature plants:* 18 inches. *Cultural requirements:* medium rich, well drained soil, average moisture, in partial shade; in full sun the plant sunburns like chervil or parsley in summer; sow seed as soon as ripe or shortly afterward and seedlings will be up 3 or 4 inches in early spring; this plant is not to be confused with American sweet cicely (*Osmorhiza longistylis*).

Uses: Seed—(industrial) oil in Chartreuse. Root—(culinary) boiled, eaten with oil and vinegar in salads.

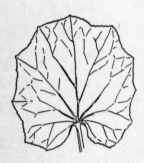

COLTSFOOT—Son Before Father (*Tussilago Farfara*). *Propagation:* by seed; by cuttings of underground running roots. *Nature of plant:* flat orange flower heads appear in early spring before any of the leaves; leaves have a thin, waxy transparent covering membrane; spreading habits of plant make it a popular ground cover for waste spaces. *Spacing of mature plants:* 6 or 8 inches apart but will wander about. *Cultural requirements:* grows under almost any conditions; prefers full sun.

Uses: Leaf and Flower—(medicinal) cough medicine, smoked with other herbs for asthma, poultices, in sweet, glutinous infusion for bronchial catarrh; made into "coltsfoot rock," fluted light brown candy sticks flavored with oil of anise or of dill; dried leaves as tobacco substitute, main part of plant used is the leaf but flowers sometimes are added.

CORIANDER — (*Coriandrum sativum*). *Propagation:* by seed, easy germination, viable for five years. *Nature of plant:* grown for its savory seeds, not suitable for flower garden because of evil smell of foliage and of fresh seed, foliage is delicate and lacy and flower umbels beautiful pinkish white, ripe seeds are fragrant and become more so as they dry. *Spacing of mature plants:* 10 inches. *Cultural requirements:* average, dry, light, medium rich soil in full sun, when plants are 3 inches high, thin to 10 inches by pinching off seedlings at ground, delicate root systems hinder any transplanting, sow thinly as per cent of germination normally is very high, seed must be harvested as soon as ripe because they are so heavy that they will fall to the ground and self-sow freely.

Uses: Seed—(culinary) sugar-coated as confection, powdered or ground in bread, gingerbread, biscuit, cookie, cake, baked apple, sausage, frankfurter, cheese, sauce for wild game, poultry stuffing, in vinegar for beets, crushed and dropped in demitasse; (industrial) to improve taste of cheap grades of cocoa, in Chartreuse, vermouth, and other liqueurs, in gin distilling, curry powder, toilet water, lily-of-the-valley perfume; (medicinal) stomachic, oil added to medicines corrects nauseating and griping qualities.

CORNFLOWER—Bachelor's Button (*Centaurea Cyanus*). *Propagation:* by seed, easy germination, self-sows. *Nature of plant:* stems 2 feet high topped by bright blue flowers make it decorative for garden and for flower arrangements. *Spacing of mature plants:* usually placed in clumps for effect, individual plants from 6 to 8 inches apart. *Cultural requirements:* light moderately rich garden soil in sunny location.

Uses: Flower—(household) blue ink from the expressed juice; (industrial) added to fumigation powders; (medicinal) cordial, tonic, for diseases of eyes and fevers.

COSTMARY—Bible Leaf, Mint Geranium, Sweet Mary, Alecost (*Chrysanthemum Balsamita*). *Propagation:* by seed; by division of rapidly spreading roots. *Nature of plant:* aromatic, grows 3 or 4 feet tall, luxuriant, light green, fragrant foliage makes it attractive for flower border, flowers are yellow rayless buttons. *Spacing of mature plants:* the whole plant is a constantly enlarging mass of fragrant leaves on stalks rising from running roots, individual plant 3 feet apart will grow together in 2 or 3 years. *Cultural requirements:* dry soil in sun or shade but in shade there will be luxuriant foliage and no flowers, plant should be divided every 3 years or it will spread widely and become scraggly.

Uses: Leaf—(culinary) in beer, negus and floated in strawberry shrub; (medicinal) infusion for catarrh.

CRUSADER'S HERB—see WORMWOOD

DIGITALIS—see FOXGLOVE

DILL—(*Anethum graveolens*). *Propagation:* by seed, easy germination, self-sows readily and resulting plants are much stronger than from first sowing. *Nature of plant:* grown from seed, 3 feet tall, feathery foliage, flower umbels. *Spacing of mature plants:* 10 inches. *Cultural requirements:* avoid transplanting because of delicate root system; average moderately rich, sandy, well drained soil in sunny spot; must be cultivated and weeded to produce thriving plants; needs protection from wind; individual plants may be staked when 18 inches high.

Uses: Leaf—(culinary) in cottage and cream cheese, fish sauce, potato salad, cream sauce for chicken, tomato soup, sprinkled over steaks and chops, thinned-out seedlings may be used. Seed head—in pickles and vinegar. Seed—(culinary) in apple pie, pastry, spiced beets, Scandinavian bean and beet soup, gravy; (industrial) oil to scent perfume and soap; (medicinal) carminative.

DITTANY OF CRETE—Hop Marjoram (*Origanum Dictamnus*). *Propagation:* by seed; by cuttings, very easily rooted. *Nature of plant:* a foot high, branching plant with soft woolly gray round leaves, suitable for edging of gray gardens, though not hardy in cold climates, spikes of pink hoplike blossoms against the gray foliage are attractive. *Spacing of mature plants:* 7 inches. *Cultural requirements:* plants do better in winter in small pots, slightly pot-bound, many prefer to put it

out in pots, even in summer; requires dry, sandy soil in full sun.

Uses: Whole Plant—(medicinal) in fomentations for scrofula, oil on cotton for toothache. Flower—(culinary) considered a satisfactory substitute for ordinary tea.

DROPWORT—see Meadowsweet

ELECAMPANE—Horseheal (*Inula Helenium*). *Propagation:* by seed, germination about 15 days; by root division in spring; in the fall by offsets with 1 bud and 1 eye, taken from the parent root and set out. *Nature of plant:* 10 feet high, sturdy, almost unbranching plant with huge leaves, broad at the base and tapering to a point; small orange flower disks bordered with a shaggy fringe. *Spacing of mature plants:* 2½ feet. *Cultural requirements:* light sandy soil, moderately moist; keep free from weeds; seeds when ripe can be planted in cold frame for winter; commercial growers increase stock rapidly by cutting roots of mature plants into 2-inch pieces, setting them in enriched sandy soil in a warm place.

Uses: Root—(culinary) candy, pudding; (industrial) for flavoring absinthe, vermouth, herbal tobacco, in blue dye; (medicinal) in cough medicines, treatment of asthma and skin diseases, veterinary medicine.

FENNEL—Several interesting varieties include perennial wild fennel (*Foeniculum vulgare*), a cultivated garden form of the wild (*F. vulgare* var. *dulce*), another variety of which the stalks are used like celery and called carosella and an annual

dwarf variety of the wild, sold in vegetable markets under the name finocchio. They all have bright green feathery foliage and vary in height from the 2-foot annual variety to the 4-foot wild fennel. None of the varieties can stand transplanting. *Propagation:* by seed. *Nature of plant:* both the wild and the garden fennel with their bright foliage and yellow umbels of flowers are useful for the border. Except in cold climates, both are hardy perennials and harvesting seeds does not destroy plants. *Spacing of mature plants:* 12 inches. *Cultural requirements:* sow seed thinly where plants are to grow; light, limy, moderately fertile soil in dry, sunny spot; tall varieties must be sheltered from the wind or individual plants staked when 18 inches tall; pile up the soil around finocchio to blanch the bulbous base as soon as it is the size of an egg; gather just before flower umbels form; finocchio needs a richer soil than other forms.

Uses: Root—(culinary) bulbous base of finocchio leaves is eaten raw or boiled, served with sauce made of meat stock, used to flavor wine. Stem—(culinary) stems of the carosella are cut and eaten like celery. Leaf—(culinary) fish sauce, garnish, soup, salad, in soft cheese, spiced beets. Seed—(wild or garden fennel) (culinary) pudding, soup, cake, spiced beets, German sauerkraut; (medicinal) carminative, pectoral, in eye lotions, corrective for unpleasant medicines; (industrial) oil in soap for flavoring absinthe and other liqueurs, in confectionery, perfume.

FENNEL FLOWER—Black Cumin, Roman Coriander (*Nigella damascena*). *Propagation:* by seed. *Nature of plant:* 1-foot high plant with clear blue flowers is welcome in the border or blue garden, desirable for flower arrangements. *Spacing of mature plants:* 8 inches. *Cultural requirements:* sow seed in moderately rich soil in sunny spot where plants are to remain, does not transplant; thin by pinching off seedlings.

Uses: Seed—(culinary) pungent black seeds with aromatic odor and spicy taste like nutmeg, used like dill and poppy seeds on bread, in cake, for flavoring wine; (industrial) oil in perfume; (medicinal) in snuff tobacco, expectorant, corrective of unpleasant medicines.

FENUGREEK—Bird's Foot, Greek Hay Seed (*Trigonella Foenum - Graecum*). *Propagation:* by seed. *Nature of plant:* largely of interest because of uses and the resemblance of the seed pods to elongated string beans; a legume; seedlings resemble an erect almost branchless sweet clover; grows to 15 or 18 inches. *Spacing of mature plants:* 4 inches. *Cultural requirements:* moderately fertile, deeply dug, well drained, dry loam, keep weeded.

Uses: Seed—(industrial) ground seeds give maple flavor to confectionery, in making curry; (medicinal) ointments, plasters, reputed equal in virtue to quinine for fevers, mucilaginous material from soaking in water for inflamed stomachs and intestines, poultices, decreases nauseating and griping effects of purgatives, plant and seed as fodder in veterinary medicine.

FEVERFEW — Featherfew, Featherfoil (*Chrysanthemum Parthenium*) by seed, germination 20 days, self-sows freely; by root division in spring; by cuttings from young shoots at base of plant with a heel of the main plant. *Nature of plant:* attractive for flower border; much branching yellow-green foliage like chrysanthemum; daisylike heads of flowers; aromatic leaves; good for high edging, about 18 inches. *Spacing of mature plants:* 12 inches. *Cultural requirements:* heavy, enriched soil in sun or shade; plants spread freely by base shoots.

Uses: Whole Herb—(medicinal) infusion for fevers, for colic pains, tincture applied immediately to skin bites to relieve pain, tincture diluted with water applied to skin to keep off insects. Flower—(medicinal) infusion to relieve nervous pains, neuralgia, earache, dyspepsia, rheumatism.

FLAG—Several plants are called flags that technically are not flags and do not belong to the same botanic family. Sweet Flag (*Acorus Calamus*) belongs to the Arum family, while blue (*Iris versicolor*), white (*I. florentina*) and yellow (*I. Pseudacorus*) "flags" belong to the Iris family. These so-called flags are grown industrially and medicinally chiefly for rhizomes. In the home garden they are grown for beauty of flower and leaf and for flower arrangements. *Propagation:* usually by division of rhizomes. *Nature of plant:* Blue Flag or Water Flag, likes a wet, rich, well drained soil but will grow in an average moist shady spot in the garden; the swordlike, blue-green leaves are about 1

inch wide and 2½ feet long; flowers are small, outer segments being about 2½ inches long; they are a vivid purplish blue, variegated with white, yellow and green markings and purple veins; this plant makes a vivid border for a brook or pool. Sweet Flag or Sweet Grass grows almost in water but will grow in a shady spot, normally moist; leaves have wavy margins and a conspicuous midrib a little off center, are about 1 inch wide and from 3 to 5 feet long, have a lemony, aromatic odor; the rhizome has the hot taste of ginger (another choice plant for the edge of a brook). Yellow Flag or European Wild Flag, called Fleur de lys, prefers much water but will grow in a moist, shady spot in the garden; leaves are 1 inch wide and 3 feet long; flowers are small, bright yellow veined with brown, outer segments 2 or 2½ inches long; particularly suitable for a natural pool or along a water course. White Flag is the Florentine Iris, White Flower de luce; flowers are really a pale blue, outer segments about 3½ inches long; wide, light green leaves about 3½ feet in length; very ornamental for flower garden. *Spacing of mature plants:* Sweet Flag 1 foot, others 18 inches. *Cultural requirements:* about every 3 years, in spring or fall, dig up plants and divide or cut rhizomes so that each piece has at least 1 good bud; in cooler climates this should be done right after blooming so that plants will get established for winter.

Uses: Rhizome—(medicinal) Blue Flag —cathartic, emetic in large doses, used in jaundice; Sweet Flag—infusion for fevers, used for dyspepsia; White Flag—emetic

and cathartic in large doses; (culinary)
Sweet Flag—cut up fresh rhizome, boil in
syrup and cool for confection, for flavoring cream, custard, rice pudding, because
of spicy taste is often substituted for ginger, cinnamon or nutmeg; Yellow Flag—
roasted, ground and used like coffee. (Do
not use Blue Flag for any culinary purpose); (household) White Flag—thrown
in fireplace to give pleasant odor, held in
mouth as a breath sweetener to disguise
garlic, liquor, tobacco; Sweet Flag—dried
and used as a preventive against moths
and other insects, laid among clothes and
furs for the same purposes. Powdered
root—(industrial) Sweet Flag—to scent
hair powder and tooth powder, as snuff,
oil of root improves flavor of gin, some
kinds of beer, bitters, tonics, Benedictine,
Chartreuse, vermouth, other liqueurs and
cordials; White Flag—orris powder, basis
of powders with violet scent (*Iris pallida*
and *I. germanica,* also used) in violet perfumes. Leaf—Sweet Flag—for making
mats and baskets. Flower—Yellow Flag
—used instead of galls in making ink and
for yellow dye.

FLAX—Common Flax (*Linum usitatis-
simum*). *Propagation:* by seed, germination 8 days. *Nature of plant:* annual, 18
inches high, single light blue flowers, decorative for flower border or blue garden,
narrow blue-green foliage is decorative,
flowers delicate. *Spacing of mature plants:*
12 inches. *Cultural requirements:* cultivated for flax fiber or seed; seed crops
need deeply dug, moist, rich loam, sun.
    Uses: Seed—(medicinal) crushed seed

with hot water for poultices, for inflammation, and chest colds, whole seed as laxative, in cough medicine, for burns, with other seeds in veterinary medicine and for bird food; (industrial) source of linseed oil for paints, varnishes, putty, in making oilcloth and linoleum, in furniture polish, in rubber manufacture and tanning, flax seed oil and charcoal rubbed over Parmesan cheese for shiny coating. Stem and Fiber—(industrial) source of linen thread and cloth.

FOXGLOVE—Thimble Flowers, Gloves of Our Lady (*Digitalis purpurea*). *Propagation:* by seed, slow and uncertain germination. *Nature of plant:* unbranching stalk 3 feet high, erect with 2 inch long thimble-like flowers, purple, yellow or white, in a one-sided spray along the stalk and opening first at bottom of spray and finally at tip; very effective in groups in flower garden and useful in flower arrangements; the true medicinal foxglove has only dull deep pink or magenta flowers, never pale colors. *Spacing of mature plants:* about 10 inches. *Cultural requirements:* in rich, peaty, moist, but absolutely well drained soil in sun or shade; for commercial growing the area must be sunny, preferably protected, as the drug obtained from the leaves will develop only in the sun; as the plant is biennial, seeds must be sown each year to produce flowers every season; the tiny seeds should be mixed with sand to insure thin enough planting; sow in summer for the next season's bloom; enrich the soil around the plants and cover lightly after the ground has frozen; if covered too heavily the plants tend to winter-kill.

Uses: Leaf—(medicinal) heart diseases, dropsy, a narcotic, sedative, stimulant in lack of blood circulation.

FRAXINELLA—Gas Plant, Burnish Bush, Bastard Dittany (*Dictamnus albus*). *Propagation:* by seeds sown as soon as ripe; by root cuttings 3 inches long in spring but difficult. *Nature of plant:* grows 3 feet high; has dark shiny, leathery foliage resembling the ash tree; flowers in terminal racemes have many oil glands which release oil at the touch of a lighted match on a still, hot night; decorative for flower garden and useful in flower arrangements; both flower and foliage when crushed have lemony odor. *Spacing of mature plants:* 18 inches. *Cultural requirements:* moderately rich, somewhat light soil, deeply dug; sun or partial shade; established plants should not be moved as flower stems grow taller each season if not disturbed; seeds are shiny, black balls; cover seeds with 1 inch of soil when sowing; the next spring when seedlings appear, keep weeded; when seedlings are 2 years old, they may be transplanted; flowers will appear the fourth year.

Uses: Root—(medicinal) in fevers, hysteria. Leaf—(culinary) a refreshing tea.

FUMITORY—Earth Smoke (*Fumaria officinalis*). *Propagation:* by seed, self-sows freely. *Nature of plant:* low, sprawly plant with weak stems and finely divided leaves; whole plant has a grayish, blue-green, hazy appearance which has been likened to smoke coming out of the ground;

flowers in pinkish spikes, rosy purple at top; a wonderfully soft edging but far too fine to conceal an artificial boundary. *Spacing of mature plants:* 9 inches. *Cultural requirements:* dry, light, sandy soil, grows best in full sun.

Uses: Whole Herb—(medicinal) laxative, tonic, blood purifier, smoked like tobacco for head disorders. Flower—infusion for dyspepsia; (household) yellow dye for wool from flowers.

GARLIC—(*Allium sativum*). *Propagation:* by seed; by bulb division. *Nature of plant:* bulb is made of many bulblets called cloves, held together by a whitish skin; leaves are flat; flowers top a stalk that comes from the bulb and are massed into small, white umbels; sometimes bulbils are among the parts of the umbel. *Spacing of mature plants:* 6 inches. *Cultural requirements:* rich, sandy soil, moderately moist, in a sunny spot; cloves are planted about 2 inches deep, in drills like onions; harvest in late summer when leaves die down; keep free from weeds and hoe up soil about plants now and then.

Uses: Bulb—(medicinal) expectorant, rubifacient, diaphoretic in bronchitis, coughs and colds, antiseptic much used in first World War, the expressed juice diluted with water and applied with swabs of sterilized sphagnum moss, ointments and lotions, veterinary medicine, anthelmintic, for bringing boils and ulcers to a head.

GAS PLANT—see FRAXINELLA

GERMANDER—Wall Germander (*Teucrium Chamaedrys*). *Propagation:* by seed, takes 30 days for germination; by root divisions in fall; by cuttings in spring or summer. *Nature of plant:* much branched, low plant with dark green, glossy leaves like tiny oak leaves hiding stems and blossoming out in rosy flowers in leaf axils; beautiful edging plant or as clumps in flower bed; roots spread quite rapidly. *Spacing of mature plants:* 12 inches. *Cultural requirements:* prefers rich, light, well drained soil in sunny spot but will adapt itself to almost any condition.

Uses: Whole herb (medicinal) antiscorbutic, used in fevers.

GOOD KING HENRY—Fat Hen (*Chenopodium Bonus-Henricus*). *Propagation:* by seed, slow and uncertain but the best method; by root division in spring. *Nature of plant:* a cluster of deep green foliage at the ground with spikes of inconspicuous green flowers; interesting for flower arrangements because of leaves shaped like arrow-heads, but not spectacular for flower borders; useful for filling in around bare lower stalks of other plants. *Spacing of mature plants:* 12 inches. *Cultural requirements:* in rich, deeply dug, well drained soil in sun or shade, preferably shade, plants will grow luxuriantly after the first year; then leaves may be cut but do not strip the plant; avoid transplanting after cutting leaves.

Uses: Whole herb—(culinary) potherb like spinach; (medicinal) cooling infusion, laxative, applied to inflamed areas for soothing effect.

HEN-AND-CHICKENS—see HOUSELEEK

HERBA-BARONA—see THYME

HOLLYHOCK—(*Althaea rosea*). *Propagation:* by seed, easy germination, 5 days; by roots buried in sand deep enough to cover crown; many suckers can be taken off and rooted. *Nature of plant:* a time-honored garden plant for tall, colorful backgrounds against white picket fences, for concealing unsightly spots, bare walls of garages, houses, for grouping at a corner spot; usually from 5 to 6 feet tall but reaches as high as 15 feet in preferred locations. *Spacing of mature plants:* about 2 feet. *Cultural requirements:* rich, well drained soil, deeply dug, in full sun; if planted in unprotected spots, stalks should be supported against heavy winds and rains; plants of one summer's sowing may be removed to a permanent place the next spring; be sure roots are pointing downward and crown is below surface of ground; earth up soil about plants after rains so that root will not be exposed; winterkilling of plants comes from exposed roots heaved out of ground, good root systems will not develop in dry, sandy soil.

Uses: Flower—(industrial) for coloring wine, provides coloring matter for indicator in volumetric analysis; (medicinal) emollient, demulcent, in chest diseases.

HOLY THISTLE—see BLESSED THISTLE

HOREHOUND—(*Marrubium vulgare*). *Propagation:* by seed, germination from 14 to 20 days; by root division. *Nature of plant:* somewhat decumbent habits; good for edgings of a gray garden except for its tendency to winterkill. *Spacing of mature plants:* 9 inches. *Cultural require-

ments: prefers dry, poor, light, chalky well drained soil in sun or partial shade; sow seed every other season to be sure to have plants as some will winterkill; in autumn, cut off old stalks to keep the bed thick.

Uses: Leafy top—(medicinal) in an infusion for bronchitis, coughs, colds, in lozenges and candy; in jaundice and dyspepsia.

HORSEHEAL—see ELECAMPANE

HOUSELEEK—Hen-and-Chickens, Roof Houseleek (*Sempervivum tectorum*). *Propagation:* by offsets; by leaves cut to the base with an eye on the stem. *Nature of plant:* a natural plant for rock gardens, niches or top of walls, very hardy. *Spacing of mature plants:* 6 inches. *Cultural requirements:* in good, well drained soil; do not let plants flower because the rosette is apt to die; to start new plants from offsets, place them where they are to grow and cover with moist earth.

Uses: Leaf—(medicinal) bruised leaves applied as cooling applications to burns and other external inflammations, juice is supposed to cure warts.

HYSSOP—(*Hyssopus officinalis*). *Propagation:* by seed, easy germination; by root division in spring; by cuttings. *Nature of plant:* a sub-shrub, almost evergreen, invaluable for low hedges; flower spikes of blue, pink or white for flower arrangements; can be trimmed like box but, of course, will not flower if tops are cut off; aromatic foliage. *Spacing of mature plants:* 12 inches. *Cultural requirements:* prefers light, well drained, well limed, warm soil

in sun or partial shade; cut back after flowering to keep little bushes from growing straggly; often there is a second, late flowering; when old plants get too woody, fill in with younger plants.

Uses: Leafy top—(medicinal) in dyspepsia, coughs and colds, cathartic, induces perspiration; (industrial) in toilet waters, in Chartreuse.

INDIGO—Wild Indigo (*Baptisia tinctoria*), with loosely clustered pealike yellow blossoms and False Indigo (*B. australis*) with similar clusters of blue flowers, commonly called Baptisia, are both attractive in the garden and are important herbs for medicine and commerce. *Propagation:* by seed; by root division in spring. *Nature of plant:* becomes a tall bushy clump, often reaching 4 or 5 feet in height, with much branching stems and terminal spikes of blossoms changing into spectacular pods; useful for flower arrangements. *Spacing of mature plants:* 4 feet. *Cultural requirements:* both varieties grow in dry, sandy soil in full sun for free blooming, slow growing and resent moving.

Uses: Root—(medicinal) Wild Indigo —in typhoid and scarlet fevers, diphtheria, emetic, externally and as a gargle in sore throat, ulcers, gangrene, antiseptic; False Indigo—emetic. Woody stalk—(industrial) blue dye as inferior substitute for indigo.

JERUSALEM OAK—Ambrosia, Feather Geranium (*Chenopodium Botrys*). *Propagation:* by seed, self-sows freely; crowds of seedlings must be thinned ruthlessly.

Nature of plant: when small, plant is bushy with inch long leaves like oak leaves in shape and appearance, even turning red and yellow like oak leaves; as plant grows to 2 or 3 feet high, leaves diminish to almost nothing and feathery branches develop; useful for flower border; very fragrant spikes. Good for cutting. *Spacing of mature plants:* 12 inches. *Cultural requirements:* prefers dry, sandy soil; once planted anywhere in the garden, innumerable seedlings will appear in many other places every spring, seeds are very small and should be mixed with sand when sowing.

Uses: Whole Herb—(medicinal) anthelmintic, pectoral.

JOE-PYE WEED—see BONESET

LARKSPUR—Lark's-heel, Forking Larkspur (*Delphinium Ajacis*). *Propagation:* by seed, germination easy, self-sows. *Nature of plant:* vivid blue, violet-blue or white blossoms in spikelike racemes make the plant beautiful for gardens and flower arrangements; grows from 3 to 4 feet tall; effective in masses. *Spacing of mature plants:* 6 inches. *Cultural requirements:* sandy, well drained soil is best; after flowers have faded, cut off spike for a second blooming.

Uses: Seeds—(medicinal) poisonous, in asthma, for pediculi. Flowers—poisonous, in dysentery, dropsy, gout.

LAVENDER—Three varieties of lavender used in industry, medicine and in household preparations are beautiful additions to the garden picture. These are Spike (*Lavandula Spica*), True or English (*L.*

vera), or French (*L. Stoechas*). The last is easiest to identify. It is a small shrub with long, narrow, gray-green leaves; flowers are dark purple on spikes, topped by purple bracts; smells somewhat like Spike, but is not hardy in cold climates. Spike lavender differs from True by broader, spatulate, green-gray leaves, more compact inflorescence, and bracts in axils where flowers are found are narrower. Stems of Spike are very long, interrupted and branching way above the body of the plant; flowers yield 3 times as much oil (called Spike oil) but inferior in quality to True, and has a piny note to the fragrance. It is often adulterated with oil of turpentine. True lavender has narrow, blunt, blue-green leaves and comparatively large blue flowers in spikes on square stems; flowers are arranged in groups of from 6 to 10 in whorls, lower ones far apart from upper ones. Young leaves are apt to be found in groups in axils and are a downy, greenish white. True lavender is quite hardy and Spike less so unless protected. *Propagation:* by seed, not easy and slow germination; by root division in spring; but cuttings, very easy. *Nature of plant:* suitable for gray and for fragrant gardens; both flowers and leaves are fragrant. *Spacing of mature plants:* from 12 inches to 3 feet, depending on the climate. In mild geographic locations, lavenders will grow to 3 feet in height but in temperate and colder places, the normal height is about 1 foot, with spikes of Spike lavender a foot or 18 inches higher. True lavender will spread if undisturbed. *Cultural requirements:* light, gravelly or sandy soil in a sunny spot; dig in lime or chalk about roots several times a season. Plants must be grown in poor soil to produce the most fragrance; in good soil plants grow more luxuriantly but fragrant essential oils are lacking. Good drainage is essential or plants will winterkill. From a few established plants cuttings may be taken in early spring and rooted; the next spring, roots may be divided, and so on to increase stock. Cuttings should be about 6 inches and are best taken by ripping a branch down quickly, thus getting a heel from the parent stalk. When roots have developed, dig the soil deeply and set plant well down. Old plants must be well pruned every year for they become woody; prune after flower stalks have been cut. Keep young plants from blossoming the first year in order to bush them. In fall, clear the ground around plants, dig in wood ashes, cover with salt hay or leaves. French lavender must be taken in and Spike is best taken in. Lavenders are subject to shrub disease shown by yellow shoots in the spring, and affected plants must be burned.

Uses: Flower—(industrial) Spike for making oil of lavender and lavender water; True for making oil of aspic to dilute delicate colors for china painting, in varnish, spray to keep moths from clothes, liqueurs, herbal tobacco, snuff, toilet water, to perfume soaps and clean paint brushes; French for an inferior grade of oil (household) packed away with clothes as moth preventive, to polish floors—(medicinal) spirit of lavender used as stimulant and carminative when diluted and sweetened, oil rubbed on skin for ticks, as nervine and antiseptic to swab wounds, French for chest complaints.

LAVENDER COTTON—see SANTOLINA

LEMON BALM—see BALM

LILY-OF-THE-VALLEY—May Lily, Our Lady's Tears (*Convallaria majalis*). *Propagation:* by root division. *Nature of plant:* a high ground cover for a moist, shady spot; attractive in early spring; cut flowers much prized. *Spacing of mature plants:* 6 inches. *Cultural requirements:* rich, sandy, deeply dug soil in a moist, shady place; plants require deep cultivation and rich earth to produce large blossoms; should be transplanted every 3 or 4 years; dig up roots with soil, cut into 3 or 4 inch squares and reset; mulch with manure before winter sets in.

Uses: Root—(medicinal) as a heart stimulant, cardiac dropsy. Flower and Leaf emetic, cathartic, cardiac tonic.

LOVAGE—Has been known as Smallage and our grandmothers called it "Smellage" (*Levisticum officinale*). *Propagation:* by seed as soon as ripe; by root division in spring. *Nature of plant:* handsome, tropical, background plant; grows 7 feet high; has aromatic leaves. *Spacing of mature plants:* 3 feet. *Cultural requirements:* prefers rich, deeply dug, moist soil in sun or part shade; seeds may be sowed in September and seedlings transplanted the following spring.

Uses: Rhizome—(medicinal) carminative, infusion produces perspiration. Leaf —(culinary) fresh or dried, similar in odor and taste to celery and used in place of it. Fruit—(seed) used in confectionery and cordials. Leaf Stalk and Stem—blanched and used like celery, for a fragrant tea. Flowering Top and Leaf—(industrial) oil used to flavor some tobaccos, in perfumery.

MADDER—Dyer's Madder (*Rubia tinctorum*). *Propagation:* by seed; by root division. *Nature of plant:* grown mostly for its long fleshy root; decumbent nature permits the 4-foot-long stems to lie on the ground; in second year flowers like spikes of tiny yellow stars, rise from joints in stem; rough, spiny leaves and stems. *Spacing of mature plants:* 10 inches. *Cultural requirements:* light, sandy soil; prefers sun; puts out underground runners profusely.

Uses: Root—(medicinal) deobstruent; (industrial) depending upon what mordant is used, will dye turkey red, pink, lilac, purple, brown, orange, black. Leaf and Stem—(industrial) spiny nature of the whorls of leaves and stems has made them useful in polishing metal work.

MARJORAM—Four useful marjorams, Pot Marjoram (*Marjorana Onites*), Wild Marjoram (*Origanum vulgare*), Sweet Marjoram (*M. hortensis*) and Showy Marjoram (*O. Pulchellum*) are perennials but in cool climates Sweet Marjoram has to be treated as an annual; they may be used as culinary seasonings but Sweet is most fragrant, though Pot, as its name indicates, is widely used. Wild is used mostly for medicinal purposes. *Propagation:* by seed; Sweet and Pot are very slow to germinate; Wild and Showy self-sow freely;

by root division and by cuttings of hardy varieties in spring. *Nature of plant:* Sweet or Knotted Marjoram is an erect little bush, narrow leaves, white flowers, and green bracts; grown for leaves to be used in the kitchen but is a delightful plant for the fragrant garden; it is not spreading. Wild Marjoram grows to a leafy bush, about 2½ feet high, with pale pink flowers in loose clusters; its oval leaves are broader than those of other varieties, about ⅜ inch across and ½ inch long. Pot Marjoram is about 1½ feet high and is inclined to sprawl and layer itself, soon forming a beautiful mound; flower clusters and bracts are purplish and suitable for flower arrangements. Showy Marjoram is most decorative for the garden, with broad yellow-green leaves and pink flower clusters; it forms a round little bush about 16 inches high completely covered with foliage. *Spacing of mature plants:* Sweet 10 inches, others 15 inches. *Cultural requirements:* all varieties should be planted in light, medium rich, chalky soil, average dry in full sun. Sweet Marjoram seedlings require shade until well started; since all varieties are slow growing, they require frequent weeding and cultivation.

Uses: Leaf—(culinary) in vinegar, soup, dressing, vegetable cocktail, meat pie, roast lamb, cheese, salad, chopped meat, pudding, egg dishes, peas, beans, tomatoes, in white sauce for boiled fish and as a garnish. Flowering Top—(industrial) Sweet Marjoram oil is used to scent soap and perfume pomades; Wild Marjoram in tobacco; (household) in dyes. Whole Plant—(medicinal) Sweet Marjoram infusion for nervous headaches, oil to hasten eruptions in measles, in microscopy; Wild Marjoram stimulant, oil on cotton for toothache, in fomentations.

MARSHMALLOW—(*Althaea officinalis*). *Propagation:* by seed, sow as soon as ripe. *Nature of plant:* sturdy, erect root stalks with 3-lobed, soft, downy, gray-green leaves, flowers are a light rose, about 1 inch across, found in the leaf axils. Not spectacular but suitable for back of border or for a gray garden. *Spacing of mature plants:* 18 inches. *Cultural requirements:* in friable, moderately moist soil, deeply dug; young seedlings must be protected and mulched for winter as they tend to winterkill; well established plants are hardy.

   Uses: Root—(medicinal) excipient for pills, decoction for inflammation of mucous membranes as in coughs, colds, bronchial troubles; (industrial) liquid from root is a base for commercial mucilage. Flower and Leaf—(medicinal) in poultices.

MEADOWSWEET—Several plants called Meadowsweet are found in the garden but only two varieties are truly herbs which have medicinal value and are Dropwort (*Filipendula hexapetala*) and Queen-Of-The-Meadow (*F. Ulmaria*). *Propagation:* by seed; by root division in spring. *Nature of plant:* both are additions to any garden and useful for flower arrangements. The flower stalk of Dropwort rises to 18 inches in height, has tufted clusters of creamy white fragrant flowers rose tinted inside; fernlike foliage; makes a splendid

lacy edging plant since foliage is in rosettes at base of flower stalks. Queen-Of-The-Meadow grows to 5 or 6 feet with large 3- or 5-lobed terminal leaflets, slightly hairy underneath; white flowers in rather dense clusters; odor of leaf and flower are different; resemblance of the leaf to the elm leaf gives the botanical name. *Spacing of mature plants:* Dropwort 10 inches; the other about 15 inches. *Cultural requirements:* Queen-Of-The-Meadow likes rather rich, moist soil in partial shade; Dropwort prefers drier soil in full sun with a little lime.

Uses: Leaf—(medicinal) Dropwort infusion for colds; Queen-Of-The-Meadow astringent; (culinary) Dropwort gives delicate flavor to soup. Root—(industrial) both contain tannic acid, used in tanning; (medicinal) Queen-of-the Meadow in diarrhea. Flower—oil of both is similar to oil of wintergreen, flowers have to a small extent the virtues of salicylic acid and in form of a decoction are used as diuretic and tonic.

MILFOIL—see YARROW

MINT—About a dozen of the 30 odd species found in the North Temperate Zone are grown for use in medicine, cooking, household preparations and industry. All mints have an aromatic, refreshing odor, though each one is distinctive. This odor comes from the essential oil for which most mints are grown. Sometimes the distilled oil is used, sometimes leafy tops containing the oil in its natural state. All mints are characterized by their square stems, purplish flowers either in whorls or in terminal spikes, and shallow, creeping, underground roots. *Propagation:* by seed; by cutting up of runners and resetting. *Nature of plant:* Apple Mint (*Mentha rotundifolia*) is also called woolly mint because of the soft woolly, round leaves, about 1 inch broad, on erect stems 18 inches high; it is often confused with *M. sylvestris* which grows much taller and whose leaves are not round. Apple Mint has lilac flowers in thick, interrupted spikes; because of the hairy leaves is not good for culinary use. American Apple Mint (*M. gentilis* var. *variegata*): low growing plant with smooth, green leaves streaked with yellow cream color, pale purple flowers in whorls on leaf axils, has a fruity, refreshing odor and taste. Corn Mint (*M. arvensis*): freely branching, hairy stems and leaves, very pale, lilac flowers in whorls in leaf axils, leaves are a rounded oblong, in Europe it is often grown with peppermint and deteriorates the oil of the latter. Curly Mint (*M. spicata* var. *crispata*): crinkly, heavily veined, broad leaves, pale purple flowers in terminal spikes, stems are hairy, long and weak so that the plant in late summer has sprawling tendencies. Orange or Bergamot Mint (*M. citrata*): reddish green branching stems with egg-shaped, smooth, dull green leaves edged with purple; the first whiff of odor is like lavender, purple flowers in axils and short spikes. White Peppermint (*M. piperita* var. *officinalis*)—leaves and slender stems smooth, light green, purple flowers in dense terminal spikes, produces finest oil. Black Peppermint (*M. piperita* var. *vulgaris*)—thicker stems than the

white variety and grows higher, stems are purple, leaves are dark green tinged with purple, reddish purple flowers in terminal spikes, more prolific in oil and stronger than white variety. Spearmint (*M. spicata* var. *viridis*)—called garden mint or lamb mint; erect stems are reddish, often light green at top, leaves are glossy, narrow, heavily veined, ending in a sharp point and have toothed indentations around the edge, pale purple flowers in whorls on stems. Water Mint (*M. aquatica*)—hairy stems, oval shaped leaves, pale purple flowers in terminal spikes, very pungent odor, found along banks of streams and lakes. *Cultural Requirements:* need rather rich soil, not necessarily shady, if moderately moist; keep weeded, enrich soil after cutting, renew beds every 3 or 4 years. For small beds, instead of plowing or harrowing in spring, chop up the whole area with a sharp edging tool or spade deep enough to cut through runners; water well and cover with a thin layer of enriched soil, this will start new plants and avoid a tangled mat of roots; if bed gets too crowded, thin by pulling up runners. Cutting plants improves the growth, do not permit flowering stalks to go to seed before cutting as quite often plants will die; spearmint is subject to rust and the ground should be burned over to eradicate the rust; manure is apt to cause rust and other fertilizer should be used when any is required.

Uses: Leafy top—(medicinal) Corn is used as an infusion for colicky spasms, remedy for rheumatic pains; Apple as a stomachic, stimulant, carminative, substituted for spearmint or peppermint in colic;

Peppermint as an infusion to relieve nausea, colic, headache, to correct nauseating or griping effects of other medicines, for heat prostration; Curly, Spearmint, Water Mint used in colic, flatulence, cholera, diarrhea; Orange Mint as an infusion to produce perspiration, relief of nervous headaches; (culinary) Spearmint, Apple Mint, Orange Mint used in lamb and fish sauces, apple sauce, fruit cup, iced beverages, confectionery, sprinkled over vegetables, in pea soup, currant jelly, mint jelly, vinegar, teas, in French dressing for green salads, in chopped cabbage (Apple Mint and Orange Mint are more delicate in flavor than Spearmint and generally preferred); (industrial) Orange Mint used as oil in perfume, Chartreuse, a source of bergamot oil; Peppermint used in chewing gum, confectionery, menthol is the distinctive oil in oil of peppermint and much used, oil also used in dental preparations, toilet waters, moth mixtures; soaps, foot bath preparations, in paste as a preservative, in many liqueurs including Benedictine, Chartreuse, *crême de menthe,* used for testing steam boilers for leaks and in testing gas masks; Spearmint used in teas, confectionery, chewing gum, toilet water; (household) to keep mice away.

MONKSHOOD—see ACONITE

MUGWORT—Three plants called Mugwort are useful in medicine and industry— Common Mugwort (*Artemisia vulgaris*), White Mugwort (*A. lactiflora*) and Western Mugwort (*A. ludoviciana*); all are ornamental garden plants. *Propagation:* by seed; by root division in spring; by cut-

tings. *Nature of plant:* Common Mugwort—sturdy, much-branching stalks with a tinge of purple; grows to a height of 4 feet; leaves are divided into several segments, the underside being slightly downy; yellow flowers are in spiked panicles; suitable for back of garden border. White Mugwort, Hawthorn-scented Mugwort, resembles the Common Mugwort, slightly taller, but has white panicles of very fragrant flowers; good for backgrounds, high hedges and it has been suggested that they be grown in tubs as they are so decorative; flower stems are useful in flower arrangements both for fragrance and grace. Western Mugwort sometimes called White Sage; has creeping underground roots, gray stems between 2 and 3 feet high; deeply cut, almost white leaves, which to the touch resemble felt, like beach wormwood; flower heads are inconspicuous, small panicles; suitable for a gray garden. *Spacing of mature plants:* Western about 8 inches, others 2 feet. *Cultural requirements:* average moist soil in full sun; to produce luxuriant flowers, White Mugwort needs rich soil; a treatment of soapsuds or nicotine spray is occasionally required.

Uses: Whole Herb including Root—(medicinal) Common used in epilepsy, tapeworm; White used similar to Common; Western as a hair stimulant.

MULLEIN—Two useful varieties of Mullein are far apart in size; Great Mullein (*Verbascum Thapsus*), also called Our Lady's Flannel, Hag's Taper, and some 30 other local names, grows to a height of 8 or 9 feet when brought into the garden while the delicate stalk of Moth Mullein (*V. Blattaria*) grows not over 4 feet high. *Propagation:* by seed, germination 10 days, self-sows freely. *Nature of plant:* Great Mullein—sturdy, erect stalk from 7 to 8 feet high with huge velvety leaves from 16 to 18 inches long in a big rosette at the foot but much smaller leaves on stalk; flower spikes thick with small, golden yellow flowers; when dried and dipped in oil, stalks burn like tapers; it is too coarse and large for a small flower garden but of interest in a large gray garden. Moth Mullein—leaves about 2 inches long, flowers ¾ inch across, yellow with lilac-colored centers, on short stems or pedicels appear to be clinging to the 18-inch stalk; decorative for gardens and good for height in flower arrangements. *Cultural requirements:* poor, dry soil anywhere; unless seed head of Great Mullein is cut, ground will be matted the following spring with seedlings. *Spacing of mature plants:* Great Mullein 3 feet; Moth Mullein 10 inches.

    Uses: Leaf—(medicinal) in cigarettes for asthma; infusion for pulmonary diseases, vulnerary, poultices, oil has softening and soothing properties.

MUSTARD—Both Black (*Brassica nigra*) and White Mustard (*B. alba*) are grown for medicinal and culinary uses of seeds, while White produces foliage much prized as a salad and potherb. *Propagation:* by seed, easy germination, self-sows freely. *Nature of plant:* Black Mustard grows to 4 feet with yellowish green, smooth leaves and racemes of small yellow flowers. White Mustard is a smaller plant than the black,

not over 18 inches high; these plants self-sow too freely for introduction to the flower garden but are an addition to the culinary plot. *Spacing of mature plants:* 12 inches. *Cultural requirements:* poor, sandy soil in full sun.

Uses: Seed—(industrial) Black Mustard seeds mixed with White Mustard seeds, crushed and moistened with water, produce official oil of mustard used in manufacture of oleomargarine, soap, liniment, salad oil and lubricants; (medicinal) Black as a sterilizing agent, deodorizer, antiseptic, laxative, in foot-baths and for headaches, White in an infusion for bronchitis, rheumatism, gargle, for flatulency, hemorrhoids, laxative; (culinary) White used in pickles. Leaf—(culinary) White in salad, potherb.

NASTURTIUM — (*Tropaeolum majus*) *Propagation:* by seed, germination about 8 days. *Nature of plant:* much loved, low plant with round or kidney-shaped leaves; flowers in many colors from yellow, orange to brownish and red; used for flower arrangements and in garden borders. *Spacing of mature plants:* 8 inches. *Cultural requirements:* in light, sandy, moderately rich soil in sunny spot; subject to aphids which should be treated with nicotine spray or soap suds; thinning of leaves by cutting out badly affected ones is advised; a moth ball placed at the foot of each seedling is said to discourage insects.

Uses: Seed—(culinary) half-ripened seeds in mustard pickles. Leaf and Flower —(culinary) in salads. Juice—(medicinal) a remedy for itching.

NETTLE, DEAD—Bee Nettle, Blind Nettle (*Lamium maculatum* var. *album*).
Propagation: by seed; by division of roots
in spring. *Nature of plant:* a hardy, low-
growing, decumbent plant with dull, light
green, pebbly, heart-shaped leaves; white
flowers 1 inch long are in terminal clusters; a variegated form has a streak of
white along midrib; good for border edging and rock gardens. *Spacing of mature
plants:* 12 inches. *Cultural requirements:*
light, well drained soil in full sun.

   Uses: Plant—(medicinal) in hemorrhages.

OLD MAN—see SOUTHERNWOOD

OLD WOMAN—see WORMWOOD

ORACH—French Spinach, Mountain Spinach. This annual, a popular potherb from
the sixteenth to the nineteenth century,
might well be re-introduced as a beautiful
addition to the garden and there are green
(*Atriplex hortensis*) and red (*A. hortensis*
var. *atrosanguinea*) varieties. *Propagation:* seed, self-sows. *Nature of plant:*
both varieties grow sturdily erect to about
4 feet, unbranching, and so can be planted
in masses to make a spectacular spot; the
arrow-shaped leaves have wavy margins
and are soft textured, large at base and
smaller as they ascend the stem; one variety has vivid, light, yellow-green leaves
and stem and the other unbelievably bright
crimson foliage and stem and seeds which
droop in loose terminal clusters; against a
background of a gray wall or of tall, gray
leaved artemisias like wormwood, it is
most striking; good for flower arrangements. *Spacing of mature plants:* 8 inches.

Cultural requirements: in light, well drained soil in full sun; water during drought to develop foliage.

Uses: Whole plant—(medicinal) soothing for inflammations. Seed—emetic.

OSWEGO TEA—see BERGAMOT

PARSLEY—(*Petroselinum hortense*).*Propagation:* by seed, very slow and uncertain germination. *Nature of plant:* there is a curly and a fern-leaved variety, both pleasing in garden, the vivid green foliage of the curly variety being particularly beautiful as an edging. *Spacing of mature plants:* 6 inches. *Cultural requirements:* medium rich, deeply dug, average soil in partial shade; not satisfactorily transplanted; germination period may be shortened by soaking seeds for 24 hours before planting and sowing on the surface and tamping them firmly with a flat board; thin by pinching out unwanted seedlings (which may be used for garnish) and keep leaves clipped for thick growth; flower stalks appear in spring of second season and should be cut off to preserve plants; enriched soil can then be spread around plants and dug in; most growers prefer to sow seed in autumn as resulting plants are less liable to winterkill; fern-leaved variety is less liable to winterkill than curly.

Uses: Leaf—(culinary) in soup, stew, creamed vegetables, salad, over eggs, chicken stock, in melted butter for potatoes; (medicinal) in treatment of wounds. Whole Herb—(industrial) for coloring wines and in sage cheese, planted between rows of onions and of carrots to counteract odor and lessen the attraction of attacking flies; (household) oil to destroy vermin. Seed—(medicinal) to dispel fever. Root—(medicinal) for kidney troubles, mild laxative.

PASQUE FLOWER—Anemone (*Anemone Pulsatilla*). *Propagation:* by seed. *Nature of plant:* a little 10-inch high plant, flowers in April blue to reddish purple, about 1½ inches across; leaves and seed pods have silky hairs which give it a grayish cast; a red-flowered variety is somewhat smaller and a variegated form with pale purple flowers blooms in May; excellent for flower border edgings, in clumps and in flower arrangements. *Spacing of mature plants:* 8 to 10 inches. *Cultural requirements:* deeply dug, light, gravelly, well drained soil; add lime.

Uses: Flower—(household) juice of purple sepals yields a green color used to color Paschal or Easter eggs; not a permanent dye. Whole Plant—(medicinal) in syphilis, asthma, rheumatism, coughs, catarrh.

PENNYROYAL—There are two plants of this name: one is English Pennyroyal or Pudding Grass (*Mentha Pulegium*) and the other is American Pennyroyal or Squaw Mint (*Hedeoma pulegioides*). Both are very strong and pungent with a clean, cool, refreshing, minty odor. *Propagation:* American by seed, slow to germinate from sown seed but self-sows freely; English by seed, by division of roots in fall or spring. *Nature of plant:* American—stiffly erect little annual, 10 inches high and much branched, light green leaves, about 1 inch long and sharp

pointed, standing out stiffly at right angles to stem, pale blue flowers in axillary clusters, grown for its aromatic oil; English— prostrate in habit, stems about 14 inches long, leaves are deep green, somewhat hairy, and oval in shape, about ½ inch long, tiny lilac-colored flowers in axillary whorls, useful ground cover in warmer climates but apt to winterkill in cold climates, plant can be taken up for a trailing house plant. *Spacing of mature plants:* from 5 to 6 inches. *Cultural requirements:* English likes clay, moist soil in partial shade; American prefers light, sandy, dry soil in full sun.

Uses: Whole plant—(medicinal) American in infusions to produce perspiration, used in colic, emmenagogue; English in infusions for spasms, an emmenagogue.

PERILLA—Beefsteak Plant (*Perilla frutescens* var. *crispa*). *Propagation:* by seed, easy germination, self-sows from year to year plentifully. *Nature of plant:* erect, growing to 2 feet, with broad, wrinkly, purple-bronze leaves 3½ inches long; small pink flowers in axillary and terminal racemes; gives an odd, different color to border and to flower arrangements. *Spacing of mature plants:* 9 inches. *Cultural requirements:* moderately dry, partly sunny spot; sow seeds very thinly in a shallow furrow and cover with soil; percentage of germination very high.

Uses: Seed—(industrial) oil is used in Japan in manufacture of paints, paper umbrellas, and for same uses as linseed oil; in United States widely used as a drying oil for paint.

PIMPERNEL—Poor Man's Weathergrass (*Anagallis arvensis*). *Propagation:* by seed. *Nature of plant:* stem so weak that it lies on the ground with leaves and flowers always facing up; flowers stay open only in sunny weather and usually close by mid-afternoon; one variety has scarlet flowers, the other blue. *Spacing of mature plants:* 6 inches. *Cultural requirements:* light, warm, well drained, dry soil in full sun; transplanting difficult.

Uses: Whole Herb—(medicinal) infusion to produce perspiration; expectorant, nervine; household remedy for rabies, epilepsy, dropsy.

POPPY, OPIUM (*Papaver somniferum*). *Propagation:* by seed. *Nature of plant:* annual with bluish green stems, flowers 3 to 4 inches across, in color from bluish white to blue; seeds in round, oval pods vary from white to slate gray; opium is obtained from the shell of seed pod but seeds have no soporific qualities; decorative plant for garden. *Spacing of mature plants:* 8 to 10 inches. *Cultural requirements:* fairly rich, average moist soil in a sunny spot; under good conditions plant is said to grow almost as tall as the flaming oriental poppies but I have never found it so.

Uses: Juice from seed pod—(medicinal) source of morphine. Seed—(industrial) gray seeds called "maw" sold for birds' food; oil used as a substitute for olive oil; (culinary) used for breads and cakes.

POT MARIGOLD—see CALENDULA

PRIMROSE (*Primula veris*). *Propagation:* by seed; by root division. *Nature of plant:* makes an attractive edging for a border since the plant grows not much higher than 8 or 9 inches; after the lovely yellow flowers have gone, the yellow-green foliage still makes a bright accent for an edging; beautiful in large masses. Suitable for rock gardens and for flower arrangements. *Spacing of mature plants:* 10 inches. *Cultural requirements:* rich, well drained, moist soil in a shady or semi-shady spot; require watering in hot weather; crowns of plants must not stay above ground; if necessary, dig up and replant; protect with a light covering in winter.

Uses: Root and Leaf—(medicinal) emetic, anodyne, used as a sternutatory.

PYRETHRUM—(*Chrysanthemum cinerariaefolium*). *Propagation:* by seed but difficult, should be started in seed bed where soil has been sterilized; by root division in spring. *Nature of plant:* well known, 2-foot high plant with beautiful white or pink daisylike flowers on slender stems; excellent in masses for a bright spot in the garden and for flower arrangements; white variety found more in botanic gardens, the pink being the garden favorite; after flowers have passed, cut back to obtain a second blooming. *Spacing of mature plants:* 6 inches. *Cultural requirements:* well drained, limy soil, not too heavy, in open sunny borders; keep free from weeds and cultivate during growing season; avoid watering seedlings too much; after plants are established they need no extra water; in starting from seed, mix with sand, sow thinly on ground surface and tamp down but do not cover.

Uses: Flower—(industrial) the flowers are used in most insecticides, white variety is considered superior and produce more flowers.

RAMPION — (*Campanula Rapunculus*). *Propagation:* by seed. *Nature of plant:* sturdy, erect stems to 2½ feet high; leaves 1 to 3 inches long. Bell-like flowers vary from reddish purple, blue to white, are about ¾ inch long, ½ inch across, in narrow terminal racemes; gives soft, colorful accent to flower border or rock garden; grown for culinary purposes, fleshy taproot being edible. *Spacing of mature plants:* 6 inches. *Cultural requirements:* full sun in average sandy or limy moist soil; if grown for root, earth up around base of plant to blanch root and do not let it flower; a biennial, therefore seed must be sown each year; in flower border plant is made perennial by cutting off flower heads before they go to seed; seeds are tiny, should be mixed with sand, sown on the surface, pressed down but not covered; not readily transplanted.

Uses: Root—(culinary) raw in salads or young shoots blanched and eaten like asparagus, boiled and eaten like parsnips. Leaf—(culinary) raw in salads, cooked and eaten like spinach.

ROSE—Many varieties of roses are grown not only for their beauty in the garden and for bouquets and flower arrangements, but also for their use in industry, medicine and to some extent in culinary dishes. The most common for these purposes are the very

fragrant four: Apothecaries' Rose or Rose de Provins (*Rosa gallica*), Cabbage Rose or Provence Rose (*R. centifolia*), Dog Rose or Wild Brier (*R. canina*) and Kazanlik (*R. damascena trigintapetala*), a variety of Damask Rose (*R. damascena*). *Propagation:* by grafting. *Nature of plant:* Apothecaries' Rose grows to 4 feet, flowers are single and of a purplish red color, very fragrant when dried; Cabbage requires heavy fertilizing and close pruning, flowers about 3 inches across and each has 100 or more petals, must be seen fully opened to be appreciated, pink and droop heavily from stem; Dog is a shrub with long curving branches sometimes to 10 feet, flowers are white or pink, single, and about 2 inches across, much used as stock for grafting; Kazanlik is a rosy pink semi-double flower of 30 petals as the botanic name (*trigintapetala*) indicates, source of Attar of Roses. *Spacing of mature plants:* for most roses of these types 3 feet is a minimum and 4 or 5 feet much better. *Cultural requirements:* many books have been written on rose culture and these should be consulted; in general they require a firm or clay soil, well enriched and well drained and during the growing season should be further enriched and well watered; they should be in a bed by themselves away from roots of trees and dripping roofs; the sunniest spot in the garden will produce the most fragrant blooms; in cool climates, they should be mulched after a final digging in of manure.

Uses: Flower—Apothecaries' (medicinal) astringent, in eye lotions, (culinary) in conserve; Cabbage (industrial) rose water, Attar of Roses, this Attar with sandalwood and a fixative makes Essence of White Rose, not caustic and stronger than carbolic acid as a germicide and is non-irritating and not poisonous, soap, confectionery and to flavor some types of tobacco, (medicinal) as a gentle laxative; Kazanlik (industrial) Attar of Roses; Fruit—Dog (culinary) conserve of roses, (medicinal) medium for making drugs into pills, an excipient.

ROSE GERANIUM—(*Pelargonium graveolens*). *Propagation:* by seed; by cuttings. *Nature of plant:* old-fashioned, sweet smelling favorite; a large, branching plant with inconspicuous flowers but fragrant, deeply cut leaves, more fragrant the larger they are; suitable for fragrant gardens and bouquets. *Spacing of mature plants:* 3 feet. *Cultural requirements:* light, well drained soil in full sun; in cool climates plant is tender and after cuttings are made, the severely cut back plant may be stored in cellar if watered once a week; is a beautiful houseplant, if not severely cut back.

Uses: Plant—(industrial) oil for perfume, as adulterant for oil of rose. Leaf—(household) sometimes used in jellies.

ROSEMARY — (*Rosmarinus officinalis*). *Propagation:* by seed, slow to germinate, 3 weeks or more; by cuttings; by roots, quite easily in sand or water; by layering. *Nature of plant:* a piny looking bush, slow growing year after year but will reach 4 or 5 feet in height; leaves very narrow, dark green above, gray beneath; flowers commonly pale blue, but a deep blue vari-

ety has flowers like tiny orchids, in axillary
racemes; odor of leaves spicy, pungently
aromatic and taste is warm and piny; roots
are tender and must not freeze. *Spacing of
mature plants:* 3 feet. *Cultural requirements:* light, warm, dry, limy, well drained
soil; needs extra lime or chalk dug into
soil several times a season; should be
placed in full sun in a sheltered spot; in
cool climates the plants must be brought in
for the winter or placed in a pit or cellar.

Uses: Leafy top—(industrial) ingre-
dient of Hungarian (and other) toilet
waters, tooth wash, hair preparation,
soap, perfume, liniment, ointment and vermouth; (medicinal) tea for relief of nervous headaches, smoked for asthma, throat
or lung affections; (culinary) garnish, iced
beverage, pickle; (household) in moth
mixtures, burned with juniper berries as
disinfectant. Leaf—(culinary) in jam,
sweet sauces, veal stew, soup, peas, sprinkled over pork and beef roasts, added to
deep fat for frying potatoes, chopped fine
in baking powder biscuits. Flowers—(medicinal) for spasms, in rubefacient liniment, an emmenagogue.

RUE—Herb o' Grace (*Ruta graveolens*).
Propagation: by seed, easy germination,
self-sows freely; by cuttings; by root division. *Nature of plant:* a most unusual and
beautiful 2-foot high, branching, woody
sub-shrub with lacy, blue-green leaves and
bright yellow flowers ½ inch across; excellent for hedges in small gardens or borders for paths; can be trimmed like box
but will not bloom if tips are cut; almost
evergreen, turning brown late in winter

but one of the first herbs to recover in spring, sending out tiny leaves all along bluish stalks; gives a lacy effect in flower arrangements. *Spacing of mature plants:* 18 inches. *Cultural requirements:* in poor, rather heavy but well drained soil, preferably lime, chalk or clay and average moist; needs sun; liable to winterkill in rich soil but very hardy in poor soil.

Uses: Leaf—(medicinal) for croup in poultry, for worms, hysteria and colic, juice used as disinfectant, bruised leaves for rheumatism and headache; (industrial) oil used to give odor to sweet pea perfume; (household) branches hung in room to drive out flies, Italians have used it for generations for the eyes; (culinary) sparingly chopped in sandwiches, vegetable cocktail, mixed with chicken and mushrooms, spread on Swedish bread, in salad and stew.

SAFFLOWER—American Saffron, False Saffron (*Carthamus tinctorius*). *Propagation:* by seed, easy germination. *Nature of plant:* has no connection with Saffron, a bulbous plant; stiff, erect stems grow to 2 feet or more; leaves are oval shaped with sharp, spiny points; flower heads resemble a thistle, having red florets with yellow styles; the fruit, wrongly called seed, are almost 4 sided and are shiny, pearl-white; sowed in clumps, it makes a colorful spot in the garden. *Spacing of mature plants:* 6 inches. *Cultural requirements:* in warm, light soil, needs sun, cultivate until plant is in bud.

Uses: Flower—(medicinal) produces perspiration, cathartic; (industrial) red florets used in dyeing silk from rose to red, mixed with talcum powder to make a dry rouge, substitute and adulterant for Saffron as coloring matter, colors liqueurs, cosmetics, confectionery. Seed—(industrial) drying oil for paint; (medicinal) cathartic; (culinary) oil is much used in India; (household) in India oil is used for burning.

SAFFRON—Saffron Crocus (*Crocus sativus*). *Propagation:* by division of bulbs; by seed. *Nature of plant:* leaves are like narrow grass with a heavy midrib; flowers lilac-colored like partly opened goblets, appear in fall, grow to 3 inches; plant is grown for the orange-scarlet stigmas used in industry, about 60,000 stigmas weighing one pound; much adulterated by petals of arnica, calendula or florets of safflower. *Spacing of mature plants:* 6 inches. *Cultural requirements:* it is best to buy plants since it takes 3 years to get flowers from seed; in August set the small, shiny, brown corms 6 inches deep in rich, light, well drained soil in a sheltered spot; they can be left in the ground for 3 years or taken up every year and separated.

Uses: Stigma—(medicinal) nerve sedative, promotes eruption in skin diseases; (industrial) extract for coloring sauce, cream, biscuit, cake, preserve, liquor, butter, cheese; (culinary) in bouillabaisse.

SAGE—Several varieties are used in cooking, medicine and industry. The most commonly useful are Clary (*Salvia Sclarea*), Garden (*S. officinalis*), (*S. Horminum*), Meadow (*S. pratensis*) and Pineapple Sage (*S. rutilans*). *Propagation:* all by

seed; all self-sow freely except Pineapple Sage which, in cool climates, is touched by frost before it sets seed, and is propagated by cuttings; Garden Sage is increased by cuttings, layering or root division; *S. Horminum,* once self-sown, sows so freely that it will not need to be planted again; this is true also of Clary Sage if seeds are not harvested. *Nature of plant:* Clary grows to 4 feet with broad, pebbly, gray-green leaves about 9 inches long; flowers are either rosy blue or white in terminal spikes; useful for back of border or in gray garden and for flower arrangements if stems are mashed before placing in water. Garden, a sub-shrub, 2 feet high with slender, grayish green leaves, pebbly to the touch; flowers in terminal spikes are light purple and a white flowered variety is beautiful for a white garden; both suitable in a gray garden and as a low hedge about a vegetable or herb garden. *S. Horminum* grows to 1½ feet with oblong floral leaves a vivid purple; makes a striking contrast against a background of Cinque-foil. Meadow grows to 2 feet with beautiful racemes of bright blue flowers; suitable for the blue garden and for flower arrangements. Pineapple, Bailey says that this is thought to be a horticultural form of *Salvia Splendens,* the red of the flowers is a much purer, richer red; the leaves have the delightful fragrance of fresh pineapple; it is tender, grows to 3 feet high; a much branching bush flowering late in the fall. *Spacing of mature plants:* S. *Horminum* 6 inches; Meadow 1 foot; Garden 18 inches; Pineapple and Clary about 2 feet; *Cultural requirements:* all

like limy or sandy, well drained soil in full sun; since Clary is a biennial, it flowers the second year and must be planted each year for continuous bloom; Garden Sage grows woody and should be renewed every 3 or 4 years, and if not kept well apart, plants turn yellow; requires cultivation and enrichment of soil.

Uses: Clary: Flower—(medicinal) eye diseases; (industrial) in blending perfumes. Seed—(medicinal) to pick up foreign bodies in the eye, and a mucilaginous drink made from seeds for heat prostration. Leaf—(medicinal) for spasms; (industrial) gives muscatel flavor to wine, oil for perfume blending and fixing, to adulterate digitalis. Garden Sage: Leaf—(medicinal) gargle, astringent, vulnerary, nasal sores, expectorant, produces perspiration, oil is often an adulterant for rosemary and lavender oils; (industrial) hair washes; (household) leaves rubbed on teeth as a dentifrice, can be smoked like tobacco, sage tea very popular as a drink; (culinary) in poultry stuffing, making sausage, pork dishes, soft cheese. *S. Horminum:* Seed—(medicinal) for eye diseases. Meadow: Leaf—(medicinal) to produce perspiration, expectorant. Pineapple: Leaf—(culinary) like Garden Sage but has a milder, more fragrant odor and taste.

SAMPHIRE—Sea Fennel (*Crithmum maritimum*). Not found on United States coast and not to be confused with a plant along our coasts sometimes called samphire by natives but which is Glasswort. *Propagation:* by seed as soon as ripe; by root division; by cuttings. *Nature of plant:* a low growing, salt loving herb with many branches being finely cut, blue-green (almost gray) foliage; flowers are delicate umbels of yellowish white; grown for culinary use. *Spacing of mature plants:* 18 inches. *Cultural requirements:* in sandy or rocky, well drained soil in sun; once or twice a season dig in a little rockweed or a spoonful of common salt.

Uses: Leaf—(culinary) boiled in salted water, vinegar and spice added, leaves are canned for pickles, later to be used in salad.

SANTOLINA—Lavender Cotton (*Santolina Chamaecyparissus*). *Propagation:* by seed; by cuttings; by layering. *Nature of plant:* a 2-foot high shrubby plant with spreading branches forming a dense mound; foliage resembles a tiny gray coral; the flowers are round, lemon-colored balls about ¾ inch across; both leaves and flowers contain a pungent oil; beautiful for a gray garden and pleasing in any garden. *Spacing of mature plants:* 3 feet. *Cultural requirements:* dry, light, well drained soil, moderately rich, in sunny spot; too much pruning retards growth; in winter plant must be protected so that snow does not settle on it.

Uses: Flower—(medicinal) for ringworm and as a general vermifuge. Leafy stem—(household) moth preventive; (industrial) oil for perfume.

SAVORY—Two forms of savory are used in cooking and in medicine; one is the annual Summer Savory (*Satureja hortensis*) and the other, perennial Winter Savory (*S. montana*). *Propagation:* Summer Sa-

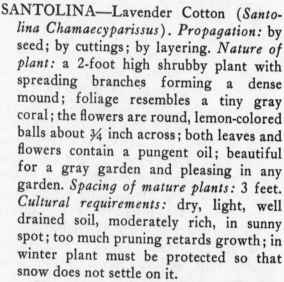

vory by seed, easy germination; Winter Savory by seed, slow germination; by cuttings in spring from side shoots; by layering. *Nature of plants:* Summer Savory is grown for culinary seasoning, grows to 18 inches, rather weak woody stems inclined to fall over when mature and easily beaten down by rain, a mass of plants in flower looks to be covered with pinkish snow; Winter Savory is a sub-shrub about 15 inches high, stems so weak that they fall over and make the plant suitable for edgings to cover artificial boundaries, selfsows and spreads so that a few plants may be the beginning of a long stretch of edging, leaves are stiff and do not blend so well in food as Summer Savory, flowers, like those of Summer Savory, are tiny and give the appearance of a plant covered with a light fall of snow, lilac in color, good for rock gardens. *Spacing of mature plants:* Summer 6 inches; Winter 1 foot. *Cultural requirements:* Summer — dry, moderately rich soil in sunny spot, leaves very narrow, ½ inch long, for a good crop make several sowings 3 weeks apart; Winter—poor, light, well drained soil in full sun, winterkills if soil is too damp or rich, keep well clipped to induce new growth.

Uses: Summer: Leaf — (culinary) in salad, sauce, meat dishes, sausage, poultry stuffing, scrambled eggs, soup, string beans, garnish; (household) crushed on bee stings to relieve pain, for aromatic baths. Winter: Leaf—(culinary) though not as delicate as Summer Savory, can be used in *bouquet garni.*

SENNA, WILD — (*Cassia marilandica*).
Propagation: by seed, difficult to grow
from old seed but self-sows freely and
gives innumerable seedlings; by root division in spring. *Nature of plant:* a tall
bushy, handsome plant, growing to 5 or 6
feet, light green leaves like those of locust,
yellow flowers with brown centers in loose
clusters, beautiful as a high spot in garden.
Spacing of mature plants: 4 feet. *Cultural
requirements:* light, moist, sandy soil in
sunny spot.

 Uses: Leaf — (medicinal) cathartic,
vermifuge.

SESAME—see BENE

SKIRRET—(*Sium Sisarum*). *Propagation:*
by seed, difficult to germinate; by root division in spring. *Nature of plant:* an old-
time potherb, interesting because of root
which grows in clusters like bunches of
little parsnips; root has a woody core that
is removed before cooking; a mature plant
under favorable conditions grows to 3 or 4
feet, has umbels of white flowers. *Spacing
of mature plants:* 1 foot. *Cultural requirements:* in quite rich, alkaline, well drained
soil; roots increase so rapidly that every
spring each plant may be taken up, divided
into smaller parts (about 3 tubers to a
clump) and reset; if wanted for winter,
roots may be dug like turnips and stored in
sand, or left in the ground like parsnips.

 Uses: Root — (culinary) boiled and
eaten with butter and salt; (medicinal)
boiled and eaten for chest diseases.

SMALLAGE—see LOVAGE

SNAKEROOT — Bugbane, Black Cohosh (*Cimicifuga racemosa*). *Propagation:* by seed; by division of roots. *Nature of plants:* a handsome plant for back of the flower border; rises to 6 or 7 feet with beautiful sprays of white flowers some 18 inches long; flower stalk is so slender and rises so far above the mass of large, deeply cut foliage that from a distance the spray seems to be waving by itself in mid-air; has an unpleasant odor, said to drive away bedbugs, hence, the name Bugbane. *Spacing of mature plants:* rich, moist soil; does not mature until the third or fourth year; resents being moved; grows in sun or shade.

Uses: Root—(medicinal) sedative, expectorant, produces perspiration, in rheumatism, fevers, asthma, dropsy, St. Vitus' Dance.

SORREL—Two sorrels should be noted, French variety (*Rumex scutatus*) and Garden Sorrel (*R. Acetosa*). *Propagation:* by seed, self-sows freely; by root division. *Nature of plant:* French, as its botanic name indicates, has shieldlike-shaped leaves larger than the Garden variety, is less acid and more fleshy, used for salads more than Garden, almost prostrate in growing habits; Garden grows to 3 feet with oblong leaves, arrow shaped at base, in early spring almost tasteless, but later in the season becomes very acid. *Spacing of mature plants:* 1 foot. *Cultural requirements:* both grow luxuriantly in heavy, somewhat moist soil in full sun; plants of Garden Sorrel should be dug up, divided and replanted every 4 or 5 years.

Uses: Leaf—(culinary) for soups and and salads; in diet for scurvy.

SOUTHERNWOOD — Old Man, Lad's Love (*Artemisia Abrotanum*). *Propagation:* by cuttings, root very easily. *Nature of plant:* very ornamental shrub with feathery, gray-green foliage and a distinctive, pungent, peculiarly lemon odor, suitable for landscaping purposes, can be trimmed to shape, flowers are inconspicuous, yellow-white in loose panicles. *Spacing of mature plants:* 5 feet. *Cultural requirements:* average soil in full sun.

Uses: Leaf—(household) in aromatic baths and poultices, in clothes to keep out moths; (medicinal) astringent, anthelmintic, deobstruent.

SPEEDWELL — (*Veronica officinalis*). *Propagation:* by seed; by root division. *Nature of plant:* useful for rock gardens and flower borders; stems grow to 16 inches but are almost prostrate, turning up only toward the tip; will grow under trees and in shady spots where grass will not grow; spreads rapidly and thus makes a good ground cover. *Spacing of mature plants:* 1 foot. *Cultural requirements:* grows in almost any soil or location.

Uses: Whole Herb—(medicinal) infusion for rheumatism, tuberculosis, gout, to induce perspiration, for hemorrhages and skin diseases; (industrial) in manufacture of vermouth.

SUCCORY—see CHICORY

SWEET CICELY—see CICELY

SWEET MARY—see COSTMARY

TANSY—Two varieties are discussed here: one the Common (*Tanacetum vulgare*) or coarse, tall plant found in field and along roadsides; the other the Fern-leaved (*T. vulgare* var. *crispum*) with rich green, more delicate foliage, fewer and larger "buttons." *Propagation:* by seed, self-sows freely; by root division. *Nature of plant:* Common Tansy useful hedge for a garden if flower heads are cut off before going to seed, stalks require staking against wind and rain, unless in a protected spot; Fern-leaved Tansy not so coarse as Common and most beautiful for flower borders, grows to about 3 feet, very decorative foliage with orange "buttons" for vivid contrast. *Spacing of mature plants:* Common about 4 feet; Fern-leaved 2½ feet. *Cultural requirements:* will adapt themselves to any soil or location not too wet; both spread rapidly into large clumps.

Uses: both varieties have similar virtues. Leafy Tip—(medicinal) sedative, to produce perspiration, for healing wounds; (industrial) in cosmetics, toilet water, liniment, ointment and in Chartreuse; (household) keeps ants away, rubbed on meat to preserve it. Seed—(medicinal) anthelmintic. Root—(household) gives a green dye.

TARRAGON, FRENCH — (*Artemisia Dracunculus*). *Propagation:* by cuttings; by root division; is not known to set seed. *Nature of plant:* grown for its leaves, tasting and smelling somewhat like anise; a rather graceful plant when full grown. *Spacing of mature plants:* 18 inches. *Cul-*

tural requirements: moderately rich, warm, well drained soil in partial shade; should be transplanted every 3 years to avoid disease; divide roots by hand; commercial growers pot up small pieces of root and set out resulting plants the following spring; will winterkill in heavy moist soil; in cool climates, protect with a mulch of leaves after heaping up soil around plants; can be bought only as plants.

Uses: Leaf—(culinary) over steaks and chops, in salads, fish sauce, preserves, pickles, mustard, mayonnaise, Sauce Bearnaise and in tarragon vinegar; (medicinal) in scurvy. Leafy Top—(industrial) flavors confectionery, perfumes, toilet waters.

THOROUGHWORT—see BONESET

THRIFT — (*Armeria maritima*). *Propagation:* by seed; by division of clumps. *Nature of plant:* an attractive edging plant; resembles a mound of dark green grass with large pink pins stuck in it; pins are about 9 inches long with pink flower heads about ¾ inch across. *Spacing of mature plants:* 10 inches. *Cultural requirements:* light, well drained, dry soil; every second year clumps may be taken up, divided and re-set.

Uses: Flower—(medicinal) for urinary troubles.

THYME—There are innumerable varieties of Thyme but only a few are used for culinary, medicinal or industrial purposes. The most commonly used are *Thymus azoricus*, Caraway (*T. Herba barona*), Garden (*T. vulgare*), Lemon (*T. citri-*

odorus), Wild (*T. Serpyllum*) and *T. Zygis. Propagation:* by seed, all but the Garden variety are difficult to germinate; by layering; by division of roots. *Nature of plant: T. azoricus*—beautiful for a rock garden and in between stepping stones; vivid, dark green foliage of oblong linear leaves in mounds which increase slowly from year to year but are liable to winterkill unless kept dry; has a citrus fruity odor; lilac-colored flowers in June. Caraway—prostrate growth; fine ground cover for sunny places as it spreads rapidly and in June is covered with rosy colored flowers; odor definitely caraway. Garden —a little shrub that grows a foot high, almost evergreen; pale lavender flowers all through June; grayish green, strongly aromatic foliage. Lemon — an excellent ground cover like a carpet with long, thick pile; golden green foliage with pinkish flowers in July; quite a rapid spreader; odor definitely lemon. Wild—also called Mother of Thyme, Mountain and Creeping Thyme; growth varies from low mats to 9-inch high mounds; the mauve-pink flowers appear in June. *T. Zygis*—a trim little shrub about 4 inches high with gray-green foliage and pale purple flowers; resembles Garden Thyme but has white hairs at base of leaves; liable to winterkill. *Spacing of mature plants:* low, spreading mat-making varieties about 10 inches apart, the more erect, shrubby thymes about 6 inches apart. *Cultural requirements:* thymes need light, sandy, limy and well drained soil in raised beds; mat varieties like to climb over rocks and prefer slopes; all thymes need full sun. Garden Thyme

should be kept well clipped to prevent its getting too woody and will have to be renewed every 3 or 4 years; several varieties of this thyme include common English thyme, the dark green, broad-leaved English thyme, and the gray-green narrow-leaved French thyme; thymes should be mulched for winter and covered so that snow will not settle on them, particularly *T. azoricus* and *T. Zygis*.

Uses: T. azoricus and *T. Zygis*—Leaf (culinary) in creams and custards. Caraway—Leaf (culinary) rubbed over meat to preserve and flavor it. Garden—Leaf (culinary) in vinegar with other herbs, in sauces for meat and fish, in cocktails, croquettes, chipped beef, fricassees, with pork, veal, in soups and chowders with onion, in cheese, carrots, peas, scalloped onions, stuffing; (household) in aromatic baths, sachets, tea; (industrial) deodorants, anesthetics, gargles, perfumes, embalming fluid, destroys mold on herbarium parasites, preserves anatomical specimens, anti-mold for paper, in herbal tobacco, Benedictine, liquid dentifrices, wounds, toothaches, masks odor of iodoform and naphthalene, hair dressings, soap; (medicinal) sedative, in bronchitis, whooping cough, indigestion, flatulence, coughs and in numerous formulas. Lemon Thyme—Leaf (culinary) in teas, baths and jellies. Wild Thyme, used about the same as Garden Thyme, oil of Serpolet made from Wild is milder than Oil of Thyme made from Garden.

VALERIAN—Garden Heliotrope (*Valeriana officinalis*). *Propagation:* by seed; by

root division spring or fall. *Nature of plant:* handsome for a sunny border; flower stalks rise from a mass of foliage and grow to 4 feet high; pinkish flowers are in loose clusters forming a rather flat head with an odor like that of heliotrope, overpowering on a hot June day; useful for flower arrangements. *Spacing of mature plants:* about 2 feet. *Cultural requirements:* in rather heavy, average moist, rich soil in full sun or partial shade; plant spreads by creeping roots which may be divided every other year; enrich soil with manure before setting out plants.

Uses: Rhizome—(medicinal) sedative, anodyne for spasms, epilepsy, fevers; (industrial) perfume. Leaf—(industrial) flavors tobacco.

VERBENA, LEMON — (*Lippia citriodora*). *Propagation:* by seed; by cuttings. *Nature of plant:* an old-time garden favorite for its fragrant and refreshing lemony-scented foliage; graceful stems are useful for flower arrangements; leaves often used in finger bowls; light lavender flowers in slender terminal spikes are inconspicuous but very attractive. *Spacing of mature plants:* in most climates about 2 feet. *Cultural requirements:* light well drained soil in full sun; plant is tender and in cool climates may be taken indoors, cut back and stored with infrequent watering; in February, cut off weaker stalks and repot in new soil; keep plants from 55 to 60 degrees; new green growth will come along stems; spray for red spider; in cutting back plants for the winter, cuttings may be rooted in sand.

Uses: Leaf — (medicinal) febrifuge, sedative, used in treatment of indigestion, flatulence; (industrial) in perfume.

WALDMEISTER—see WOODRUFF

WILD MADDER—see BEDSTRAW

WOAD—(*Isatis tinctoris*). *Propagation:* by seed, self-sows freely. *Nature of plant:* a biennial; during the first year is a rosette of long, rather narrow, blue-green leaves; the second year stalks rise to 3½ or 4 feet with panicled racemes of bright, yellow flowers; blue-green stems with flowers and later with long blue-black seeds are unusual for flower arrangements; sturdy tall plants make a gorgeous effect when in flower, for back of border. *Spacing of mature plants:* 12 inches. *Cultural requirements:* grows best in rich, well drained soil; needs some sun; once planted, will give a bright clump each year unless seeds are gathered or flowers cut before seeds are formed.

Uses: Leaf and Stem—(medicinal) astringent, to dry wounds and ulcers; (industrial) formerly much used for a blue dye but now a mordant for black dye and to fix true indigo, which it improves. Flowers—(industrial) by artists and illuminators in paint.

WOODRUFF, SWEET — Waldmeister (*Asperula odorata*). *Propagation:* by seed, very slow to germinate, usually a year, but might be lessened by planting as soon as ripe; by root division. *Nature of plant:* most beautiful ground cover for shady spots or under trees; deep green, starry whorls of 8 long, oval leaves on

slender square stems with minute hairs under the central rib; when sun strikes plants, leaves become lighter; tiny white flowers are also stars with four petals; graceful in flower arrangements. *Spacing of mature plants:* 12 inches. *Cultural requirements:* in loose, moist, well drained soil in partial shade or shade; plants spread into high mats from underground roots.

Uses: Leaf—(medicinal) pectoral tea, vulnerary; (industrial) in fancy snuffs, wines, liqueurs, sachets, spiced wines; maitrink.

WORMWOOD — Several varieties of Wormwood are used for medicinal, industrial and culinary purposes; all have inconspicuous yellow flower heads in loose panicles. *Propagation:* by seed, slow to germinate; by cuttings; by root division. *Nature of plant:* Common Wormwood (*Artemisia Absinthium*) a bushy plant 3½ to 4 feet tall with much cut, grayish, silky leaves; useful for background of border or high spot in garden. Beach Wormwood, Dusty Miller, Old Woman (*A. Stelleriana*) stems are 2 feet long but are creeping, leaves are white, broad, deeply cut and feltlike to the touch; spreads rapidly and is a good ground cover for sandy soil in a sunny spot; terminal flower clusters droop so that they look like tassels. Fringed Wormwood, Colorado Mountain Sage, Mountain Fringe (*A. frigida*), lower part of stems is woody but upper part is graceful with its soft, silvery, slender leaves; attractive in flower borders and in flower arrangements with its 18-inch high delicate, leafy stems. Roman Wormwood (*A. pontica*) much branching, little shrub, 2 feet high with finely cut, lacy, greenish gray foliage. Useful for edging of borders, particularly for a gray garden; must be trimmed and kept from spreading. Silky Wormwood (*A. mutellina*) grows to 6 inches; makes a silvery mount with its finely cut leaves; very decorative for an edging. Sweet Wormwood (*A. annua*), a yellow-green, very lacy, broad leaf, grows sometimes to 5 feet high, much branched and very fragrant; graceful for flower arrangements. *Spacing of mature plants:* Common 2 feet; Beach 8 inches; the others from 12 to 15 inches. *Cultural requirements:* all varieties thrive in rather poor, light, but well drained soil in sun or shade, though sun is preferred; special notice must be given to Common Wormwood. Soil for it must contain clay and be a little heavier than for the others and should be dug deeply because the root reaches very far below the surface. Common also likes a little more shade. Since plants grow taller they are inclined to fall and the stems twist, therefore plants should be staked in June; in the early spring older parts of plant are cut out; it is likely to winterkill unless cut back in fall and mulched with manure and leaves.

Uses: Common—Leafy Top (medicinal) in fevers and rheumatism, anthelmintic, antiseptic, stomachic; (industrial) in absinthe and liniments; (culinary) lay leafy tops along back of a roasting goose to cut grease. Beach—Whole Herb used to fatten cattle; (medicinal) anthelmintic, in fevers. Fringed—Whole Herb (medicinal) fevers, rheumatism, scarlet fever, diphtheria, induces perspiration, mild cathartic. Roman—Leafy Top (industrial) in vermouth, often used instead of Common; (medicinal) applications for swellings, produces perspiration, vulnerary, bitter stomachic. Silky — Peel of Bark (medicinal) bitter stomachic; (industrial) in absinthe. Sweet—Whole Herb (industrial) oil in perfume (gives odor like basil).

YARROW—Two varieties of Yarrow have been found useful medicinally: Common Yarrow or Milfoil (*Achillea Millefolium*) and Sneezewort (*A. Ptarmica*). *Propagation:* both varieties can be grown quite easily, Common variety spreading rapidly from creeping rootstock and both varieties increased by root division. *Nature of plant:* Common Yarrow comes up 2½ feet high from horizontal rootstock; stems are grayish green, branching toward the top; on the stem alternately are feathery, deeply cut foliage, so much cut as to give the name *millefolium* or thousand leafed; white flowers are in flat topped clusters; the whole plant is pungently aromatic; a most beautiful rosy red flowered variety, with a white center to the flower, is like an old-fashioned calico print; red yarrow grows to but 18 inches; useful in flower arrangements. Sneezewort grows to be about 2 feet. The variety called Pearl is most commonly known, has white, flat flower heads and is suitable for flower arrangements; keep old flower heads cut off for a second blooming in the season. *Spacing of mature plants:* 12 inches. *Cultural*

requirements: in moderately rich, rather moist soil in full sun.

Uses: Sneezewort—Leaf (medicinal) epilepsy, catarrh, uterine diseases. Common Yarrow—Whole Herb (medicinal) mild laxative. Flowers—(medicinal) uterine diseases, catarrh, mild sudorific tonic and astringent.

CHAPTER 18

Herb Tables

These 26 tables and lists are for convenient and quick reference. The final table lists all herbs mentioned in the book (except those in Table X), and gives the botanical name and family and whether the herb is a perennial, biennial or annual.

For the most part these tables supplement chapters of the book which deal with the same subject matter, but some of them are purely for reader interest. Table N lists herbs mentioned in this book which are mentioned in the Bible; this however is not a complete list of Biblical herbs as many of them fall outside the scope of this volume. Table X lists plants that are not mentioned elsewhere in the book. Many lavenders, thymes, mints, artemisias, pelargoniums, santolinas and other plants are not of any importance now as useful herbs, but are so attractive in the herb garden where other varieties of the same plants have an important place. Any of the thymes, for instance, would serve as useful a purpose as the ones chosen for culinary and commercial use but certain varieties, for one reason or another, are standard. The decorative herb garden need have no such limitations. The home gardener, too, will be interested in many varieties of mint that are not of commercial importance merely because there are other varieties which through the ages have been used; yet pineapple mint is probably the most decorative variety and it can be used. It seems to me preferable to the *M. rotundifolia* which is so widely used by amateur gardeners.

HERB LISTS AND TABLES

TABLE
A Herbs That Will Grow in Shade or Partial Shade
B Herbs That Will Grow in Dry Places
C Herbs That Will Grow in Moist Places
D Herbs for Low Edgings

E   Herbs for Ground Cover
F   Herbs for Crevices
G   Herbs for Hedges and High Edgings
H   Tall Herbs for Garden High Spots
I   Herbs Useful in Flower Arrangements
J   Herbs with Colorful Flowers
K   Herbs of Conspicuous Foliage
L   Continuous Bloom in Herb Garden
M   Useful and Decorative Herbs for House Plants
N   Biblical Herbs
O   Herbs That Are Almost Evergreen
P   Fragrant Herbs
Q   Herbs for a Bee Garden
R   Herbs for Green Salads
S   Potherbs
T   Herbs for Teas
U   Culinary Herbs for Flavoring
V   Herbs Used in Dyeing and Coloring
W   Herbs Used in Commerce and Industry
X   Plants Useful in Herb Garden
Y   Plant Families
Z   Table of Herbs Mentioned in Text

TABLE A

Herbs That Will Grow in Shade or Partial Shade

Aconite
Angelica
Balm, Lemon
Baneberry
Bugle-weed, Carpet
Bugloss, Italian
Chervil
Cicely, Sweet
Comfrey
Coneflower

Costmary
Good King Henry
Ground Ivy
Liatris
Lily-of-the-Valley
Lungwort
Mints (except Cat-
  nip)
Myrtle, Running
Parsley

Pennyroyal, English
St. John's Wort
Snakeroot
Tarragon, French
Turtle-Head
Valerian
Violet, Common
Violet, Sweet
Wintergreen
Woodruff, Sweet

TABLE B

Herbs That Will Grow in Dry Places

Agrimony
Alkanet, Common
Alum-root
Arnica
Bedstraw, White
Bedstraw, Yellow
Blessed Thistle
Borage
Broom, Dyer's
Broom, Scotch
Bugloss, Viper's
Burnet
Butterfly Weed
Calamint
Castor Oil Plant
Chamomile, German
Chamomile, Roman
Chicory
Chives
Coltsfoot
Cornflower

Daisy, English
Dittany of Crete
Fennel, Wild or
    Sweet
Feverfew
Fleabane
Geranium, Wild
Germander
Golden Rod
Houseleek
Lavender (all
    kinds)
Lungwort
Maudlin, Sweet
Mullein, Great
Mullein, Moth
Nettle, Dead
Pasque Flower
Pennyroyal, American
Perilla
Primrose

Primrose, Evening
Rosemary
St. John's Wort
Sage (all kinds)
Santolina, Gray
Savory, Winter
Senecio
Sneezewort
Soapwort
Southernwood
Speedwell
Spiderwort
Star-grass
Sunflower
Teasel
Thrift
Thyme (all kinds)
Violet, Birdsfoot
Wormwood (all
    kinds)
Yarrow, Common

TABLE C

Herbs That Will Grow in Moist Places

Angelica
Bergamot
Boneset
Bugloss, Italian
Cardinal Flower
Celandine

Christmas Rose
Cicely, Sweet
Coneflower
Dropwort
Elecampane
Flag, Blue

Flag, Sweet
Flag, Yellow
Flax
Glasswort
Joe-Pye Weed
Lady's Mantle

Liatris
Loosestrife
Lovage
Marshmallow
Mints (except Cat-
nip)
Myrtle, Running

Parsley
Pennyroyal, English
Poppy, Opium
Primrose
Prunella
Rampion
St. John's Wort

Senna, Wild
Snakeroot
Speedwell
Turtle-Head
Valerian
Violet, Common
Violet, Sweet

TABLE D

Herbs for Low Edgings

Basil, Dwarf green
Basil, Dwarf purple
Bugle-weed, Carpet
Calamint
Chives

Germander
Nettle, Dead
Parsley
Pennyroyal
Primrose

Savory, Winter
Thrift
Thyme, Garden
Thyme, Zygis
Woodruff, Sweet
Wormwood, Beach

TABLE E

Herbs for Ground Cover

Calamint—sun or partial shade
Carpet Bugle-weed—sun or par-
tial shade
Chamomile, Roman (English)
—sun
Coltsfoot—in waste places—sun
Ivy, Ground—in waste places—
sun or partial shade
Johnny Jump-up—partial shade
Lily-of-the-Valley—shade

Myrtle, Running—shade
Nettle, Dead—sun
Speedwell—shade
Thyme, Caraway—sun
Thyme, Lemon—sun
Thyme, Wild—sun
Violet, Common—partial shade
Wintergreen—shade
Woodruff, Sweet—partial shade
Wormwood, Beach—Sun

TABLE F

Herbs for Crevices

Chamomile, Roman (English)	Thrift
Thymes	Woodruff, Sweet

TABLE G

Herbs for Hedges and High Edgings

Basil, Sweet	Rosemary
Basil, Sweet (Purple variety)	Rue
Feverfew	Sage, Garden
Germander	Santolina
Hyssop	Southernwood
Lavender, True	Wormwood, Roman

NOTE: Rosemary is tender. Hyssop, Rosemary, Rue and Southernwood may all be clipped like a box hedge. Hyssop and Rue will not flower if tops are cut off, but either makes a beautiful flowering hedge, if not trimmed except at sides. All plants mentioned in the table are hardy perennials except the basils.

TABLE H

Tall Herbs for Garden High Spots

Aconite	Liatris	Pokeweed
Angelica	Loosestrife	Sage, Clary
Bay, Sweet	Lovage	Senna, Wild
Castor Oil Plant	Marshmallow	Snakeroot
Elecampane	Mugwort, Common	Sunflower
Fennel, Sweet	Mugwort, White	Tansy
Fennel, Wild	Mullein, Great	Teasel
Hollyhock	Myrtle, Erect	Wormwood

NOTE: Angelica, Elecampane, Lovage, Common Mugwort under favorable conditions grow to 7 or 8 feet tall. Hollyhock and

Sunflower grow to 10 or 15 feet high. Wild Senna will make a 6 foot high spreading bush each year. Great Mullein will have a single stalk from 8 to 10 feet high. The remainder will be from 3 to 4 feet high, though erect myrtle will not reach that height for several years.

TABLE I

Herbs Useful in Flower Arrangements

Aconite
Agrimony
Alum-Root
Arnica
Bedstraw, White
Bedstraw, Yellow
Bergamot
Boneset
Bugloss, Italian
Butterfly Weed
Calendula
Cardinal Flower
Coneflower
Cornflower
Dill
Dropwort
Fennel
Fennel Flower
Feverfew
Flag, Blue
Flag, Yellow

Flag, White
Foxglove
Fraxinella
Geranium, Wild
Heliotrope
Hyssop
Jerusalem Oak
Joe-Pye Weed
Larkspur
Lavenders
Liatris
Lily-of-the-Valley
Loosestrife
Marjoram, Pot
Mugwort, White
Nasturtium
Orach, Red
Pasque Flower
Pelargonium, Rose
Perilla
Pimpernel, Scarlet

Primrose, Evening
Pyrethrum
Queen of the
    Meadow
Rocket, Dames
Sage, Clary
Sage, Meadow
Salvia Horminum
Sea Holly
Sea Lavender
Senecio
Speedwell
Tansy, Fern-leaved
Teasel
Thrift
Turtle-Head
Woad (flowers and
    seeds)
Woodruff, Sweet
Wormwood, Sweet
Yarrow, Common

TABLE J

Herbs with Colorful Flowers

Red: Bergamot, Cardinal Flower, Hollyhock, Scarlet Pimpernel
Purplish rose: Germander, Joe-Pye Weed, Pyrethrum, Apothecaries' Rose, Yarrow

Light Purplish rose: Daphne, Wild Geranium, Valerian

Pink: Alum-Root, Dames Rocket, Dittany of Crete, Hollyhock, Hyssop, *Origanum Pulchellum,* Clove Pink, Damask Rose, Dog Rose, Kazanlik Rose

Orange: Butterfly Weed, Calendula, Coltsfoot, Elecampane, Golden Rod, Nasturtium, St. John's Wort, Common Tansy, Fern-leaved Tansy

Yellow: Nasturtium, Primrose, Rue; Brownish Yellow: Yellow Flag, Wild Senna; Bright Yellow: Arnica, Yellow Bedstraw, Wild Indigo, Evening Primrose

Light Blue: Rosemary, Speedwell; Grayish Blue: Sea Holly; Clear Vivid Blue: Chicory, Cornflower, Fennel Flower, Hound's Tongue, Meadow Sage; Opens Rose, Turns to Blue: Borage, Italian Bugloss, Lungwort; Deep Blue: Aconite, Blue Flag, Hyssop, False Indigo, Spiderwort; Dark Purplish Blue: Larkspur, Stoechas Lavender, Violets; Light Purplish Blue: Spike Lavender, True Lavender

Rosy Lavender: Chives; Heliotrope: Heliotrope; Purple: Coneflower, Pasque Flower, *Salvia Horminum;* Magenta: Foxglove

White: White Bedstraw, Boneset, Dames Rocket, Feverfew, Fraxinella, Lily-of-the-Valley, White Mugwort, Pyrethrum; Creamy White: Dropwort; Bluish White: White Flag, Opium Poppy.

TABLE K

Herbs of Conspicuous Foliage

Alum-Root
Angelica
Balm, Lemon
Baneberry
Basil, Dwarf (Green and Purple)
Basil, Sweet (Green and Purple)
Bedstraw, White
Bedstraw, Yellow
Bergamot
Blessed Thistle
Borage
Bugle-weed, Carpet
Bugloss, Italian
Burnet
Cardoon
Castor Oil Plant
Celandine
Chamomile (German and Roman)
Chervil
Cicely, Sweet
Coltsfoot
Comfrey
Costmary
Dill
Dittany of Crete
Dropwort
Elder, English

Elecampane
Fennel, Wild and
Sweet
Feverfew
Fraxinella
Fumitory
Germander
Glasswort
Horehound
Indigo, False and
Wild
Jerusalem Oak
Lady's Mantle
Lavenders
Lovage
Lungwort
Madder
Marshmallow
Mints:

Apple mint
American apple
mint
Orange mint
Black peppermint
Mugwort, Western
Mullein, Great
Orach, Green and
Purple
*Origanum
pulchellum*
Pasque Flower
Perilla
Pokeweed
Primrose
Queen-of-the-
Meadow
Rose Geranium
Rosemary

Rue
Sage, Clary
Sage, Pineapple
Samphire
Santolina, Gray
Sea Holly
Senecio
Senna, Wild
Snakeroot
Southernwood
Tansy, Common
Tansy, Fern-leafed
Thyme, Azores
Thyme, Lemon
Woodruff, Sweet
Wormwood: Sweet,
Beach, Fringed,
Roman, Silky

Table L

Continuous Bloom in Herb Garden

Early to Late Spring: Celandine, Coltsfoot, Lily-of-the-Valley, Pasque Flower, Primrose, Violets.

Late Spring to Early Summer: Alum-Root, Carpet Bugle-weed, Italian Bugloss, Sweet Cicely, Dames Rocket, Daphne, Drop-wort, Flags, Fraxinella, Lady's Mantle, Lungwort, Running Myrtle, Pyrethrum, Queen-of-the-Meadow, Rosemary, Sweet Woodruff.

Early Summer to Mid-Summer: Arnica, Bedstraws, Borage, Chamomiles, Cornflower, Dittany of Crete, Feverfew, Foxglove, Fumitory, Wild Geranium, Germander, Heliotrope, Hollyhock, Hound's Tongue, Indigo (False and Wild), Larkspur, Lavenders, Marjorams, Nasturtium, Orach, Clove Pink, Opium Poppy, Evening Primrose, Roses, Rue, Clary Sage, *Salvia Horminum*, Gray Santolina, Sea Holly, Sneezewort, Speedwell, Valerian, Yarrow.

Mid-Summer to Autumn: Aconite, Bergamot, Boneset, Butterfly
Weed, Calendula, Chicory, Coneflower, Autumn Crocus, Elecampane, Fennel Flower, Golden Rod, Hyssop, Joe-Pye Weed,
Liatris, Loosestrife, Scarlet Pimpernel, Pokeweed, Saffron, Pineapple Sage, St. John's Wort, Wild Senna, Common Tansy, Fern-
leafed Tansy.

NOTE: Some plants can be kept blooming all season by cutting
off old flowers; others will bloom a second time, if cut back after
first bloom.

TABLE M

Useful and Decorative Herbs for House Plants

Balm, Lemon	Fennel (Sweet and	Parsley
Basil, Dwarf	Wild)	Pennyroyals
(Green and Pur-	Germander	Rose Geranium
ple)	Good King Henry	Rosemary
Basil, Sweet	Heliotrope	Rue
(Green and Pur-	Hyssop	Sage, Garden
ple)	Lavenders	Savories
Borage	Marjoram, Sweet	Tarragon
Burnet	Mints:	Thymes:
Chervil	American apple	Azores
Chives	mint	Garden
Dill	Orange mint	*Zygis*
Dittany of Crete	Peppermint	Verbena, Lemon

TABLE N

Biblical Herbs

Anise	Hyssop	Rue
Coriander	Mandrake	Saffron
Cumin	Mint	Wormwood
Garlic	Pasque Flower	

TABLE O

Herbs That Are Almost Evergreen

Bugle-weed, Carpet
Burnet
Calamint
Chamomiles (Self-
  sown fall plants)
Ground Ivy

Horehound
Hyssop
Nettle, Dead
Rue
Sage
Santolina, Gray

Savory, Winter
Southernwood
Thyme, Caraway
Thyme, Garden
Thyme, Wild

TABLE P

Fragrant Herbs

Ground Covers or Low Mats: Calamint, Johnny Jump-up, English
  Pennyroyal, Thymes, Violets, Sweet Woodruff.
Medium Low: Dwarf Basil (green and purple), Chamomile (Ger-
  man and Roman), Stoechas Lavender, Sweet Marjoram, Nas-
  turtium, American Pennyroyal, Winter Savory.
Medium High: Sweet Basil (green and purple), Burnet, Feverfew,
  Heliotrope, Hyssop, Lavender (Spike and True), Marjoram
  (Pot, *O. Pulchellum,* Wild), Sweet Maudlin, Mints, Clove
  Pinks, Dames Rocket, Rose Geranium, Rue, Sage, Tarragon,
  Yarrow.
Medium Tall: Lemon Balm, Bergamot, Sweet Cicely, Costmary,
  Daphne, Dill, Dropwort, Sweet Flag, Jerusalem Oak, Erect
  Myrtle, Queen of the Meadow, Apothecaries' Rose, Cabbage
  Rose, Kazanlik Rose, Southernwood.
Tall: Angelica, Sweet Bay, Fennel (Wild & Sweet), Lovage,
  White Mugwort, Dog Rose, Pineapple Sage, Common Tansy,
  Fern-leafed Tansy, Valerian, Sweet Wormwood.

TABLE Q

Herbs for a Bee Garden

Balm, Lemon
Basils
Bergamot, Red
Borage
Bugloss, Italian
Butterfly Weed
Catnip
Chamomile
Chicory
Cicely, Sweet

Daphne
Dropwort
Fennel
Foxglove
Germander
Ground Ivy
Hyssop
Lavenders
Marjorams
Melilot

Nettle, Dead
Queen-of-the-
    Meadow
Rosemary
Sage
Savory, Winter
Teasel
Thymes

TABLE R

Herbs for Green Salads

Anise—leaves
Balm, Lemon—leaves
Basil—leaves
Borage—young leaves
Burnet—leaves
Calendula—flower petals
Caraway—leaves
Cardoon—blanched inner leaf
    stalk and top of stalk
Chervil—leaves
Chicory (Witloof)—leaves
Chives—leaves
Dill—leaves, flowering umbels
Fennel—leaves, flowering um-
    bels, stalks of carosella

Houseleek—leaves
Lovage—leaves
Marjoram, Sweet—leaves
Mustard, White—seedlings,
    young leaves
Nasturtium—leaves, petals,
    pickled seeds
Rampion—leaves, boiled roots
Rose—petals
Samphire—pickled shoots
Savory, Summer—leaves
Sorrel—leaves
Tarragon—leaves
Thymes—leaves
Violet, Sweet—flower petals

TABLE S

Potherbs

Borage—leaves
Cardoon—blanched inner leaf stalks
Chervil—leaves
Chicory—leaves
Cicely, Sweet—leaves and roots
Glasswort—shoots are pickled
Good King Henry—leaves
Hops—young shoots
Lovage—leaves
Mustard, White—seedlings
Orach—leaves
Pokeweed—young shoots
Rampion—roots and leaves
Samphire—shoots are pickled
Skirret—roots
Sorrel—leaves

NOTE: These herbs are boiled as vegetables.

TABLE T

Herbs for Teas

Agrimony
Angelica
Anise (seeds)
Balm, Lemon
Bergamot
Boneset
Calamint
Caraway (seeds)
Catnip
Chamomile
Costmary
Dill (seeds)
Fennel (seeds)
Feverfew
Ground Ivy
Horehound
Lovage
Marjoram, Sweet
Mints:
   American golden apple mint
   Orange mint
   Peppermint
   Spearmint
Pennyroyals
Rosemary (green sprigs)
Saffron (stigmas)
Sage, Garden
Speedwell
Thyme, Garden
Thyme, Lemon
Verbena, Lemon
Wintergreen
Yarrow

NOTE: Many of the herb teas are used medicinally. Some of them, however, are delightful and refreshing and have long been used as beverages.

TABLE U

Culinary Herbs for Flavoring

FOLIAGE PLANTS

Angelica
Basils (Italian & Sweet)
Bay, Sweet
Borage
Burnet
Chervil
Chives
Lovage
Marjoram, Sweet
Mints:
    American golden apple mint

Orange mint
Spearmint
Parsley
Rosemary
Sage, Garden
Sage, Pineapple
Savory, Summer
Savory, Winter
Tarragon, French
Thyme (all varieties)

SAVORY SEEDS

Anise
Bene (Sesame)
Caraway
Coriander
Cumin

Dill
Fennel
Mustard, White
Nasturtium
Poppy, Opium

TABLE V

Herbs Used in Dyeing and Coloring

Agrimony
Alkanet
Bedstraw, Yellow
Broom, Dyer's
Broom, Scotch
Calendula
Cardoon

Chicory
Cornflower
Daphne
Elecampane
Elder
Flag, Yellow
Fumitory

Golden Rod
Hops
Hollyhock
Hyssop
Indigo, Wild
Madder
Marjoram, Wild

Parsley
Pasque Flower
Pokeweed
Safflower
Saffron

St. John's Wort
Sunflower
Tansy
Teasel
Toadflax

Violet
Woad
Yarrow

TABLE W

Herbs Used in Commerce and Industry

Angelica
Anise
Balm, Lemon
Bedstraw, Yellow
Bene (Sesame)
Bergamot
Blessed Thistle
Bugloss, Dyer's
Calendula
Caraway
Cardoon
Chamomile
Chicory
Cicely, Sweet
Coriander
Cornflower
Dill
Elecampane
Fennel, Wild &
    Sweet
Fenugreek
Flax
Flag, Sweet

Flag, White
Hollyhock
Hyssop
Indigo, Wild
Lavenders
Lovage
Madder
Marjoram, Sweet
Meadowsweet
    (Dropwort)
Mints:
    Orange mint
    Peppermint
    Spearmint
Mustard, Black
Mustard, White
Parsley
Perilla
Poppy, Opium
Pyrethrum
Rose, Cabbage
Rose, Kazanlik
Rose Geranium

Rosemary
Rue
Safflower
Saffron
Sage, Clary
Sage, Garden
Santolina, Gray
Tansy, Common
Tansy, Fern-leafed
Tarragon, French
Thyme, Garden
Valerian
Verbena, Lemon
Woad
Woodruff, Sweet
Wormwood, Common
Wormwood,
    Roman
Wormwood, Silky
Wormwood, Sweet

NOTE: The specific uses of these important industrial herbs will be found in the tabular paragraphs (Chapter 17).

TABLE X

Plants Useful in Herb Garden

COMMON NAME	BOTANICAL NAME	FAMILY	REMARKS
Bergamot, Wild	*Monarda fistulosa*	Labiatae	Lavender flowers
Betony, Woolly	*Stachys lanata*	Labiatae	Soft, woolly leaves, "Lamb's ears"
Camphor Plant			See note below
Fennel, Bronze	*Foeniculum vulgare* (variety of)	Umbelliferae	Like Wild Fennel with bronze foliage
	Lavandula delphinensis	Labiatae	Blue dwarf variety, short spikes
	L. dentata	"	Fine scalloped leaves, dark blue
	L. pedunculata	"	Sprawling, large dark purple flowers
	L. pinnata	"	Old-fashioned jagged lavender, annual
Mint, Corsican	*Mentha Requieni*	"	Flat mat, vivid green
Mint, Pineapple	*M. rotundifolia*, var. *variegata*	"	Leaves blotched with creamy white
Pelargoniums, Sweet leaved	Many names	Geraniaceae	Some 75 available in U. S.
	Santolina pinnata	Compositae	Soft green needlelike foliage
	Santolina tomentosum	"	Soft gray foliage
Santolina, Green	*Santolina viridis*	"	Vivid green coral-like foliage
Silver King	*Artemisia albula*	"	Finely divided gray leaves, slender branching stems
Tansy, Huron	*Tanacetum huronense*	"	Like skeleton-leaf fern, few large buttons
Thymes, Many varieties		Labiatae	Low plants, flowers of many shades and colors
Yarrow, Fernleaf	*Achillea filipendulina*	Compositae	Brilliant yellow flat flower heads

NOTE: All are perennials except Bronze Fennel and Lavender pinnata which is treated as an annual. None of the plants are of great importance in industry, medicine or cooking. Camphor plant is not named by any modern authority although frequently confused with a variety of costmary.

TABLE Y

Plant Families

The numbers are arbitrary but correspond to those in Table Z.

1. ARACEAE—Sweet Flag
2. COMMELINACEAE—Spiderwort
3. LILIACEAE—Autumn Crocus, Chives, Garlic, Lily-of-the-Valley, Star Grass
4. IRIDACEAE—Blue Flag, White Flag, Yellow Flag, Saffron
5. MORACEAE—Hops
6. POLYGONACEAE—French Sorrel, Garden Sorrel
7. CHENOPODIACEAE—Glasswort, Good King Henry, Jerusalem Oak, Green Orach, Red Orach
8. PHYTOLACCACEAE—Pokeweed
9. CARYOPHYLLACEAE—Clove Pink, Soapwort
10. RANUNCULACEAE—Aconite, Baneberry, Christmas Rose, Fennel Flower, Larkspur, Pasque Flower, Snakeroot
11. LAURACEAE—Sweet Bay
12. PAPAVERACEAE—Celandine, Opium Poppy
13. FUMARIACEAE—Fumitory
14. CRUCIFERAE—Black Mustard, White Mustard, Dames Rocket, Woad
15. CRASSULACEAE—Houseleek
16. SAXIFRAGACEAE—Alum-Root
17. ROSACEAE—Agrimony, Salad Burnet, Dropwort, Lady's Mantle, Queen-of-the-Meadow, Apothecaries' Rose, Cabbage Rose, Damask Rose, Dog Rose, Kazanlik Rose
18. LEGUMINOSAE—Dyer's Broom, Scotch Broom, Fenugreek, False Indigo, Wild Indigo, Melilot, Wild Senna
19. GERANIACEAE—Wild Geranium, Rose Geranium
20. TROPAEOLACEAE—Nasturtium
21. LINACEAE—Flax
22. RUTACEAE—Fraxinella, Rue
23. EUPHORBIACEAE—Castor Oil Plant
24. MALVACEAE—Hollyhock, Marshmallow
25. HYPERICACEAE—St. John's Wort

26. VIOLACEAE—Johnny Jump-Up, Birdsfoot Violet, Common Violet, Sweet Violet
27. THYMELAEACEAE—Daphne
28. LYTHRACEAE—Purple Loosestrife
29. MYRTACEAE—Erect Myrtle
30. ONAGRACEAE—Evening Primrose
31. UMBELLIFERAE—Angelica, Anise, Caraway, Chervil, Sweet Cicely, Coriander, Cumin, Dill, Wild Fennel, Florence Fennel, Lovage, Curly Parsley, Fernleaved Parsley, Samphire, Sea Holly, Skirret
32. ERICACEAE—Wintergreen
33. PRIMULACEAE—Scarlet Pimpernel, Primrose
34. PLUMBAGINACEAE—Sea Lavender, Thrift
35. APOCYNACEAE—Running Myrtle
36. ASCLEPIADACEAE—Butterfly-Weed
37. BORAGINACEAE—Common Alkanet, Borage, Dyer's Bugloss, Italian Bugloss, Viper's Bugloss, Comfrey, Heliotrope, Hound's Tongue, Lungwort
38. VERBENACEAE—Lemon Verbena
39. LABIATAE—Lemon Balm, Bush Basil, Italian Basil, Sweet Basil, Bergamot, Carpet Bugle-Weed, Calamint, Catnip, Dittany of Crete, Germander, Ground Ivy, Horehound, Hyssop, French Lavender, Spike Lavender, True Lavender, Pot Marjoram, Pulchellum Marjoram, Sweet Marjoram, Wild Marjoram, Apple Mint, American Apple Mint, Corn Mint, Curly Mint, Orange Mint, American Peppermint, English Peppermint, Spearmint, Water Mint, Dead Nettle, American Pennyroyal, English Pennyroyal, Perilla, Prunella, Rosemary, Clary Sage, Garden Sage, *Salvia Horminum*, Meadow Sage, Pineapple Sage, Summer Savory, Winter Savory, *Thymus azoricus*, Caraway Thyme, Garden Thyme, Lemon Thyme, Wild Thyme, *T. Zygis*.
40. SCROPHULARIACEAE—Foxglove, Great Mullein, Moth Mullein, Speedwell, Toad Flax, Turtle-Head
41. PEDALIACEAE—Bene
42. RUBIACEAE—White Bedstraw, Yellow Bedstraw, Madder, Sweet Woodruff
43. CAPRIFOLIACEAE—English Elder
44. VALERIANACEAE—Valerian

45. DIPSACACEAE—Teasel
46. CAMPANULACEAE—Rampion
47. LOBELIACEAE—Cardinal Flower
48. COMPOSITAE—Arnica, Blessed Thistle, Boneset, Calendula, Cardoon, German Chamomile, Roman Chamomile, Chicory, Coltsfoot, Purple Coneflower, Cornflower, Costmary, English Daisy, Elecampane, Feverfew, Fleabane, Golden Rod, Joe-Pye Weed, Liatris, Sweet Maudlin, Mugwort, Western Mugwort, White Mugwort, Pyrethrum, Safflower, Gray Santolina, Senecio, Sneezewort, Southernwood, Sunflower, Common Tansy, Fernleaf Tansy, French Tarragon, Beach Wormwood, Common Wormwood, Fringed Wormwood, Roman Wormwood, Silky Wormwood, Sweet Wormwood, Yarrow

TABLE Z

Table of Herbs Mentioned in Text

COMMON NAME	BOTANICAL NAME	BOTANICAL FAMILY	ANNUAL, BIENNIAL OR PERENNIAL
Aconite	*Aconitum Napellus*	10	P
Agrimony	*Agrimonia Eupatoria*	17	P
Alkanet, Common	*Anchusa officinalis*	37	B or P
Alum-Root	*Heuchera americana*	16	P
Angelica	*Angelica Archangelica*	31	B or P
Anise	*Pimpinella Anisum*	31	A
Arnica	*Arnica montana*	48	P
Autumn-Crocus	*Colchicum autumnale*	3	P
Balm, Lemon	*Melissa officinalis*	39	P
Baneberry	*Actaea alba*	10	P
Basil, Bush	*Ocimum minimum*	39	A
Basil, Italian	*O. crispum*	39	A
Basil, Sweet	*O. Basilicum*	39	A
Bay, Sweet	*Laurus nobilis*	11	P
Bedstraw, White	*Galium Mollugo*	42	P
Bedstraw, Yellow	*G. verum*	42	P

COMMON NAME	BOTANICAL NAME	BOTANICAL FAMILY	ANNUAL, BIENNIAL OR PERENNIAL
Bene	*Sesamum orientale*	41	A
Bergamot	*Monarda didyma*	39	P
Blessed Thistle	*Cnicus benedictus*	48	A
Boneset	*Eupatorium perfoliatum*	48	P
Borage	*Borago officinalis*	37	A
Broom, Dyer's	*Genista tinctoria*	18	P
Broom, Scotch	*Cytisus scoparius*	18	P
Bugle-Weed, Carpet	*Ajuga reptans*	39	P
Bugloss, Dyer's	*Alkanna tinctoria*	37	P
Bugloss, Italian	*Anchusa azurea*	37	P
Bugloss, Viper's	*Echium vulgare*	37	B
Burnet, Salad	*Sanguisorba minor*	17	P
Butterfly Weed	*Asclepias tuberosa*	36	P
Calamint	*Satureja alpina*	39	P
Calendula	*Calendula officinalis*	48	A
Caraway	*Carum Carvi*	31	A or B
Cardinal Flower	*Lobelia cardinalis*	47	P
Cardoon	*Cynara Cardunculus*	48	P
Castor Oil Plant	*Ricinus communis*	23	A
Catnip	*Nepeta Cataria*	39	P
Celandine	*Chelidonium majus*	12	P
Chamomile, German	*Matricaria Chamomilla*	48	A
Chamomile, Roman	*Anthemis nobilis*	48	P
Chervil	*Anthriscus Cerefolium*	31	A
Chicory	*Cichorium Intybus*	48	P
Chives	*Allium Schoenoprasum*	3	P
Christmas Rose	*Helleborus niger*	10	P
Cicely, Sweet	*Myrrhis odorata*	31	P
Coltsfoot	*Tussilago Farfara*	48	P
Comfrey	*Symphytum officinalis*	37	P
Coneflower, Purple	*Echinacea purpurea*	48	P
Coriander	*Coriandrum sativum*	31	A
Cornflower	*Centurea Cyanus*	48	A

COMMON NAME	BOTANICAL NAME	BOTANICAL FAMILY	ANNUAL, BIENNIAL OR PERENNIAL
Costmary	*Chrysanthemum Balsamita*	48	P
Cumin	*Cuminum Cyminum*	31	A
Daisy, English	*Bellis perennis*	48	P
Daphne	*Daphne Mezereum*	27	P
Dill	*Anethum graveolens*	31	A
Dittany of Crete	*Origanum Dictamnus*	39	P
Dropwort	*Filipendula hexapetala*	17	P
Elder, English	*Sambucus nigra*	43	P
Elecampane	*Inula Helenium*	48	P
Fennel, Wild	*Foeniculum vulgare*	31	P grown as A
Fennel, Florence	*F. vulgare* var. *dulce*	31	A
Fennel Flower	*Nigella damascena*	10	A
Fenugreek	*Trigonella Foenum-Graecum*	18	A
Feverfew	*Chrysanthemum Parthenium*	48	P
Flag, Blue	*Iris versicolor*	4	P
Flag, Sweet	*Acorus Calamus*	1	P
Flag, White	*Iris florentina*	4	P
Flag, Yellow	*I. Pseudacorus*	4	P
Flax	*Linum usitatissimum*	21	A
Fleabane	*Erigeron pulchellus*	48	P
Foxglove	*Digitalis purpurea*	40	B
Fraxinella	*Dictamnus albus*	22	P
Fumitory	*Fumaria officinalis*	13	A
Garlic	*Allium sativum*	3	P
Geranium, Wild	*Geranium maculatum*	19	P
Germander	*Teucrium Chamaedrys*	39	P
Glasswort	*Salicornia europaea*	7	A
Golden Rod	*Solidago odora*	48	P
Good King Henry	*Chenopodium Bonus-Henricus*	7	P
Ground Ivy	*Nepeta hederacea*	39	P
Heliotrope	*Heliotropium arborescens*	37	P
Hollyhock	*Althaea rosea*	24	B or semi-P

COMMON NAME	BOTANICAL NAME	BOTANICAL FAMILY	ANNUAL, BIENNIAL OR PERENNIAL
Hops	*Humulus Lupulus*	5	P
Horehound	*Marrubium vulgare*	39	P
Hound's Tongue	*Cynoglossum officinalis*	37	B
Houseleek	*Sempervivum tectorum*	15	P
Hyssop	*Hyssopus officinalis*	39	P
Indigo, False	*Baptisia tinctoria*	18	P
Indigo, Wild	*B. australis*	18	P
Jerusalem Oak	*Chenopodium Botrys*	7	A
Joe-Pye Weed	*Eupatorium purpureum*	48	P
Johnny Jump-Up	*Viola tricolor* var. *hortense*	26	A or P
Lady's Mantle	*Alchemilla vulgaris*	17	P
Larkspur	*Delphinium Ajacis*	10	A
Lavender, French	*Lavandula Stoechas*	39	P
Lavender, Spike	*L. Spica*	39	P
Lavender, True	*L. vera*	39	P
Liatris	*Liatris spicata*	48	P
Lily-of-the-Valley	*Convallaria majalis*	3	P
Loosestrife, Purple	*Lythrum Salicaria*	28	P
Lovage	*Levisticum officinale*	31	P
Lungwort	*Pulmonaria officinale*	37	P
Madder	*Rubia tinctorum*	42	P
Marjoram, Pot	*Marjorana Onites*	39	P
Marjoram, Showy	*Origanum pulchellum*	39	P
Marjoram, Sweet	*Marjorana hortensis*	39	P grown as A
Marjoram, Wild	*Origanum vulgare*	39	P
Marshmallow	*Althaea officinalis*	24	P
Maudlin, Sweet	*Achillea Ageratum*	48	P
Melilot	*Melilotus officinalis*	18	P
Mint, Apple	*Mentha rotundifolia*	39	P
Mint, American apple	*M. gentilis*	39	P
Mint, Corn	*M. arvensis*	39	P
Mint, Curly	*M. spicata* var. *crispata*	39	P

Common Name	Botanical Name	Botanical Family	Annual, Biennial or Perennial
Mint, Orange	M. citrata	39	P
Mint, American pepper-	M. piperita officinalis	39	P
Mint, English pepper-	M. piperita var. vulgaris	39	P
Mint, Spear-	M. spicata var. viridis	39	P
Mint, Water	M. aquatica	39	P
Mugwort	Artemisia vulgaris	48	P
Mugwort, Western	A. ludoviciana	48	P
Mugwort, White	A. lactiflora	48	P
Mullein, Great	Verbascum Thapsus	40	B
Mullein, Moth	V. Blattaria	40	B
Mustard, Black	Brassica nigra	14	A
Mustard, White	B. alba	14	A
Myrtle, Erect	Myrtus communis	29	P
Myrtle, Running	Vinca minor	35	P
Nasturtium	Tropaeolum majus & T. minus	20	A
Nettle, Dead	Lamium maculatum var. album	39	P
Orach, Green	Atriplex hortensis	7	A
Orach, Red	A. hortensis var. atrosanguinea	7	A
Parsley, Curly	Petroselinum hortense var. crispum	31	B
Parsley, Fern-leaved	P. hortense var. filicinum	31	B
Pasque Flower	Anemone Pulsatilla	10	P
Pennyroyal, American	Hedeoma pulegioides	39	A
Pennyroyal, English	Mentha Pulegium	39	P
Perilla	Perilla frutescens var. crispa	39	A
Pimpernel, Scarlet	Anagallis arvensis	33	A

Common Name	Botanical Name	Botanical Family	Annual, Biennial or Perennial
Pink, Clove	*Dianthus Caryophyllus*	9	P
Pokeweed	*Phytolacca americana*	8	P
Poppy, Opium	*Papaver somniferum*	12	A
Primrose	*Primula veris*	33	P
Primrose, Evening	*Oenothera biennis*	30	B
Prunella	*Prunella vulgaris*	39	P
Pyrethrum	*Chrysanthemum cinerariae-folium*	48	P
Queen-of-the-Meadow	*Filipendula Ulmaria*	17	P
Rampion	*Campanula Rapunculus*	46	P
Rocket, Dames	*Hesperis matronalis*	14	P
Rose, Apothecaries'	*Rosa gallica*	17	P
Rose, Cabbage	*R. centifolia*	17	P
Rose, Damask	*R. damascena*	17	P
Rose, Dog	*R. canina*	17	P
Rose, Kazanlik	*R. damascena* var. *triginti-petala*	17	P
Rose Geranium	*Pelargonium graveolens*	19	P
Rosemary	*Rosmarinus officinalis*	39	P
Rue	*Ruta graveolens*	22	P
Safflower	*Carthamus tinctorius*	48	A
Saffron	*Crocus sativus*	4	P
Sage, Clary	*Salvia Sclarea*	39	B
Sage, Garden	*S. officinalis*	39	P
Sage, Horminum	*S. Horminum*	39	A
Sage, Meadow	*S. pratensis*	39	A
Sage, Pineapple	*S. rutilans*	39	Tender P
St. John's Wort	*Hypericum perforatum*	25	P
Samphire	*Crithmum maritimum*	31	P
Santolina, Gray	*Santolina Chamaecyparis-sus*	48	P
Savory, Summer	*Satureja hortensis*	39	A
Savory, Winter	*Satureja montana*	39	P
Sea Holly	*Eryngium maritimum*	31	P

Common Name	Botanical Name	Botanical Family	Annual, Biennial or Perennial
Sea Lavender	*Limonium vulgare*	34	P
Senecio	*Senecio Cineraria*	48	P
Senna, Wild	*Cassia marilandica*	18	P
Skirret	*Sium Sisarum*	31	P
Snakeroot	*Cimicifuga racemosa*	10	P
Sneezewort	*Achillea Ptarmica*	48	P
Soapwort	*Saponaria officinalis*	9	P
Sorrel, French	*Rumex scutatus*	6	P
Sorrel, Garden	*R. Acetosa*	6	P
Southernwood	*Artemisia Abrotanum*	48	P
Speedwell	*Veronica officinalis*	40	P
Spiderwort	*Tradescantia virginiana*	2	P
Star Grass	*Aletris farinosa*	3	P
Sunflower	*Helianthus annuus*	48	A
Tansy, Common	*Tanacetum vulgare*	48	P
Tansy, Fern-leaved	*T. vulgare* var. *crispum*	48	P
Tarragon, French	*Artemisia Dracunculus*	48	P
Teasel	*Dipsacus sylvestris*	45	B
Thrift	*Statice Armeria*	34	P
Thyme, Azores	*Thymus azoricus*	39	P
Thyme, Caraway	*T. Herba-barona*	39	P
Thyme, Garden	*T. vulgare*	39	P
Thyme, Lemon	*T. citriodorus*	39	P
Thyme, Wild	*T. Serpyllum*	39	P
Thyme, Zygis	*T. Zygis*	39	P
Toad Flax	*Linaria vulgaris*	40	P
Turtle-Head	*Chelone glabra*	40	P
Valerian	*Valeriana officinalis*	44	P
Verbena, Lemon	*Lippia citriodora*	38	Tender P
Violet, Birdsfoot	*Viola pedata*	26	P
Violet, Common	*Viola papilionacea*	26	P
Violet, Sweet	*Viola odorata*	26	P
Wintergreen	*Gaultheria procumbens*	32	P
Woad	*Isatis tinctoria*	14	B
Woodruff, Sweet	*Asperula odorata*	42	P

COMMON NAME	BOTANICAL NAME	BOTANICAL FAMILY	ANNUAL, BIENNIAL OR PERENNIAL
Wormwood, Beach	*Artemisia Stelleriana*	48	P
Wormwood, Common	*A. Absinthium*	48	P
Wormwood, Fringed	*A. frigida*	48	P
Wormwood, Roman	*A. pontica*	48	P
Wormwood, Silky	*A. mutellina*	48	P
Wormwood, Sweet	*A. annua*	48	A
Yarrow	*Achillea Millefolium*	48	P

Index

About the Author

ROSETTA E. CLARKSON also authored *Green Enchantment* and *Magic Gardens*, both about the history of gardening. She was also the publisher of *The Herb Journal*. Her own gardens at Salt Acres, on the Connecticut shore, furnished rare herb seeds to re-stock English seed companies during World War II, and her library of ancient herbals and gardening books was one of the choicest of its kind in the world.

GERTRUDE B. FOSTER and her husband, Philip, published *The Herb Grower Magazine* from 1947 to 1984. Mrs. Foster is also the author of *Herbs for Every Garden*.